P9-AFO-807

# MULTIPLE SPACES:
# THE POETRY
# OF RAFAEL ALBERTI

SALVADOR JIMENEZ-FAJARDO

# MULTIPLE SPACES:
# THE POETRY
# OF RAFAEL ALBERTI

TAMESIS BOOKS LIMITED
LONDON

Colección Támesis
SERIE A - MONOGRAFIAS, CVI

Depósito legal: M. 8333-1984

Printed in Spain by Talleres Gráficos de SELECCIONES GRÁFICAS
Carretera de Irún, km. 11,500 - Madrid-34

for
TAMESIS BOOKS LIMITED
LONDON

*To the Memory of my Father*
*and*
*To the Future of his Grandchildren*

«Sueñe el bosque su verde transparencia
su voz el mar, la cumbre alta su frente,
la llama el corazón de su pasado.»
  (RAFAEL ALBERTI: «Elegía a una vida
clara y hermosa»)

# TABLE OF CONTENTS

# TABLE OF CONTENTS

# PREFACE

In the brilliant poetic pleiad of 1925,[1] Rafael Alberti's voice rose from the start as that of a born poet. Although with less formal education than any member of his famous generation —he did not complete his *bachillerato*— he displayed almost immediately a mastery and elegance reached only, in most cases, after long and arduous efforts: his very first collection was awarded the National Literary Prize. Almost from the outset, he knew to sift out of the poetic movements of the day those elements that best suited him, and even when it came to the willed exaltation of Góngora, what he wrote was not an imitation but purest Alberti accented by Góngora.

Because of his facility, his responsiveness to the intellectual concerns of his time, and his emotional receptivity, he seemed always to escape the molds into which readers and critics would seek to encase him. How is it that the poet who had written the light-hearted verse of *Marinero en tierra* and *La amante* and the folk ballads of *El alba del alhelí* could burst upon the scene with, almost simultaneously, poetry as formally complex as that in *Cal y canto* and as sharp-edged as that in *Sobre los ángeles?* Some readers saw but the fluctuating appearance and thought that Alberti's style was inconstant, but these mutable surfaces were sustained by a tense effort of exploration, the systematic mapping of a personal imaginative space.

Alberti wrote his very first lines of poetry pressed by the need to formulate the loss of his father. This bereavement brought into sharp focus the earlier loss of his Andalusian seascape which he had left as an adolescent when his family moved to Madrid. It is this idealized geography that he seeks to recreate in his early poetry, rendered metaphorically as the space of the sea, forever forbidden, and nevertheless necessary to the poet. The same effort of recuperation of a lost scene or the need to establish emotional links with a new one will characterize all of his lyric poetry. Whether in joyful recreation of past shores or in bewildered anguish when his poetic and existential horizons are threatened from within, in the passionate reliving of his artistic awakening or in

---

[1] Much current opinion tends to dispute the value of the «generational» concept in Spanish literature, with special reference to these poets. The term *grupo poético* is offered instead of *generación* to suggest that there was less theoretical cohesiveness among the poets than the latter term assumes. Cf. Ricardo Gullón's introductory essay to *At Home and Beyond: New Essays of Spanish Poets of the Twenties*, edited by S. Jiménez-Fajardo and John Wilcox (SSAS, Lincoln: 1983).

yearning remembrance of lost instants, his work is ever an exploration, a bridging of the distance that separated the main occasions of his life.

The vast body of Alberti's verse imposed from the first the need to select and to organize. Of these two tasks, the first was the most difficult because of the exceptional value of considerable portions of his poetry. There are peaks of excellence, however, that rise unquestionably above the sustained quality of the rest. Following an initial chapter on Alberti and his generation, in which I try to emphasize the formative components of his experience, I have focused in chronological order on principal moments in the poet's work as vantage points from which to survey its extensive prospect.

Alberti's first and most important contact with the world is visual —he painted before he wrote and has now returned to painting— his most urgent, recurring need to make the world without congruent with his poetic vision. This is the task of his earliest poetry, from *Marinero en tierra* to *El alba del alhelí,* to which I devote the second chapter of this essay. This is also a period of learning where, although there is a predominance of short lyrics in a folk vein, the temptation of other innovative techniques is at times perceptible. It is during the spiritual crisis recorded in *Sobre los ángeles* that Alberti finds his definitive, highly personal voice, an idiom with which to question the sudden disjunction between inner and outer worlds, when the chaos within seems to undermine the very supports of external reality. The principal part of Chapter III is a reading of *Sobre los ángeles* with introductory and concluding excursions into respectively, *Cal y canto,* as a high point of the poet's disposition to classical form, and *Yo era un tonto y lo que he visto me ha hecho dos tontos,* as a corresponding decision to experiment.

To the convulsive inner journey recorded in *Sobre los ángeles* answers the ordeal of the poet's involvement in the civil strife of Spain and his subsequent exile, an ordeal that he tries both to contain and to express in *Entre el clavel y la espada,* the center of Chapter IV. Chapter V attends mainly to the extraordinary, vigorous lyricism born of the poet's return to painting —entitled *A la pintura*— occasioned by his intense yearning for a past artistic experience and the endlessly suggestive transformations of esthetic space achieved by pictorial art. In Chapter VI an equally powerful impulse originates in Alberti's yearning for the lost regions and instants of the past in *Retornos de lo vivo lejano,* followed by the effort to find in his new American homeland a source of poetically suggestive myth in *Baladas y canciones del Paraná.* With Chapter VII, I conclude my study of Alberti's strictly lyrical work. Again, I find the notion of space essential for an understanding of *Abierto a todas horas,* in which the poet turns once more to his surroundings. In *Roma, peligro para caminantes* and *Canciones del alto valle del Aniene,* Alberti exults in the discovery of a newly congenial reality with robust, satirical joy in the Eternal City and serenity in the Italian countryside.

Alberti's life has been one of unstinting commitment to his responsibilities as a poet and a man. He has plunged into the discord of his times, fought and suffered, recording his struggles in poetry of a civil cast; he has also taken radical political positions and placed his art at the service of these ideas. With like intent, Alberti turned to the theater as to a more immediately effective mode of communication, a public medium for the confrontation of both political and poetic ideas. Chapter VIII attempts an overview of Alberti as «poeta en la calle», and dramatist, facets of his work which, though certainly important in their own right, must take second place to his more pervasive voice. For Rafael Alberti is primarily a lyrical poet, and this consideration has been the main thrust of my study.

Alberti made use of all the resources of his language in highly inventive ways. Therefore, I have also presented the complete Spanish original of a small number of poems, when my analysis required it. With respect to my reading of Alberti's work in general, while I try to place it in the context of the poet's life, the focus of my attention is always the text itself.

I want to thank my wife, Lisa, for her expert perseverance in typing the earliest forms of this manuscript and for the unfailing perceptiveness of her suggestions. I am grateful to President Robert S. Eckley, the Personnel Council and Illinois Wesleyan University for the generous grant that made possible the final preparation of this study.

CHAPTER 1

PAINTER TO POET

I. *From Childhood to Early Achievements*

On April 27, 1977, Rafael Alberti returned to Spain after thirty-eight years of exile. He had left Spain in March, 1939, at the age of thirty-seven. By then he was an accomplished poet, having published some of his best work, *Marinero en tierra, Cal y canto* and *Sobre los ángeles,* and demonstrated singular brilliance among a group of poets of impressive gifts. He had also participated in the political turmoil of the Spain of the 1930's as a writer (through political poetry and plays) and an activist (he became a member of the Communist party in the early years of that decade). Alberti was never a man to remain above the fray. If his life within Spain was tumultuous, a result of his nature as well as of historical circumstances, it was hardly less energetic without. He maintained his political affiliations, continuing to write commited poetry and theatre; he returned to his early interest in painting and also published poetry that ranks with his best (e.g., *Retornos de lo vivo lejano, A la Pintura*). He traveled widely through Latin America (he settled in the Río de la Plata region in the 1940's and remained there until 1963), to the Soviet Union, China, Italy (where he lived for fourteen years).

Fortunately, Alberti resided in a Spanish-speaking country for the longer period of his absence from Spain and in a country of congenial customs and a sister tongue, Italy, for the rest. He remained immersed in the language of his poetry, retaining the great inventiveness that had marked it from the start; he has maintained an absorbing interest in the world around him wherever he has been and drawn energy from it for his art. As he stated in a recent interview: «El enemigo grande no es el país donde estás, el enemigo grande es la artiesclerosis...»[1] Even now, in his eighties, Alberti is free of such creative rigidity.

Rafael Alberti Merello was born December 16, 1902, in Puerto de Santa María, near Cádiz. His Italian greatgrandparents (one grandmother was Irish) settled in the region and came to own vast vineyards, later lost to, among others, such now well-known concerns as Osborne and

---

[1] LUIS PANCORBO, «Rafael Alberti: Más años fuera que dentro de España». Interview, *Revista de Occidente,* No. 148, p. 71.

Terry. Although some of Alberti's uncles still lived in relative wealth, his own father had to work for the Osbornes, becoming eventually their general agent in Spain. Rafael rarely saw him as a child and lived chiefly under the tutelage of intransigent and fanatically Roman Catholic uncles and aunts.

At the age of ten, Rafael was admitted as a day pupil at the Jesuit «Colegio de San Luis de Gonzaga» in his native town. The Jesuits extended free tuition to the children of needy families of the town, and Alberti remembers the four years spent at this institution as years of humiliation. He considers the instruction he received then as useless, hopelessly out of date; he felt stifled by the simplistic, narrow religiosity that pervaded all activities: «Allí sufrí, rabié, odié, amé, me divertí y no aprendí casi nada durante cerca de cuatro años de externado.»[2] Rafael found deliverance from this oppressiveness in the sea and in bullfighting games with the cows and calves of his Uncle José Luis de la Cuesta. Alberti's memories of the sea of Cádiz are among the earliest he mentions in *La arboleda perdida:* «De muchos azules está llena y hecha mi infancia en aquel Puerto de Santa María. Mas ya los repetí, hasta perder la voz, en las canciones de mis primeros libros. Pero ahora se me resucitan, bañándome de nuevo. Entre aquellos azules de delantales, blusas marineras, cielos, río, bahía, isla, barcas, aires, abrí los ojos y aprendí a leer» (*A.p.,* p. 17). It was also in conjunction with the sea that Alberti's interest in painting was born. His first drawing was of a boat, the «Bahama», whose exact copy, after numerous trials, he took to his Aunt Lola, an amateur painter. She encouraged him with guidance and a gift of her paints.

In 1917 Alberti was expelled from «San Luis de Gonzaga» in consequence of a romantic indiscretion — merely a youthful letter intercepted by one of his aunts and presented to the College authorities. Soon after, he and his family moved to Madrid. He was appalled by the drabness of the capital where they arrived on a damp, gray morning: «¡Dios mío! Yo traía las pupilas mareadas de cal, llenas de la sal blanca de los esteros de la isla, traspasadas de azules y claros amarillos, violetas y verdes de mi río, mi mar, mis playas y pinares» (*A.p.,* p. 98). Alberti declared that he would not pursue his studies and would instead become a painter. He studied some of the *bachillerato,* but never, in fact, completed the required work. His days were spent making copies of the reproductions of famous sculptures found in the Casón (Felipe IV's palace) and later of paintings at the Museo del Prado.

His parents were convinced by one of Alberti's good friends, Manuel Gil Cala, to provide him with a teacher. And so his afternoons at the Prado were now lackadaisically supervised by a *maestro* whose presence had no effect whatever on the young man's work. Soon Alberti was on his own again, sketching preferably from nature and free to indulge his love for rambling in the streets and gardens of Madrid.

---

[2] RAFAEL ALBERTI, *La arboleda perdida* (Barcelona, 1975), p. 44. All future references are to this edition and will appear hereafter as *A.p.* following quotations.

Gil Cala was a poet as was another friend of Alberti's at that time, Celestino Espinosa. They introduced Alberti to the artistic circles of the capital and contributed to his growing interest in poetry. He read voraciously everything that he could find and was particularly taken with the Italian *novellini* and the Greek classics. These writers intensified his awareness of the ancestry that linked him irrevocably to the Mediterranean world of dazzling colors and luminous transparency: «... comencé a sentir... desde aquellas lecturas, el angustioso anhelo de precisión y claridad que ahora sobre todo me domina» (*A.p.*, p. 124).

In 1920 Alberti was encouraged to have a show by another friend, the painter Daniel Vázquez Díaz. Although public reaction was either angry or mocking, Alberti was heartened by this *succès de scandale* and felt, for a time, confirmed in his vocation. For, by the traditional standards of Spain's established artists, his painting was indeed thought scandalous. As he was influenced by the ideas that Vázquez Díaz had brought from France, Alberti did not join any of the new literary and artistic movements that were then beginning to define themselves in Spain. In that same year Alberti's father died. Since his relations with his father had been frequently strained, he was profoundly affected by the event. His first poem was composed during the wake, a spontaneous effusion into words of feelings which his painting could not satisfactorily express. Two other deaths marked that year and left a deep imprint on the young man's life, that of the great novelist Benito Pérez Galdós, and that of Joselito, the most admired matador of the day. Although these figures appear widely different in significance, one seemingly representing values of traditional culture and intellectual accomplishment, the other a personification of the instinctive art of the people, they remained joined in Alberti's mind by the bridge of his own intuition as symbols of two basic elements of his poetry, popular elegance and conceptual elaboration.

Alberti's careless habits, his exhausting walks, irregular eating, and perhaps some physical propensity, brought upon him the early stages of tuberculosis, the illness that claimed his father. He was sent to the Sierra de Guadarrama to recover. He went on reading voraciously, interested now as well in the more recent poetry of Spain. He continued to write poetry and attempted, though in a less radical manner, the experiments heralded by the *Ultraístas*.[3] He was particularly interested in the statements of the movement's founder, Guillermo de Torre, in the manifesto entitled *Vértice*: «un manifiesto... que me sorprendió, gusté y rechacé en un principio» (*A.p.*, p. 143). The group's indiscriminate adoption of modernity and its penchant for technical jargon could not claim the whole-hearted endorsement of a poet like Alberti, who always loved classical form and found constant inspiration in the great traditions of

---

[3] One of several «futuristic», short-lived poetic movements of the 1920's, whose theorist, Guillermo de Torre, championed the creation of a far-fetched, multiple imagery.

17

Spanish poetry. Nevertheless, his first effort to have something published was a poem he sent to *Ultra*.[4] It never did appear.

By 1922, Alberti had decided to move away from painting and to devote himself completely to poetry: «Me prometí olvidarme de mi primera vocación. Quería solamente ser poeta. Y lo quería con furia, pues a los veinte años aún no cumplidos me consideraba casi un viejo para iniciar tan nuevo como dificilísimo camino. Vi entonces, con sorpresa, que lenguaje no me faltaba, que lo poseía con gran variedad y riqueza» (*A.p.*, p. 144). From the beginning Rafael Alberti displayed great gifts as a poet; this was to prove a mixed blessing, for while he was capable of producing some of the most brilliant poetry of his generation, he has sometimes let his verse weaken, allowing artifice to take the place of vigor. Alberti's dedication to poetry was confirmed during the second summer spent in the Guadarrama mountains. As his body gained strength in that bracing climate, his absorption with poetry became total. Contrary to the common experience of beginning poets, the current vogue of *Ultraísmo* left hardly any imprint on his work, clear testimony of the self-assurance that characterized even his earliest steps as a poet. When a painter friend, Gregorio Prieto, brought him a copy of Lorca's *Libro de poemas,* while he was quite enthusiastic about many of the compositions, those of a more straightforward and popular cast, he was displeased by other pieces in which he detected rhetoricist echoes from Modernism or the nineteenth century.

Alberti returned to Madrid in October. He continued to rest and write and received friends in his drafty third-floor room —dubbed «the freezer»— windows wide open to let in the fresh air. Juan Chabás brought with him another budding poet, Dámaso Alonso, who presented him with a book of poems, *Poemas puros: Poemillas de la ciudad,* and he and Alberti quickly became good friends. Juan Chabás managed to talk Alberti into exhibiting again, at the *Ateneo.* This was to be his last show for many years (until 1947-1948), and although, to his surprise, he sold one of his paintings, he felt great relief when his canvasses were again safely ensconced in his home. Chabás also brought Pedro Garfias to see Alberti. This young poet was the director of *Horizonte,* a new magazine of poetry less strident than *Ultra* and more to Alberti's liking. It was in this magazine that Alberti's first poems appeared, next to Federico García Lorca's «Baladilla de los tres ríos», some pieces by Garfias himself and others by Antonio Machado. The desire to publish and be known had become intense for Alberti. He remembered the magazine *Alfar,* directed by the Uruguayan poet, Julio J. Casal, and open to many contemporary and traditional currents in painting and poetry, Unamuno and the *Ultraístas,* Leopoldo Lugones, Alfonso Reyes, and so on. Alberti sent off a series of short pieces entitled «Balcones» —subsequently incorporated into his *Poesía (1924-1967)* (Aguilar), together with those from *Horizonte* as «Primeros poemas (1927)»— and inspired by a little girl he would often see day-dreaming by a window across from his.

---

[4] Magazine of the *Ultraísta* School.

Alberti now began to work in earnest on a complete book of poems. The original title of the collection was to be *Giróscopo*: «Pretendía yo que a mis poemas de múltiples imágenes los compendiaba bien esta palabra, designadora de ese trompo o peón de música, rayado de colores, delicia de los niños» (*A.p.*, p. 156). Some of these poems were sent by Juan Chabás to Gabriel Miró, who, though he did not care for the title (no one seemed to) saw in them language of great beauty. Alberti's love affair with the intrinsic beauty of words had begun and would grow until 1927, the year of Góngora's tricentenary when, with the publication of *Cal y canto,* he felt that «... la belleza formal se apoderó de mí hasta casi petrificarme el sentimiento» (*A.p.*, p. 157). In this earlier period (1923) Alberti began to meet the poets who were to become the *grupo poético* of 1925, as well as writers who contributed to the intellectual atmosphere of the day. Vicente Aleixandre he would see frequently because he lived in his own neighborhood; Gregorio Prieto, who had done a portrait of Alberti, once brought the eminent critic Enrique Díez-Canedo. Prieto also prepared the way for a meeting with Lorca, an occasion that took place at the *Residencia de estudiantes* in Madrid and which Alberti remembers in great detail. The two Andalusian poets became good friends from the start.

Alberti had now begun to write a collection tentatively entitled *Mar y tierra,* in which he drew not only from the popular poetry of Gil Vicente and Barbieri's *Cancionero musical de los siglos XV y XVI,* but also from the more «literary» works of Pedro Espinosa and Garcilaso de la Vega. In those active days of dicovery, Alberti was also to meet Salvador Dalí, Luis Buñuel, Eugenio D'Ors, and Claudio de la Torre. The latter novelist suggested to Alberti that he should submit his current work to the competition for the National Literary Prize. The judges that year included Gabriel Miró, Antonio Machado, Ramón Menéndez Pidal, José Moreno Villa, Carlos Arniches and Gabriel Maura. Despite doubts, the possibility tempted him. He left Madrid for Rute, a small mountain town in Andalusia, where one of his sisters and her husband lived, to work on *Mar y tierra;* once completed, he sent it off to Madrid to his friend José María Chacón y Calvo, the Cuban novelist, asking him to present it to the competition.

Immediately Alberti set out to compose another group of poems. His stay in Rute revealed to him another Andalusia, harsher, more primitive, of clashing contrasts and somber legends. His preference was still for the ballad, but of a different, more broken rhythm. Visits to neighbors and to nearby towns disclosed to his imagination a rich fund of darkly fascinating customs together with a provincial naivete that bordered on the absurd, all eminently susceptible of poetic transformation. Nevertheless, he soon grew tired of his isolation and left for Madrid. It was not in Rute, despite Alberti's own recollections in *La arboleda perdida,* that the news of his being awarded the National Literary Prize reached him, but in Madrid according to Robert Marrast.[5] The results of the competi-

5 RAFAEL ALBERTI, *Marinero en tierra, La amante, El alba del alhelí,* ed. Robert Marrast (Madrid, 1972), p. 32.

tion appeared in the *Gaceta literaria* on June 12, 1925: «Reunido el Jurado del concurso nacional de Literatura 1924-25, acordó por unanimidad elevar a la aprobación de la Superioridad la siguiente propuesta: Primera. Que se adjudique el premio de 4.000 pesetas, correspondiente al tema primero, «Poesía Lírica», al libro inédito titulado *Mar y tierra* de D. Rafael Alberti».[6] No one would dare to think him primarily a painter! Alberti's position as a promising young poet was secure.

## II. «*A New "Golden Age"*»

At the government building where Alberti went to collect his prize money, he met Gerardo Diego, who had received the second prize in the same competition for his collection *Versos humanos*. Gerardo Diego had already written a significant amount of poetry and enthusiastically participated in the «Vanguardist»[7] movements of the previous decade. Besides his own achievement as a poet, Diego's particular significance for the *grupo poético* rests on his having been among the first to see them as an actual «generation», and to have perceived some common tendencies within their highly individual expression. His anthology *Poesía española contemporánea*, 1932, was surprisingly successful. He also became an historian and *porte-parole* to his poet friends and actively participated in their various undertakings. Because of the enthusiasm that united the poets in the salute to their great ancestor, Góngora, they have been generally gathered under the banner of the anniversary as «Generation of 1927».[8] This continues to be the most commonly used label for the group. Nevertheless, we should be wary of the danger of such labeling in that it suggests, on the part of these poets, too exclusive a bond with Góngora. While it is true that they were not averse to occasional bursts of verbal pyrotechnics or conceptual intricacies, both characteristics of the great poet of Córdoba, no lasting imprint of Góngora remained in any of them. Alberti himself, who was perhaps the one who felt the greatest affinity for formal gongoristic complexity and who wrote an entire collection under its influence, broke its grip resoundingly with the spectacular brilliance of *Sobre los ángeles,* in which inner turmoil stretches to its limit the demands of form.

This group of poets has been called a new Golden Age by readers and critics alike,[9] and it is true that not since the latter part of the sixteenth century had Spain seen such a poetic flowering. The younger poets were not united, at least at the beginning, in any common political or social concerns, as was the Generation of 1898 to some extent. In the words

---

[6] *Ibid.,* p. 32.

[7] *Ultraísmo* (see note 6 above) and *Creacionismo* are the two best known of these movements.

[8] They have also been called *generación de la dictadura,* but most of the poets (and critics) reject this label because of its pejorative connotations. See footnote 1 to Preface.

[9] Cf. HUGO FRIEDRICH, *The Structure of Modern Poetry* (Evanston, Il., 1974), p. 110.

of Dámaso Alonso «esa generación no se alza contra nada. No está motivada por una catástrofe nacional, como la que da origen al pensamiento del 98».[10] This is not to say that these poets are apolitical or indifferent to the disastrous years of Primo de Rivera's dictatorship[11] and Alfonso XIII's last years. Alberti recalls that he became aware of the prevailing undercurrents of discontent upon the news of the defeat at Annual in 1921, whose consequence was the accession of Primo de Rivera: «Nadie podía saber entonces que nuestra generación comenzaría a andar bajo ese signo. Otra generación, la del 98, también había venido bajo el signo de otra catástrofe nacional: el derrumbamiento total del viejo poderío monárquico español. Ambos acontecimientos imprimieron caracteres bien definidos a estas dos promociones de escritores» (A.p., p. 147). There is no actual contradiction between the statements of Dámaso Alonso and Alberti, for while the writings of the Generation of 1898 were from the beginning marked by the socio-political climate and aimed to some extent at a *prise de conscience,* the years during which the generation of 1925 reached its creative maturity (1924-1931) left no significant ideological traces in their work. Positions would be taken later and commitments made so that in 1939 the most important members of the group, with the exception of Aleixandre, chose to live in exile.

The concerns of the group were more strictly poetical, and yet, even in this respect, the bonds that united them were more human than esthetic. They were all good friends and gathered frequently at the *Residencia de estudiantes,* for instance, or when homage was paid to individuals such as the *Presentación* of Pablo Neruda in 1934 or the *Homenaje* to Cernuda in 1935. The tricentenary of Góngora's death in 1927 afforded just that occasion and remains as probably the moment of greatest cohesiveness that the generation achieved.

Interest in the «Angel of obscurity» (Góngora) was not a sudden mood, nor were these poets alone in reclaiming his importance. The «Ultraist» vanguard had done so before; these poets had been the first to turn their backs on the excesses of Modernism, eschewing in particular its declamatory propensities, finding singular affinities with their own efforts in Góngora's systematic use of metaphor. But the exclusive attention they gave to the articulations of intricate imagery as it reduced their field of vision soon exhausted its creative potential. Our poets went to Góngora with a wider range of interests. One of the principal promoters of the anniversary was, as we saw, Gerardo Diego, the only major poet to have participated in the «Ultraist» movement and to have successfully integrated this experience. Interest in the event was unanimous: «Por primera vez en la historia de nuestra literatura, una generación entera ha rendido al poeta de las *Soledades* el tributo que se le debía».[12] Alberti participated enthusiastically in the organization of the festivities and gave free rein, in his own verse, to an already marked tendency

---

[10] DÁMASO ALONSO, *Poesía contemporánea* (Madrid, 1958), p. 172.
[11] *La dictablanda* as it used to be called.
[12] DÁMASO ALONSO, *Estudios y ensayos gongorinos* (Madrid, 1970), p. 562.

toward classical form and sumptuous imagery. But the poets of 1925, or for the moment of 1927, saw that Don Luis had much more to offer than a panoply of finely chiseled metaphors. There was also the powerful development of the long period, the demands made by the discipline of such verse, happily met by this singularly gifted, self-confident Pleiad. For Alberti these difficulties were as joys: «... mientras tanto, la lección —entiéndase bien—, el ejemplo de Góngora sigan amaneciendo cada mañana con nosotros. Contra las repetidas facilidades de un hoy ya casi anónimo versolibrismo suelto, contra los falsos hermetismos prefabricados, contra la dejadez y la desgana, contra ese sin ton ni son de tantos habladores sacamuelas, se alce de nuevo la mano de don Luis, su dibujo exigente, su rigurosa disciplina» (*A.p.*, p. 252).

But the admiration for Góngora could lead to the dangers of stylistic petrification, where mannerisms are all that remain of a vibrant source —Alberti felt, near the completion of *Cal y canto,* that the manner was stifling his expression. Yet the danger was not too great. All these poets had sunk their roots in a tradition that held Góngora and also, before him, Garcilaso de la Vega, Manrique, Juan Ruiz, Gonzalo de Berceo. They wrote sonnets unaffectedly, not merely because Góngora had written them, but also because Garcilaso wrote them, Francisco de Quevedo wrote them, and because *they* wanted to write sonnets, the *décima,* the *lira.*[13] The return to classicism involved the adoption of forms and inspirations, their adaptation to current needs rather than any reductive prescriptions. Concentration on the properties of language reduced to its pure poetic content drew them early to the work of Jiménez even more than that of Machado whom they also admired greatly. The high regard that the poetry of Unamuno would inspire grew more slowly; still, for the most part, they would go far towards agreeing with Cernuda, who has called Unamuno the greatest Spanish poet «en lo que va de siglo»,[14] a statement that causes today much less surprise than it would have forty or forty-five years ago.

It is difficult to define the specific impact that the Vanguardist movements of the teens and early twenties of the century, *Ultraísmo* and *Creacionismo,*[15] in particular, had on our poets. But, as we pointed out earlier, these experiments were to some extent responsible for the break with Modernism and, by freeing the poetry of the period from its weight, prepared the way for another important arrival, that of Surrealism. This movement had been introduced to the artists and writers of the day

[13] The *décima* is a traditional verse form of ten octosyllabic lines; it was practiced with notable success among our poets, by Cernuda and Guillén in particular. The classical *lira* was a strophe of five lines, the first, third and fourth of seven syllables, the second and fifth of eleven, with rhymes in ababa. There are also *liras* of four (abba) and of six lines (ababaa). Fray Luis de León's classical *liras,* among the best in the language, gave the verse form the alternate name of *quarillas de Fray Luis.*

[14] LUIS CERNUDA, *Estudios sobre poesía española contemporánea,* p. 72.

[15] According to Philip Silver, in a paper read at the University of Virginia Conference on the Generation of 1927 (April 11-12, 1980), the impact of *Creacionismo* may have been decisive for the formation of the poets of 1925.

early in the 1920's: André Breton, its French theoretician, gave a conference at the *Ateneo* of Barcelona in November, 1922; an article by Fernando Vela on Surrealism appeared in the *Revista de Occidente* in 1924, and in 1925 Breton's «Manifeste» was published in the same review; Louis Aragon gave a lecture on the doctrines of the movement at the *Residencia de estudiantes* in Madrid on April 18, 1925. But these ideas remained dormant until some years later when their impact, though mitigated, reverberates through the poems of several important collections: Alberti's *Sobre los ángeles,* 1929; *Sermones y moradas,* 1930; Cernuda's *Un río, un amor,* 1929; *Los placeres prohibidos,* 1931; Lorca's *Poeta en Nueva York* not published until 1940, but written in 1929-1930; Aleixandre's *Pasión de la tierra,* written in 1928, which appeared in 1936, *Espadas como labios* in 1932, and *La destrucción o el amor* in 1935.

For poets of Andalusia aware of its folklore, such as Alberti and Lorca, the spontaneous creations of the *cante jondo* could not appear too different, in origin or expression, from much Surrealistic writing. It was then as a form of liberation that Surrealism was principally felt by the Spanish poets. Lorca could free himself from the label of «Gypsyism» and write the intense «poesía de abrirse las venas»,[16] while Aleixandre finds the freedom and the language to embrace joyfully his internal chaos. Alberti tunnels inward also, to discover himself: «... aquel pozo de tinieblas, aquel agujero de oscuridad, en el que bracearía casi en estado agónico, pero violentamente, por encontrar una salida a las superficies habitadas, al puro aire de la vida» (*A.p.,* p. 263). All would have agreed with Guillén's oft-quoted words that «There is no babble quite so empty as that of the subconscious left to its triviality».[17] For if one overarching concern united them all, it was their total commitment to the exaltation of their art; their not-at-all rebellious «goal... was that exact expression which fitted what they were trying to say».[18] Alberti's own poetic career manifests unwavering attention to such exact expression, which is why his first published volume, *Marinero en tierra,* 1925, reads immediately like the work of a seasoned poet.

## III. *Success and Turmoil*

After receiving the National Prize, Alberti undertook to thank personally the members of its jury, looking forward in particular to visiting Machado, of whose vote he was especially proud, and Gabriel Miró, for whom he felt great respect. He could not meet Machado, who was at that time absent from Madrid, but he was received with much fondness by Miró, whose simplicity and kindness impressed him greatly. Yet the most important encounter of that time, for Alberti, was with Juan Ramón Jiménez. Jiménez had praised Alberti's poetry consistently for some time

---

[16] F. G. Lorca, «Carta a Jorge Zalamea». *Obras completas* (Madrid, 1964), p. 1664.
[17] Jorge Guillén, *Language and Poetry* (Cambridge, Mass., 1961), p. 204.
[18] *Ibid.,* p. 212.

and warmly welcomed the younger poet. Subsequently, he published a selection of the poems of *Marinero en tierra* in the journal *Sí,* which he was editing as *El andaluz universal.* In another issue appeared his eulogistic letter on the poems of *Marinero en tierra,* which Alberti has always included in the various editions of this collection.

José Ruiz Castillo offered to publish *Marinero en tierra* in his *Biblioteca nueva.* Although some of the poems of the collection had even become popular songs —«La corza blanca», with music by Ernesto Halffter was particularly successful, «Cinema» and «Saliero» were also widely sung— the work had not yet appeared in book form. Meanwhile, Alberti took a trip across Spain and towards the Cantabrian coast. During the trip he would write his second volume of poetry, *La amante,* a series of ballads and songs in remembrance of a friend of the past, linking the Southern and the Northern seas. On his return *Marinero en tierra* appeared. The critical reception was highly favorable; a relationship to Lorca was immediately established: «La batalla Lorca-Alberti había estallado, una batalla larga en la que los contendores casi llegaron a las manos, mientras los dos capitanes se las estrechaban, amigos, en sus puestos» (*A.p.,* p. 227).

Alberti's poems were now being translated in France and England. But the poems on Rute had not yet been completed, and he decided to spend some time there in order to conclude this project. After finishing this book, *El alba del alhelí,* he visited Emilio Prados and Manuel Altolaguirre in Málaga at their offices for *Litoral.* He left there his manuscript of *La amante* which *Litoral* would publish in 1926. Back in Madrid with Góngora's tercentenary approaching, Alberti began work on what would become *Cal y canto,* provisionally entitled *Pasión y forma,* a collection inspired by the great Andalusian ancestor: «Sometería el verso métrico a las presiones —y precisiones— más altas. Perseguiría como un loco la belleza idiomática, los más vibrados timbres armoniosos, creando imágenes que a veces, en un mismo poema, se sucederían con una velocidad cinematográfica...» (*A.p.,* p. 234). Some of these poems first appeared in the *Revista de Occidente* and *Litoral,* eliciting mixed reviews. Some readers were uneasy at this neoclassical turn in the poetry of someone they had safely pegged within the folklorist tradition. In April, 1926, the project of celebrating the third centennial of Góngora's death took form in conversations between Alberti, Diego, Salinas, and Melchor Fernández Almagro. The project involved the compilation of testimonials as well as of the works of the poet in twelve volumes or notebooks that, as agreed to by Ortega y Gasset, the *Revista de Occidente* would publish. Celebrations were planned including concerts, the presentation of a theatrical work by Góngora, exhibitions, conferences, and so on. Alberti was named secretary to the group promoting these activities.

It was at this time that Alberti met Ignacio Sánchez Mejías, bullfighter and friend of poets, who would also become known as a dramatist through his play *Sinrazón,* performed in 1928 with noted success. He invited Alberti to Seville some time before the Góngora celebrations and introduced him to another poet, Fernando Villalón, who was to remain a great friend of Alberti, until he died four years later, in 1931. He also met Luis

Cernuda, reticent, meticulous, destined to become one of the most important poets of the generation. Alberti's friendship with Sánchez Mejías grew to the point where he persuaded Alberti to join his *cuadrilla* in the entrance parade preliminary to a bullfight.

The last poems of *Cal y canto* were written under the shadow of Alberti's oncoming crisis. Not only did his inner world enter a prolonged period of turmoil, his visible behavior also appeared to change: «Un poeta antipático, hiriente, mordaz, insoportable, según los rumores que me llegaban» (*A.p.,* p. 265). Alberti suddenly felt that he had irretrievably lost a youthful Paradise. His health was again faltering, and he felt trapped, alone, attacked from within by dark angers and resentments. He turned these obscure forces into the angels that people his next book, *Sobre los ángeles.* Still, seeking escape from his nightmares he accepted José María de Cossío's invitation to visit with him at his estate in Tudanca. There he continued to write of his anguish but with less tension, a change reflected in the gradual transformation of his poetic line which became more developed, acquired longer breath. Later, Alberti left his manuscript of *El alba del alhelí* with Cossío, who had promised to publish it in his collection *Libros para amigos.* It appeared in 1928.

That year Alberti continued to write in the same vein, what has been called his «Surrealistic» style, and completed *Sermones y moradas,* where he experiments with the versicle form, and the play *El hombre deshabitado,* whose imagery harks back to several poems of *Sobre los ángeles. Revista de Occidente* published *Cal y canto* in 1928, but hardly had it begun to be noticed by the critics when *Sobre los ángeles* came on the scene, coincidentally with the beginnings of the political unrest that was to usher in the Republic in 1931. Azorín praised *Sobre los ángeles* as a work of the highest lyrical excellence, and it has remained the most admired of Alberti's works to this day. But now other events were beginning to absorb Alberti's interest and poetic rebellion was to be followed by a rebellion against, as he viewed it, the moral, political and intellectual decay then prevalent in Spain. In this Alberti accepted the Surrealist tenet whereby poetic concerns must be taken to the street, since Surrealism represents an attack on all aspects of society. He delivered his famous lecture entitled «¡Palomita y galápago, no más artríticos!» at the Ladies' Lyceum Club, an occasion that was mostly a Surrealistic event. Alberti, after rudely mocking writers from the previous generation and other highly respected intellectual values, concluded by letting loose a pigeon and firing six shots from a revolver.

Alberti now turned to politics, adopting leftist ideas, and participated in demonstrations against Primo de Rivera's regime. One night the manuscript of Pablo Neruda's *Residencia en la tierra* was brought to Alberti by Alfredo Condón, secretary to the Chilean Embassy. Neruda, Chilean consul in Java, had sent it as a poet's appeal from his confinement. Alberti would try for years to have the manuscript published, to no avail, but he entered into a correspondence with Neruda that would become a lifelong friendship. This same year of 1930 Alberti met María Teresa León, also a writer. They traveled to Mallorca, eliciting the inevitable comparison with Chopin and George Sand. Soon they married. To Alberti, this new relationship represented the strongest possible affirmation of hope after the night of *Sobre los ángeles* and *Sermones y moradas.*

*El hombre deshabitado* was performed with success; this tempted Alberti into continuing to write for the theater. On April 14, 1931, Spain became a Republic. Alberti was in Andalusia. Upon his return to Madrid he proposed to the famous actress Margarita Xirgu that she present his *Fermín Galán,* a play based on a recent event, preceding the proclamation of the Republic, the rebellion of two young officers. It was meant to recall the street ballad style in which historical or sensational events were recited across the streets of Spain. The play was presented and caused such a scandal that the metallic curtain —used only in theaters when fire broke out— had to be lowered. Alberti traveled to France with his wife where they spent a summer at the island of Port-Cross with the French poet, Jules Supervielle. In Paris that winter they befriended Picasso. They also met Alejo Carpentier, Miguel Angel Asturias, César Vallejo, Henri Michaux, and others. The couple obtained a grant to study the European theater of the day. They traveled to Germany, to the USSR, where they met Gorki, to the Scandinavian countries, and then returned to France and to Spain.

## IV. *Exile and Return*

In 1934 Alberti and María Teresa León founded the literary and revolutionary review *Octubre* in which were to collaborate among others, Luis Cernuda and Antonio Machado. That year Alberti met Miguel Hernández, who was also a good friend of Neruda's, then in Madrid. Alberti returned to Russia with his wife, where they learned of the death of Ignacio Sánchez Mejías in the bullring. The Rightist government of Gil Robles came to power. Alberti and María Teresa remained abroad, traveling to America on a tour to raise money for the striking miners of Asturias. In America, Alberti wrote the political poetry of *13 bandas y 48 estrellas.* In Mexico, he published *Verte y no verte* in 1935. Alberti had now become a *poeta en la calle* and, back in Spain after the victory of the Popular Front in 1936, he recited revolutionary poetry to the masses. During the Civil War, Alberti directed the review *Mono Azul* for the Alliance of Antifascist Intellectuals for the Defense of Culture, and became a member of the Air Force but did not fly. His adaptation of Cervantes's *Numancia* was intended to reflect the present Spanish circumstances. During the siege of Madrid, he was charged with the evacuation of art treasures from the Museo del Prado. He and his wife remained in Spain until the very end of the war, being evacuated to Oran with the Air Force General Hidalgo de Cisneros in March, 1939. From Oran they traveled by boat to Marseilles and then by train to Paris, obtaining a position as speakers for the Station Paris-Mondial on programs to Latin America. In Paris, Alberti wrote *Vida bilingüe de un refugiado español en Francia* and began *Entre el clavel y la espada.*

From France the couple proceeded to Buenos Aires. Alberti had begun writing *La arboleda perdida* and *De un momento a otro,* a play. Rafael and María Teresa arrived in Argentina on March 3, 1940, penniless. The publisher Losada offered the poet royalties of 300 pesos per month for the publication of his poetry. Alberti, still anguished over the recent cataclysm, managed to conclude *Entre el clavel y la espada.* To supplement their limited income, he and his wife collaborated in the writing of movie scripts. In 1941 their daughter Aitana was born, the most joyful event of Alberti's *émigré* life. Several plays were completed, including *El trébol florido, El adefesio,* his most successful play so far, and *La Gallarda.* Interest in poetico-musical arrangements, such as the last part of *Pleamar,* «Invitación a un viaje sonoro», dates from this period. In 1944 *Numancia* and *El adefesio* are performed by Margarita Xirgu.

Alberti continued to work on his book of memoirs, *La arboleda perdida,* as well as on his poetry. *A la pintura* appeared in 1948, and *Retornos de lo vivo lejano* was published in 1950. In 1947 he had returned to painting. His first exhibition took place in Montevideo that year, and he also became interested in joining graphics and poetry; he continues to exhibit to this day, frequently presenting extraordinary combinations of words and drawings. As he says in *Diario de un día:* «Sin duda, yo soy un poeta para quien los ojos son las manos de su poesía.»[19]

Alberti's effort to perceive and encompass the vast extensions of America is expressed in *Baladas y canciones del Paraná,* 1953-1954. Another play appears in 1956, *Noche de guerra en el Museo del Prado.* Traveling to Europe, he met Bertold Brecht, who agreed to include the play in the repertoire of the Berliner Ensemble. Unfortunately, the dramatist died before being able to undertake the performance. In 1957 Alberti and María Teresa spent four months in China. The book *Sonríe China,* 1958, in which María Teresa collaborates, with illustrations by Alberti, recalls the joys of their visit and their admiration for the Chinese people. The year 1959 sees the publication of *La arboleda perdida,* Books I and II. In 1963 Alberti and his wife return definitively to Europe, settling in Rome. In 1965 he received the Lenin Prize for Peace; and this first exhibition in Rome takes place that same year. Entitled *Roma, peligro para caminantes,* it consisted of poems and graphics. The collection of poems bearing the same title appeared in 1968 in Mexico. Alberti was very much at home in the Italian capital; the people enchanted him as did the city with its mixture of the grandiose and the near sordid. His work was now born of immediate contacts with the bubbling vitality of the people: «Es gente auténtica, generosa, estruendosa, política, muy política también. Gente que grita hasta el delirio, estalla en risas y carcajadas, con una libertad absoluta...»[20]

Alberti had already expressed his admiration for Picasso's work in *A la pintura.* Now he would compose *Los ocho nombres de Picasso,* 1970, a pictorial and poetic attempt to capture facets of the great painter's

---

[19] RAFAEL ALBERTI, *Poesía (1924-1967)* (Aguilar: Madrid, 1972), p. 854.
[20] In MANUEL BAYO, *Sobre Alberti* (Madrid, 1974), p. 94.

work. In 1972 an exhibition in homage to Alberti's seventieth birthday was held in Rome. The opening was attended by thousands of people, many from Spain, and a Spanish feast followed the event. Exhibitions of Alberti's graphic work are now not infrequent throughout Europe, combining painting, poetry, music, calligraphy. But his work as a poet continues unabated, vigorous, more hopeful at times, given the proximity to Spain. *Canciones del alto valle del Aniene,* which appeared in Buenos Aires in 1972, includes poetry that precedes *Marinero en tierra* as well as his most recent work, the *Canciones* proper.

When, in 1977, Alberti returned to Spain, political ferment awaited him there. But once more, he found life, activity, an awakening from the torpor of thirty-six years of dictatorship for his country, a return to the source for him after thirty-seven years of absence.

CHAPTER 2

FROM *MARINERO EN TIERRA*
TO *EL ALBA DEL ALHELI:* EXPLORATIONS

I. *Introduction*

In 1972, Alberti's seventienth year, Losada published *Canciones del alto valle del Aniene,* a collection encompassing the poet's work since 1964, and comprising also, for the first time, those earliest of his poems which his niece, María Alberti, had been able to assemble. Very few pieces preceding *Marinero en tierra* had been available before: none were included in Becco's 1961 Losada edition of the complete poetry, and only four poems —the last one being the triptych «Balcones»— appeared in the 1967 Aguilar volume prepared by Aitana Alberti, the poet's daughter. «Balcones» is one of the few early poems by Alberti actually published before *Marinero en tierra,*[1] and the poet notes in the introductory essay to the *Canciones...* volume: «Apenas dos poemas —'Balcones' y 'La noche ajusticiada'— lograron a través de tan larga y sostenida distancia abrirse paso hasta mi destierro argentino».[2] These same two poems appear in *La arboleda perdida.* «Balcones», the longest of Alberti's early compositions, contains elements important to all of his pre-exile poetry.

At the end of Chapter Three in Book II of his memoirs, Alberti dwells fondly on the circumstances surrounding the poem. It was inspired by Sofía, a little girl of twelve or thirteen who lived one floor down and across the street from the poet's rooms. He would see her tracing with a finger the coasts and rivers of an atlas or embroidering, «tras los cristales encendidos de su ventana» (*A.p.,* p. 155). This memory remained with him for some time «llegando a penetrar hasta en canciones de mi *Marinero en tierra*» (*A.p.,* p. 156). Later, she was «sólo un bello nombre enredado en los hilos de mis poemas» (*A.p.,* p. 156).

José Luis Tejada, in his compendious volume on Alberti's early poetry, devotes several pages to an examination of «Balcones», highlighting in particular the autobiographical element, as well as other objective aspects of the poem which he characterizes as a «salutación inspirada en las jacu-

---

[1] In the magazine *Alfar,* La Coruña, May, 1924.
[2] *Canciones del alto valle del Aniene* (Buenos Aires, 1972), p. 193.

latorias y plegarias de la tradición cristiana...»[3] The poem is in three parts; the first establishes Sofía's role as intercessor, the second describes her intimacy with elements of nature or of a scene, the third is more specifically a supplication by the speaker and concludes with an invocation of the child as light, now making explicit a relationship adumbrated at the beginning.

The first part of the composition describes Sofía in terms of light and as a middle-term between our world and that above. The name Sofía is saturated with connotations of the neoplatonic, mystical tradition, wherein Sofía is this world's intercessor to God. Neither neoplatonism nor gnosticism exerted as sustained an influence on Alberti's poetry as they did, for instance, on Cernuda's. In fact, there is little esoteric content of any sort in his work, except perhaps for the mild pythagoreanism of *A la pintura* with its emphasis on numbers and proportion. So specific a reference as early as «Balcones» is then all the more surprising, and we would not link it to the hermetic tradition were it not for the latter's elucidative role.

The poem opens with a vision of Sofía saluted by angels, a being of light in our world: «Te saludan los ángeles, Sofía, / luciérnaga del valle». God himself acknowledges her privileged character: «La estrella del Señor / vuela de su cabaña / a tu alquería». Sofía's nature is given by four lines in apposition, in which what was first mere light in darkness («luciérnaga del valle») gradually becomes not only light, but direction («linterna de los llanos»), then fragile beauty as well («Mariposa en el túnel») and finally, the poet's own guide («sirenita del mar, Sofía: »). Now, as the speaker's own muse, she leads his seaborne, dream voyage: «para que el cofrecillo de una nuez / sea siempre en sueños nuestro barco». Throughout this first part of the triptych, Sofía's aspect as mediatrix has been tempered by elements taken from a child's world: «la manzana picada» instead of evil; «los erizos del castaño» instead of pain; and also the diminutive, «sirenita». The result is to project an image of wisdom in innocence, or perhaps wisdom because of innocence.

In the second part of the triptych, the realm of childhood manifests itself fully in a dreamlike atmosphere where earth and sky make playful offerings to Sofía. Whereas previously the child was a center of interest, she is now the center of movement in a game. The ground skates around her and snow, as the sky's emissary, sings to her. The central pair of lines of the poem, «Yo traigo el árbol de Noel / sobre mi lomo de papel», manifests the speaker's hope of the last two lines of Part one («Para que... barco»). Part three widens the scope of Sofía's activity through the poet's own invocation: «Deja la aguja, Sofía. / En el telón de estrellas». She is man's emissary to heaven, and our fondest remembrance of fairyland «tú eres la Virgen María / y Caperucita encarnada»; she is everyone's familiar inspiration «Todos los pueblos te cantan de tú»; she is light,

[3] José Luis Tejada, *Rafael Alberti, entre la tradición y la vanguardia (Poesía primera: 1920-1926)* (Madrid, 1977), p. 131.

the light of poetic intelligence and of wisdom «De tú, / que eres la luz / que emerge de la luz»[4].

Among the important elements of this poem which later receive fuller development is the appearance of the muse, Sofía, in this case, other feminine beings later, objects of love or even of hate (as in *Sobre los ángeles*), imagined or remembered women, sirens, seabrides. The muse, or the siren, will be guide or companion on a longed-for sea voyage, often to snow-pure northern lands, to worlds transformed or liable to transformation. The voyage then is another motif of importance anticipated here, one that remains essential to Alberti's poetry until now. A third topic is the poetic activity itself, that is, the writing of the poem as the poem's subject. Here it becomes explicit in the lines «Yo traigo el árbol de Noel / sobre mi lomo de papel.» The dark upright fir on a white expanse accurately pictures writing on a blank page, and Christmas is antonomastic for myth in general, source of poetry and its issue. A fourth, anticipatory element is the introduction of angels whose significance comes to full fruition in the collection *Sobre los ángeles,* where they are thoroughly desacralized.

From the stylistic point of view, Alberti here uses skilfully techniques which will be frequent hallmarks of his work: (1) the radical transformation of elements of nature, giving them life and speech; (2) dramatization, in this instance, an aspect of (1); (3) imagery of ice and snow to denote purity and ethereal beauty, an unadulterated beyond; (4) the world of the child as a source of poetry and as a corollary to it; (5) the realm of the very small, an undiscovered, delicately intricate universe: «luciérnaga», «erizos del castaño», «cofrecillo de una nuez», «dedal» («En tu dedal bebía esta plegaria, / esta plegaria de tres alas:»). Although all these facets of Alberti's poetry, conceptual and stylistic motifs together, make their full appearance in the three books of poetry that will concern us now, the topic of the voyage forms the axis of this chapter. We shall examine first *Marinero en tierra* in terms of projected navigations, *La amante* as a realized itinerary, and *El alba del alhelí* as a landward exploration.

## II. *Marinero en tierra:* Chartings

In the letter that prefaces Part three of *Marinero en tierra* sent by Juan Ramón Jiménez to Alberti, and which Alberti has had included in almost all the editions of the collection,[5] Jiménez observes: «es una orilla, igual que la de la bahía de Cádiz, de ininterrumpida oleada de hermosura, con una milagrosa variedad de olores, espumas, esencias y músicas». Jiménez was peculiarly apt to capture all the echoes of these

[4] RAFAEL ALBERTI, *Poesía (1924-1967)* (Madrid, 1972), pp. 6-8. I quote from this *Aguilar* edition of Alberti's poetry and will so indicate following each citation.
[5] This letter does not appear in the Homage edition of *Marinero en tierra* (Madrid: Biblioteca Nueva, 1968), where it is replaced by a prefatory note by Miguel Ruiz Castillo.

compositions, the breezes and sceneries of that sea, because he had lived there himself as a child, he even attended the same Jesuit college. «Poesía 'popular', pero sin acarreo fácil: personalísima; de tradición española, pero sin retorno innecesario: nueva; fresca y acabada a la vez; rendida, ájil, graciosa, parpadeando: andalucísima» he recalls (*Aguilar*, pp. 56-57).

As it was presented to the jury of the National Prize for Literature, *Marinero en tierra* did not have the form in which it appears today. Juan Ramón's letter, of course, was a later addition as were the sonnets that now compose Part I. In *La arboleda perdida*, Alberti describes *Mar y tierra*, the volume that was awarded the prize: «Como su nombre daba a entender, *Mar y tierra* se dividía en dos partes. La primera agrupaba los poemas debidos directamente a la serranía guadarrameña, junto a otros de diversa temática, y la segunda —que titulaba *Marinero en tierra*—, los que iba sacándome de mis nostalgias del mar de Cádiz, de sus esteros, sus barcos y salinas» (*A.p.*, p. 163). In its present state, *Marinero en tierra* consists of an introductory poem, «Sueño del marinero»; Part I, comprising twelve sonnets, three of them on García Lorca grouped as composition Number 4; Part II with thirty-three poems in short, songlike verses; Part III, consisting of sixty-three lyrical compositions of varying length including three sonnets. The most frequent line is the octosyllable.

The book was well received, often enthusiastically, and Alberti was promptly set next to García Lorca as an exponent of poetry in a popular vein. Nevertheless, it was already noted that Alberti's «popularity» was in a traditional, literary style and that much of his verse was decidedly classical and even manneristic. Indeed, «Sueño del marinero» is a rather classical piece in twelve hendecasyllable tercets and a concluding quatrain, evincing the characteristic elusiveness of the poet, ever versatile, submitting to no tenets but those of exacting craftsmanship and a demanding vision. As the title indicates, the poem is the transcription of a dream, the dream of a seaborne voyage:

> Yo, marinero, en la ribera mía,
> posada sobre un cano y dulce río
> que da su brazo a un mar de Andalucía,
>
> sueño en ser almirante de navío,
> para partir el lomo de los mares
> al sol ardiente y a la luna fría.
>
> (*Aguilar*, p. 15)

Although quiet, this introduction contains a gradation that anticipates the launching, the movement that is to follow. The last two lines prepare us for the agitation of the ensuing two stanzas, where, amidst exclamation points, the dreamer roams from «los yelos del sur» to «las polares / islas del norte», through the «estío tropical, rojo, abrasado». But this is as yet merely an expectation. The heart of the dream, the voyage proper, begins with stanza five, in greater calm: «Mi sueño, por el mar condecorado, / va sobre su bajel, firme, seguro, / de una verde sirena enamorado.» In the central lines of the poem, the poet requests the siren's gift, a species of baptism, asking that she leave her grotto:

> a sembrarme en el pecho tu lucero.
>
> Ya está flotando el cuerpo de la aurora
> en la bandeja azul del océano
> y la cara del cielo se colora
>
> de carmín. Deja el vidrio de tu mano
> disuelto en la alba urna de mi frente,

The next step of the ritual is the dream wedding: «Gélidos desposorios submarinos» after which siren and sailor may roam their world: «El mar, la tierra, el aire, mi sirena, / surcaré atado a los cabellos finos // y verdes de tu álgida melena» (*Aguilar*, pp. 15-16).

The poem recounts not merely the dream of voyaging, but the poet's betrothal to his chosen muse, the siren — we recall Sofía of «Balcones», who was also asked «Ora por el lucero perdido». The siren is not only guide, but also motive force of the poet's ship. The voyage of creation is at this stage inseparable from the sea, and Alberti's poetry will always, in fact, look to the sea as a major source of energy. But another interesting aspect of the poem is that the dream of the poem and the dream of the voyage should be so clearly linked that poetry appears as a rediscovery of space. Also of some interest at this juncture is the presence of a somewhat «Gongoristic» vocabulary, an early glimmer of the metaphorical and lexical brilliance including Alberti's compositions in homage to Góngora as the most dazzling of his generation. Here he uses certain classical terms clearly reminiscent of the Cordovan poet such as «cano», «gélidos», «alga de nácar», «álgida».

Similar classical reminiscences inform several of the sonnets that follow «Sueño del marinero» and pursue the theme of future sea voyages. Sonnet I, «A un capitán de navío» is in alexandrines[6] hailing a seafaring friend initiated in the mysteries and joys of the voyager — the stranded poet asks to be liberated from the land's chains and taken out to sea: «todos los litorales amarrados, del mundo, / pedimos que nos lleves en el surco profundo / de tu nave, a la mar, rotas nuestras cadenas» (*Aguilar*, p. 19).

As epigraph to the poem, Alberti wrote the first line of Baudelaire's «L'Homme et la mer»: «Homme libre, toujours tu chériras la mer!»,[7] pointing to the equation, sea = freedom = poetry. In Rimbaud's poem «Le bateu ivre», the boat seems one aspect of the poet and some of the images that express liberation as a surrender to the sea are close anticipations of Alberti's: «... Et les Péninsules démarrées / N'ont pas subi tohu-bohus plus triomphants» recalls (los litorales amarrados... rotas nuestras cadenas»; «L'eau verte pénétra ma coque de sapin»[8] brings to mind the first line of the sonnet: «Sobre tu nave — un plinto verde de algas marinas.» This sug-

---

[6] The Spanish alexandrine is a line of fourteen syllables.
[7] From FRANCIS SCARFE's volume *Baudelaire* (Baltimore, 1961), p. 151.
[8] From *Rimbaud* (Paris: ed. Pierre Moreau and Michel Décaudin, 1958), pp. 120-123.

gests a parallel intuition of the liberated sea-borne voyage as an initiation to the poetic enterprise. While in Rimbaud's poem the initiation is a surrender, in Alberti's vision of himself as a «litoral amarrado» there is further the hope of being able to join reality, the land, and poetry, the sea, to achieve a harmonious unity. The same wish to join land and sea is expressed in Sonnet 2 «A Claudio de la Torre, de las Islas Canarias», where the friend's home is seen cruising towards the poet's: «Yo sé, Claudio, que un día tus islas naturales / navegarán con rumbo hacia la playa mía» (*Aguilar*, p. 19).

Charting the sea, crossing all its latitudes, is but one way of conquering or knowing its space. Another is simply to choose it as one's dwelling or personal domain. In «Jardinero» all the ocean's fathoms and surface become the lover-poet's home. He asks the gardener to cultivate in gradual ascension the depths beneath the polar ice, sky-reaching trees on the friend's island and to set mastlike trees in his own heart: «Y en mi corazón guerrero / plántame cuatro palmeras / a modo de masteleros» (*Aguilar*, p. 42). Thus will he roam over his possessions. In Poem 5 of «Marinero en tierra» proper, that is, Part III of the collection, the speaker exclaims: «Branquias quisiera tener, / porque me quiero casar. / Mi novia vive en el mar / y nunca la puedo ver» (*Aguilar*, p. 61). Here the wish expresses just as strongly the poeticization of the sea's space, and by contrast, the prosaic conditions of the poet's inland dwelling. This dwelling acquires the characteristics of a true prison when it is not even by the shore, but in the depths of the city, where the mitigating aspects of rural life are absent: «El mejor día, ciudad, / a quien jamás he querido, / el mejor día —¡silencio!— / habré desaparecido» (*Aguilar*, p. 94).

At the origin of the poet's desire to chart a future seascape is also his backward glance, a nostalgia for those years spent along the beaches of the Cádiz sea and for childhood in general. Only later, in moments of crisis, will he recall the less pleasant side of those years, the envies and angers of his days at the Jesuit *Colegio*, the narrowness of his family upbringing. For the moment he still remembers himself clear-eyed and free. There are comparatively few specific memories of his childhood that he chooses now to set down in verse; rather, the fondness of his gaze on the past comes through in the general settings of his lyrics along the shores of home and, of course, in the deeply felt longing for the sea. Also, by extension, he wishes to set to new poetry the charm of the old ballads as well as the continuing joy that he finds in the pristine songs of Gil Vicente, the clear sonorities of Garcilaso. His predilection for the latter classic was of a more familiar nature than would be his later preference for Góngora; there is affection and youthful enthusiasm in these now famous lines on the soldier-poet: «Si Garcilaso volviera, / yo sería su escudero; / que buen caballero era» (*Aguilar*, p. 80).

It is not uncommon to find side by side the playful evocation of a dreamworld and a nostalgic remembrance. In each case the aim is to transfigure a reality that seems too confining, but the elements of whose recreation are at hand, part of his real world. The act of naming, or representing, already elevates the named object above its actual conditions and sets it in a primary invented space: «—¡Por el mar, la primavera! / ¡A bordo va! // —¿De qué barco, compañero? / —Del 'Florinda', compañera» (*Aguilar*, p. 73).

The rhetoric of amplification and exclamation is freely used so that many poems seem to be but one graduated ejaculation of joy: reality acquires a new dynamism. The poet allows the transforming power of his own words to carry him along, building up to the moment of dreamed departure: «¡Alegría! / Ya mi sueño marinero / —¡alegría!— va a zarpar» (*Aguilar*, pp. 94-95). His imagination is so full of the vision of the sea that a mere ripple of wind on grass is sufficient to set his ship sailing. The exchange of landscape for seascape takes place in both directions, but more frequently, it is the sea that becomes the locale of activities generally carried out on land. These activities are often gardening or harvesting. In «Jardinero» fruit trees were to be planted as in «Pregón submarino»:

> ¡Tan bien como yo estaría
> en una huerta del mar,
> contigo, hortelana mía!
>
> En un carrito tirado
> por un salmón, ¡qué alegría
> vender bajo el mar salado,
> amor, tu mercadería!
>
> —¡Algas frescas de la mar,
> algas, algas!

> (*Aguilar*, p. 62)

This is more of a fond wish than an actual cry of exultation, but again the poet lets his words carry him through to the edge of conviction, so that by the last two lines, the poet feels that his escape into the sea is almost a reality and calls out in jubilation.

Again we meet the sea-bride, siren, muse, here gardener («hortelana») of the sea floor. Although the poet's imagined or remembered or anticipated «brides» undergo numerous transformations, these «sea changes» occur only within well-defined limits. Most frequently, the female figure will be linked to water in some way. Sonnet 7, «Rosa-Fría, patinadora de la luna», views the girl in a realm of ice and silence: «Ha nevado en la luna, Rosa-fría. / Los abetos patinan por el yelo; / tu bufanda rizada sube al cielo, / como un adiós que el aire claro estría» (*Aguilar*, pp. 24-25). As in «Balcones» a dynamic transposition endows the scenery around the girl with her own flight. Northern imagery is linked to a yearning for purity, the white background to which is added the simplicity of a space that contains only horizontal and vertical strokes. In a manner somewhat reminiscent of Mallarmé, the cold muse presides at the moment when the page is still blank, the poetic thought so virginal that its setting down on paper is a diminishing of its candor. The imagery of snow is even not infrequently linked to the otherwise life-giving force of the sea: «Sin nadie, en las balaustradas, / mi niña virgen del mar / borda las velas nevadas» (*Aguilar*, p. 89). Almost invariably there is some obstacle to the union of the speaker and his beloved. Often the poet and his chosen bride or lover exist in different elements, land and sea. At other times she is of so ethereal a nature that a mere touch might mar her:

> Amada de metal fino,
> de los más finos cristales.
>
> —¿Quién la despertará?
>
> —El aire,
> sólo el aire.
>
> (*Aguilar*, p. 35)

But in his effort either to join the bride, find her or remember her, Alberti in *Marinero en tierra* embarks on a series of poetic voyages whereby he defines a vast poetic space, a semantic and metaphorical foundation, the dreamed-of adventure of «El Sueño del marinero». The distance that remains between him and the lover of the sea, his childhood or his poetic future, will remain a constant in his poetry. The other shore may change, but the ocean to cross does not. In the next collection of poems this distance is the geography of the Peninsula itself, and Alberti's hope is to join his memory of the sea of Cádiz to his expectation of the sea of northern Spain.

## III. *La amante*: Landfall

The joy which marked many compositions of *Marinero en tierra* permeates *La amante*. In the morning of his manhood, secure in his poetic vocation, brimming with enthusiasm, Alberti's infectious happiness became a predominant aspect of his personality. José Bergamín called him «El Alegre», noting «... la alegría de su risa, juvenil y humana, derramándose claramente de todo y llenándolo todo, en su locura, como si se hubiese roto su cañería conductora y no tuviésemos a mano ninguna consigna mágica para evitarlo» (*Aguilar*, p. 98). The poems of *La amante* seem frequently explosions of joy, strong affirmations of the sensuous pleasure of existing.

*La amante* was carefully planned, tracing a journey undertaken with the specific purpose of staking out a poetic topography: «Todavía el marinero en tierra era quien se lanzaba a recorrer llanos, montes, ríos y pueblos... Rítmico, melodioso, ligero, recorrí con aquella amante ya perdida más de una centena de pueblos... Itinerario jubiloso, abierto en casi todo instante a la sonrisa» (*A.p.*, p. 221). Although Alberti states that an actual memory was the basis for the book's title, the beloved's absence as such, her inaccessibility, are the necessary ingredients of its inspiration. The itinerary does not lead to the beloved. In a sense, though absent, she is with the poet always at the source of the song.

The collection comprises four parts: «Hacia las tierras altas» (Compositions 1 to 33), «Hacia el litoral del Norte» (34 to 53), «De vuelta del litoral» (54 to 62), and «Madrid» (63 to 68). Love is the topic of more than one third of the poems, followed by what may be termed the «way-faring» motif. The sea remains as a background in a considerable number of compositions, cutting across all other themes. We will center our reading of *La amante* mainly on its amorous and geographical itineraries —the collection's very subtitle is Itinerary— both of which may be understood as metaphors for Alberti's further mapping out of his universe, essentially a continuation of *Marinero en tierra*. Characteristic of *La amante,* however, is a greater formal unity, a sustained lighthearted tone, and a consistent exploration of traditional song forms. The lyrics are short, containing frequent repetitions, exclamations and alliterations. Often, as in the opening poem, there is the clear echo of its earlier inspiration:

> Por amiga, por amiga.
> Sólo por amiga.
>
> Por amante, por querida.
> Sólo por querida.
>
> Por esposa, no.
> Sólo por amiga.
>
> *(Aguilar,* p. 103)[9]

According to the epigraph the piece was written in Madrid, that is, before departing. It stands as an emblem for the collection anticipating its playful tone and intimating the desire for unburdened affection which marks most of its love songs. This poem is a farewell song, the lover informing his lady of his intention to «travel light». Poem 2 is also a poem of departure, but it is as well a poem of arrival in that a conjectured departure calls forth a necessary return to the beloved's arms. The conclusion of the voyage is foreseen: «el aire me traería, / amante mía, / a ti» *(Aguilar,* p. 103).

This song and the next one are set in the Sierra de Guadarrama, the range of mountains that overlooks Madrid, in the heart of Castille. The poet will travel straight north through Aranda de Duero, Burgos —with smaller localities in between— to the Santander coast, turning right (east) to Bilbao, coming south to Miranda de Ebro, Aranda de Duero and back to Madrid. The relationship between the songs and their site is often slight, but rivers such as the Duero, or the Ebro, and certainly the sea, call for poems that have more perceptible links with the geography. Other settings are so significant as to make their appearance in song inevitable. Santo Domingo de Silos elicits a poem with overtones of popular religiosity, «Dialoguillo de la Virgen de marzo y el niño». The Cathedral of Burgos also dominates three compositions of which one is a *saeta.*

In the second part, «Hacia el litoral del Norte», the sea is a strong anticipated presence. The encounter takes place in Laredo, in Poem 45. The poet's eyes, full still of the memories of his other sea, fill with tears:

---

[9] The ancestor to this poem is quoted in TEJADA, *op. cit.,* p. 478, from J. CEJADOR Y FRAUCA, *La verdadera poesía castellana,* Vol. II, p. 185 (Madrid, 1924): «Si te pluguiere, señora, / conmigo te llevaría, / si quisieres por mujer, / o si quieres por amiga.»

«Perdonadme, marineros, / sí, perdonadme que lloren / mis marecitas del Sur / ante las mares del Norte!» (*Aguilar*, p. 123). Songs 45 to 53 celebrate the ocean. Song 46, one of the shortest in the book, is a ritual salute to the sea, with almost religious overtones and also a purely physical response to the ocean's immediacy: «¡Marineros, mis zapatos! // Las calles de la marina / hay que pasarlas descalzo» (*Aguilar*, p. 123).[10] Such is the familiar understanding and respect of one of the sea's intimates. In song 47, «Mi lira», the sea renews the poet's inspiration, an inspiration at once erotic and soothing, as if originating from a mythical mother-figure.[11]

Although the sea of the North, dark and turbulent, impressed Alberti greatly, there are no intrinsic differences, that is to say, differences having to do with the character of the sea itself, that mark these songs as belonging to the Cantabrian. The scenic peculiarities that stand out are manmade. «¡Ponedme la banda azul / de los mares, marineros!» (*Aguilar*, p. 125) could be another verse in that famous poem from *Marinero en tierra:* «—Madre, vísteme a la usanza / de las tierras marineras: / el pantalón de campana, / la blusa azul ultramar / y la cinta milagrera» (*Aguilar*, p. 82).

The poet's return to the heart of Castille is neatly prepared in Poem 54, where he calls on the Virgin of the Summits to bring on the dawn in order to light the way for his fisher-lass about to cross the mountain defile. The sea recedes slowly and its echo remains on the banks of the Ebro and the Duero. About to enter Madrid, the poet recalls his journey, his purpose accomplished: «Aureolado del aire / y del salitre del mar, / vuelvo de los litorales» (*Aguilar*, p. 131). By blazing a poetic road through the heart of Old Castille towards the Cantabrian, the poet turns the lands that separate him from that ocean into a familiar domain. He effects a metaphorical encounter between the two seas conceiving, as it were, a marine background for the interior.

Alberti's excursion through Castille, though it recalls the «recovery», or reaffirmation, of the Castillian countryside and traditions by the Generation of 1898, has a purpose altogether different. Theirs was an effort to unearth roots and evaluate them. Alberti's is a purely personal project. He is establishing intuitive coordinates, extracting poetry from the tension between what he sees and what he wants to see. It is in this sense also that we must view the love poetry of *La amante,* for, though it is a love-journey, the beloved remains behind and accompanies the poet only as a memory. To the departure lyrics sung for the beloved at the beginning of the book answer some homecoming songs at the end, set in Madrid. They are first a lullaby in three parts, followed by three delicately suggestive lovemaking poems. The lullaby also conveys amorous overtones: the «amante's» comb had been lost and the lover consoles her; traditionally, the connotations of the comb and women's hair have been

[10] As is well known, one must walk unshod into the Mosque and other religious precincts.

[11] The identification Sea-Great Mother is frequent and explicit in Alberti, e.g., Poem 6 y Part II of *Marinero en tierra:* «¡Marecita / madrecita; / marecita de mi sangre!»

erotic, and so they remain even within the lullaby context. Compositions 64 to 66 are more clearly erotic, as for instance, 65:

> Dormido quedé, mi amante,
> al norte de tus cabellos,
> bogando, amante, y soñando
> que dos piratillas negros
> me estaban asesinando.
>
> *(Aguilar,* p. 133)

The hair motif is joined here to that of dark eyes and the dream of water. The poet has returned home to a real or imagined lover. But he will soon leave once more, and the collection ends with a farewell love-dialog where he reasserts his Southern origins. The other, more ancient of his singing now beckons:

> ¡Al Sur,
> de donde soy yo,
> donde nací yo,
> no tú!
>
> —¡Adiós, mi buen andaluz!
>
> —Niña del pecho de España,
> ¡mis ojos! ¡Adiós, mi vida!
>
> —¡Adiós, mi gloria del Sur!
>
> —¡Mi amante, hermana y amiga!
>
> —¡Mi buen amante andaluz!
>
> *(Aguilar,* p. 135)

## IV. *«El alba del alhelí»*: Dropping Anchor

Although Alberti continues to draw inspiration from the traditional «Cancionero», there is a harshness in some of the compositions of this book that make them «... más para la guitarra que para la culta vihuela de los cancioneros» (*A.p.,* p. 183). The general impression one retains from *El alba del alhelí* —originally titled *Cales negras*— is one of brooding shadows, principally because some of the strongest poems convey this atmosphere. The folk themes that inspire many of these compositions belong to the tradition of «Andalucía la alta», the country of the High Sierras: here contrasts are not smoothed over by the tempering influence of the sea. As in most mountainous regions of the interior, links with tradition are stronger; isolation has allowed curious habits to survive. Not a large number of poems transmit specifically this atmosphere, but their impact, and their position in the central part of the book seems to affect our impression of the whole. In fact, there is a significant number of pieces that are lighthearted and playful, while almost the entire third part consists of sea-inspired poetry. The collection, though of a tenor different by and large from the two previous ones, retains many links with them and allows us to see it, with Alberti, as part of his youthful poetry.

*El alba del alhelí* has three chapters: «El blanco alhelí», comprising forty-five compositions, «El negro alhelí», also forty-five, and «El verde alhelí», with twenty-four. It is of Alberti's early collections the longest and also contains generally longer pieces. Although completed in 1926, it was not published according to José Luis Tejada until either late 1928 or more probably 1929,[12] privately, with the assistance of J. M. de Cossío. «El blanco alhelí» contains mostly light and playful poems and two interesting series of related compositions; one of fourteen «villancicos» on traditional topics such as the hardships of the Holy Family and songs of craftsmen offering their wares to the infant Jesus; another entitled «La Húngara» describing the appearance and independent spirit of a young, wandering gypsy girl. «El negro alhelí», the most intense chapter of the three, includes poems suggesting the same dramatic mystery and primitive force permeating Lorca's *Romancero Gitano*. «El verde alhelí» contains pieces on the sea, reminiscent of Alberti's earlier marine poetry.

Alberti dedicated the songs of «La Húngara» «...a una preciosa muchacha magiar, vagabunda con su familia dentro de un carro verde ornamentado de flores, pájaros y espejitos» (*A.p.*, p. 186). The ten pieces are quick impressions of her, marked by an air of distance and mystery. The idea of mutability informs most of the songs: «¡Déjame morir, vivir, / deja que mi sueño ruede / contigo, al sol, a la luna, / dentro de tu carro verde!» (*Aguilar*, p. 161). The mutability is that of life itself — the «green» of her wagon also suggests it. The last song, an echo of the first one, wherein the young gypsy has gone leaving no traces, is a series of anguished interrogations by the air itself: «¿Por qué vereda se fue? / ¡Ay, aire, que no lo sé! // ¿Por la de Benamejí? / ¿Por la de Lucena o Priego? / ¿Por la de Loja se fue? / ¡Ay, aire, que no lo sé!» (*Aguilar*, p. 165). Lightfooted, colorful and fascinating, the gypsy is a mysterious counterpart of Alberti's siren.

The mystery surrounding «La encerrada» is more oppressive, and correspondingly, the speaker's feelings are more exigent. The nine songs in this sequence trace in quick strokes aspects of the young woman's seclusion as they appear to the speaker's obsessive vision, so that his own spying becomes another lock on her door. In the first poem, the girl's imprisonment is seen as part of a conspiracy elaborated to keep the poet and his beloved separate:

> Tu padre
> es el que, dicen, te encierra.
> Tu madre
> es la que guarda la llave.
> Ninguno quiere
> que yo te vea,
> que yo te hable,
> que yo te diga que estoy
> muriéndome por casarme.

> (*Aguilar*, p. 187)

---

[12] TEJADA, *op. cit.*, pp. 531-534.

The idea of marriage introduces an element of possessiveness on the part of the suitor which suggests that the girl's liberation might be but an exchange of masters. The conspiracy keeping the suitor apart from his beloved is the central aspect of five of the nine poems. This situation appears both a product of custom and a gesture of denial specifically aimed at the intruder. The speaker's intense desire and his possessiveness belong to the same tradition as that of the girl's family and the townsmen. In the last poem through a revealing intuition, the speaker anticipates the girl's denial of his suit, and by extension, denies the power that the tradition may have on her. She makes her own choices: «—¿Qué haces tú? / —Soñando estoy / un traje para mi boda. / —¿Conmigo? / —No» (*Aguilar*, p. 192).

The poems that best transmit the oppressive, dense atmosphere of Upper Andalusia, its ancient fears and inbred narrowness are those of «Alguien». The unknown, always menacing, grows in a silence of centuries:

> Alguien barre
> y canta
> y barre
> —zuecos en la madrugada—.
> ... ... ... ... ... ... ... ...
> Algún caballo, alejándose,
> imprime su pie en el eco
> de la calle.
> ¡Qué miedo,
> madre!
>
> (*Aguilar*, p. 194)

The short, tense lines fall like an echo in the silence. In this atmosphere the familiar action of sweeping acquires sinister overtones, as if nonhuman hands brushed at the stillness in front of the door. The longer central lines are the mind, imagination, stretching out to meet the shadow. The lone horse might be death passing.

It is surprising that in «Joselito en su gloria», a poem describing the death of the famous matador in the bullring, the reigning impression is not so much of sadness, but of the bullfighter's elegance. The poem was written at the insistence of Ignacio Sánchez Mejías, the poet's friend, to whose unexpected death in the ring Alberti would later write an elegy. It is a composition in ten quatrains of assonant octosyllables. Its classical form, together with brilliant imagery anticipating at times Alberti's «Gongoristic» period, create sufficient artistic distance to mitigate the impact of the death: «Niño[13] de amaranto y oro, / cómo llora tu cuadrilla / y cómo llora Sevilla / despidiéndote del toro» (*Aguilar*, p. 209). The wounds are transformed into flowers and precious stones, traditional poetic material to which also belongs the dying man's figure. Here, as in the other

---

[13] Joselito was twenty-five years old when he was killed. Also, traditionally, matadors are frequently called «niño».

two poems on bullfighting in *El alba del alhelí,* Alberti begins to move beyond the popular forms of his early poetry, even while treating a topic that is itself in the folk style. Soon he will discard the type of poetry that this tradition had inspired.

## V. *Conclusion*

In the last song of *El alba del alhelí* entitled «Despedida», the poet envies the sailor-girl who can cry out her weariness of the sea and her yearning to live in the fields. «¡Lo que tú, quién lo dijera... / sin partir!» (*Aguilar*, p. 234). He is tired of the sea song now —the last chapter of this book, as we indicated, consists primarily of sea poetry— but needs the strength it has given him and gives him still. Ideally, he wants to sing other subjects, but to stay near the sea. «Despedida» then is a poem about the desire to write poetry other than heretofore attempted. The intense, quick vignettes, the traditional songlike lyrics, popular motifs and simple, bare language will be abandoned in favor, for a time, of intricate, learned metaphors, a dazzling verbal display, classical reminiscence.

*El alba del alhelí* concludes a well-defined period in Alberti's writing. It is a largely optimistic period, though marked by the nostalgia for past or future shores, for a world where beauty has become familiar. Alberti still appears torn between the techniques of «Vanguardist» movements and his predilection for classical form. The latter tendency comprises not only Andalusian folk forms and those of the old «cancioneros» as in *La amante* and *El alba del alhelí* and much of *Marinero en tierra,* but also the imprint of Renaissance lyricism, Garcilaso's in particular —noticeable in the sonnets of *Marinero en tierra*— the more recent influence of modernism, and the poets of 1898, notably J. R. Jiménez. Occasionally all these tendencies seem not to have been thoroughly integrated into a personal poetics. In the «Gongoristic» moment to follow, *Cal y canto,* Alberti demonstrates his virtuosity by submitting his craftsmanship to the most demanding strictures. But it will be in his «crise de conscience» and the intense exploration of this chaotic inner space —*Sobre los ángeles*— that Alberti will find a thoroughly formed, strong personal voice, suited to the needs of his divided self.

## CHAPTER 3

## CAL Y CANTO TO YO ERA UN TONTO Y LO QUE HE VISTO ME HA HECHO DOS TONTOS: A CONTAINED TUMULT

### I. Introduction

Alberti's poetry took its most decisive turn in the years 1926-28. He wanted to move beyond the folk-inspired motifs to another tradition. The more elaborate aspect of the classics —i.e., not the light, songlike lyrics of Gil Vicente or Barbieri's *Cancionero*— had already attracted him in *Marinero en tierra,* inspiring the introductory «Sueño del marinero» and the ensuing sonnets. Now, with the tercentenary of Góngora's death approaching, the great baroque poet was enthusiastically recalled.

Alberti's celebration of Góngora in his own verse had surfaced earlier in Sonnet 10 of *Marinero en tierra* «Catalina de Alberti, Italo-Andaluza», where his ancestor is termed «... honor de la estirpe gongorina» (*Aguilar,* p. 27). Remembrance of Góngora in that particular sonnet shows that he held the Cordovan poet in marked esteem, thus displaying a sensible disregard for the then current critical opinion in Spain. With respect to his own poetry and that of Lorca, Alberti recalls that «... Góngora nos llegaba muy oportunamente. Su glorificación y las infiltraciones de sus lianas laberínticas en nuestra selva poética nos ayudarían a conjurar el mal» (*A.p.,* p. 235). The evil that Alberti refers to was «Un andalucismo fácil, frívolo y hasta ramplón que amenazaba con invadirlo todo...» (*A.p.,* p. 235). To counter this, in the spirit of Góngora, Alberti would return to traditional, strophic forms, remold classical myths, and even compose a «Soledad tercera» of his own in the pattern of Góngora's first and second «Soledades».

The tricentennial was duly celebrated in 1927, a year of great achievement for Alberti and for the poets of his generation. But already, Alberti felt the early signs of an oncoming emotional upheaval: «¡Fue un gran año aquel 1927! Variado, fecundo, feliz, divertido, contradictorio (...) y una tremenda tempestad de toda índole me sacudía ya por dentro» (*A.p.,* p. 252). As did Góngora, who could be by turns «angel of light» and «angel of darkness», Alberti was to enter his own dark night, to struggle against his host of apocalyptic angels: «¿Qué espadazo de sombra me separó casi insensiblemente de la luz, de la forma marmórea de mis poemas inmediatos, del canto aún no lejano de las fuentes populares, de mis barcos, esteros y salinas...?» (*A.p.*, p. 263). Such inner turmoil could not comply with the outer structures of renovated Classicism. It demanded other, less conventional frames, whose stringencies would be internal, though equally exacting. Although Alberti was to encounter Surrealism at this time also, and some of the imagery of *Sobre los ángeles* seems to answer to the tenets of the movement, he did not quite commit himself to this vogue as yet. Certainly, there are elements in *Sobre los ángeles* recognizable as Surrealistic; Surrealism had much to do with the appearance of oneiric material in his poetry. But on the whole, his control remains too strict, the symmetries of the book too well defined. One of the main injunctions of Surrealism, unhampered, automatic writing, was patently not observed by the poet, despite his own assertion that he often wrote «con un automatismo no buscado» (*A.p.*, p. 265). The composition of these poems is too well wrought for the unconscious to have been left in complete command.

Closer to Surrealism in form and intent, but perhaps less successful from the lyrical point of view, is *Sermones y moradas,* the collection that follows *Sobre los ángeles.* In it, the versicle form, as well as the slightly declamatory tone, does not allow the sharp-edged lyricism characteristic of *Sobre los ángeles* to surge forth. Much of what in *Sobre los ángeles* had been fruitful mystery has now become obscurity.

The collection examined in the conclusion to this chapter will be *Yo era un tonto y lo que he visto me ha hecho dos tontos.* In this sequence Alberti has joined his love for the comics of silent film with some mildly Surrealistic techniques and much happy inventiveness to write a most eloquent poetic encomium of the cinema and its slapstick heroes. Within the limits it sets itself, this book of poems is among Alberti's most effective and succeeds in capturing not only an art form but a stage in the growth of our century.

Because of the exceptional importance of *Sobre los ángeles* in Alberti's work, as well as in the Spanish poetry of our era, we shall devote the larger part of this chapter to a reading of the collection with some emphasis on structure and imagery. Our examination of *Cal y canto* will underline the idea of reinventing a reality according to the tenets of formal beauty and the expression of constant tension between stability and flux.

## II.  *Cal y canto,* 1929

The title of this collection was first *Pasión y forma,* but Alberti changed it to *Cal y canto* at the suggestion of José Bergamín. Both titles describe the two basic components of these poems: the delineation of immediate reality in its profusion, but submitted to a reordering in tense moments of formal equilibrium. His song, Alberti says, would be «como en un cofre de cristal de roca, en una blanca y dura urna, aunque transparente. Sometería el verso métrico a las presiones —y precisiones— más altas. Perseguiría como un loco la belleza idiomática, los más vibrados timbres armoniosos» (*A.p.*, p. 234). The poet wanted to frame his world according to clear, esthetic guidelines and to write poetry whose subject, ultimately, was the poetic vision itself.

*Cal y canto* is divided into eight chapters of very unequal extension. The second and most elaborate one, for instance, has eleven compositions of some length —a few in several parts— while the fourth comprises only one, the «Soledad tercera». Alberti also experimented with a variety of verse forms, going from the stately, classical sonnet to free verse compositions and including the *silvas*[1] of «Soledad tercera», assonant tercets, traditional ballads, quatrains, and others. Underlying all these poems is the idea of transformation, and its corollary, renewal. Alberti's personal myth of the sea is transformed and renewed, as is traditional mythical material (Venus, Orpheus, Narcissus, Romeo and Juliet). The cosmos is redrawn according to the poet's dynamic imagination.[2] On occasion, veiled behind playful or biting irony, the edge of disillusionment appears, and already dangerous angels, «Los ángeles albañiles», are hovering; but on the whole, the collection is a strong, selfconfident celebration of the powers of the poetic word.

Because critics have been more aware of the shadow of Góngora behind this poetry than Alberti was himself, they have had some difficulty in placing *Cal y canto* within the developing curve of the poet's work. Thus Luis Felipe Vivanco, although he does make the very sound point that Alberti reinstates Góngora as a poet of the twentieth and not of the seventeenth century, would remove Parts 3, 5 and 6 from the collection and place them in *Yo era un tonto...*[3] He reasons that these chapters contain poetry of a mostly burlesque character that does not fit in the context of «belleza poética más esencial»[4] of the rest. But Alberti, as he is careful to point out, conceived of his books as totalities; the poems of Parts 3, 5 and 6, though playful on the surface conform in essence to the main axis of the book which is an effort to capture the birth of the poetic image. «Venus en ascensor» may seem whimsical, but its playfulness is underpinned by a serious self-reflective intent: an examination of the perennial and the transitory in myth, and the affirmation of poetic value in structured language *per se*. These poems present a needed contrast to those compositions of a superficially more «classical» or Gongoristic cast.

*Cal y canto* offers a perfectly coherent structure as a whole. The presence of Góngora appears in its true perspective as that of the famous

---

[1] The *silva* is a traditional verse form of hendecasyllables, alone or combined with heptasyllables. Originally, it followed no specific rhyme pattern or strophic form. It was used by Góngora in his «Soledades» (hendecasyllables) as well as by, among others, Rodrigo Caro and Quevedo.

[2] One is reminded of Rimbaud's vision in «Phrases»: «J'ai tendu des cordes de clocher à clocher; des guirlandes de fenêtre à fenêtre; des chaînes d'or d'étoile à étoile, et je danse» [*Rimbaud*, ed. by Moreau and Décaudin (Paris, 1958)], p. 205.

[3] L. F. VIVANCO, «Rafael Alberti en su palabra acelerada y vestida de luces», in *Introducción a la poesía española contemporánea* (Madrid, 1957), p. 227.

[4] *Ibid*, p. 228.

and admired ancestor to whom the present poet bows and to whom he offers his own poetry, the work of a poet of *this* century. The highest token of his admiration, the «Soledad tercera», is placed at the very center of the book as Part 4. Parts 1 to 3 are a reflection on beginnings, on a poetic past; Part 1 would be a vision of the poem as potential, with language framing the birth of the poem; Part 2 views the poet's own established myths, described in terms of movement, and his personal preference for the sea, bullfighting, the presence of Spain; Part 3 renders other aspects of these themes in the more traditional «romance» form and leads to the «Soledad». Parts 5 to 8 are a vision of the present and a glance at poetry to come. This is the myth of today's language. Part 5 corresponds to Part 1 in that it offers a thoroughly modernized, breathless rendition of beauty, ironic, centered on the idea of motion, of travel. Part 6, which opens with «Venus en ascensor» is an equally modern picture of traditional poetic material, Venus, death, dreams. It is an echo of Part 2, the poet's personal past myths. Part 7 offers today's context for myth-making, such as the «flapper» of the 1920's («Miss X...»), landmarks and sports heroics «Nadadora», and «Platko». Part 8 «Carta abierta» is a poetic program for the future, a counterpart to the ballads of Part 3 and to «Soledad tercera».

In metaphorical density, syntactical elaboration and even in the fund of imagery from which Alberti draws, the four sonnets of Part 1 are definitely Gongoristic. But there is nothing specific in them that takes one directly back to Góngora; it is more an air that pervades these pieces and makes the reminiscence inevitable. «Araceli», first of these sonnets, celebrates the constellated sky, while attempting to capture its gradual manifestation: «Ara del cielo, dime de qué eres, / si de pluma de arcángel y jazmines, / si de líquido mármol de alba y pluma» (*Aguilar*, p. 241). The last of the four sonnets, «Amaranta», is specifically linked to Góngora by its epigraph «... calzó de viento...» taken from the «Polifemo». Elsa Dehennin sees in this poem also a reference to the poetic activity: «This Gongoristic sonnet means then a species of creative *prise de conscience* that is not irrelevant, we believe, to the success of the 'Soledad tercera'. It is an allegorical sonnet that unveils for us a universe of solitude where the work accomplishes itself and where the poet learns of the passionate ties that link him to the matter he recreates».[5] «Passionate» is here the operative word, though the passion is restrained and then denied. For the desire elicited by «Rubios, pulidos senos de Amaranta, / por una lengua de lebrel limados» is inhibited by ever-watchful, personified solitude, itself suffused by the passion it thwarts in the lover: «Su cuerpo en sombra, oscuro, se le enciende, / y gladiadora, como un ascua impura, / entre Amaranta y su amador se tiende» (*Aguilar*, p. 243). This sonnet is a proper conclusion to the quartet that began with a tentative birth out of matter to reach moments of breathless, violent movement in «Busca»: «Rompe la aurora en el acantilado / su frente y por el

⁵ ELSA DEHENNIN, *La Résurgence de Góngora et la génération poétique de 1927* (Paris, 1962), p. 173. My translation.

viento marinea» (Aguilar, p. 242). «Reflejo» maintains the idea of rapidity joined to that of evanescence: «Y en el agua, cabellos, flores, plumas, // a la deriva de la ventolina, / huyendo, verdes, de la voz del faro, / coronan el mantel de las espumas» (Aguilar, p. 242), while the sense of upheaval has already diminished. All four sonnets try to capture a source of poetic imagery, to create a myth of the transitory: «Araceli» traces the nascent night sky; «Busca» seizes the meeting of dawn and a sea almost foreign to the poet who seeks in it earlier memories of another ocean; «Reflejo» depicts a morning sea viewed from far inland, carrying with it in its reflections the language of earlier poems «cabellos», «flores», «plumas».

The «Soledad tercera», which constitutes Part 4 of Cal y canto, is presented as a direct tribute to Góngora: «Homenaje a Don Luis de Góngora y Argote (1627-1927)».[6] In her book on Góngora and the Generation of 1927, Elsa Dehennin devotes a large portion of her chapter on Alberti to a study of this piece. With respect to Alberti's imitation of Góngora, she states: «Alberti has taken the Gongoristic creation to its own conclusion: thus, he has not betrayed Góngora, but he has not imitated him either. What is more, he has renovated the Gongoristic discipline, which governs many another poem of Cal y canto in terms of his own creative norms».[7] Góngora had planned on writing four «Soledades» of which the third one would be that of the woods, and Alberti duly continued the tradition by writing his own woodland «Soledad», which he subtitled «Paráfrasis incompleta». The poem's anecdotal support is appropriately slight. The wind awakens a young pilgrim and leads him into a wood. A sudden shower brings to life tree-formed dryads, further enlivened by the oreads, and these minor deities seem to form a close, loving ring around the youth. But their lascivious threat disturbs the wind, its originator; it sends in a fiery unicorn, as always the defender of virginity, who frightens the nymphs back into their previous arboreal form.

The «paraphrase» seems purest, modernized Góngora. «Hipérbaton», multi-valent vocabulary, «cultismos» in tightly interwoven complexity —Alberti had wanted in Cal y canto «una difícil carrera de obstáculos» (A.p., p. 235)— challenge the reader from the outset. And yet the «Soledad» remains a narrative poem, thin as the narration might be, whose development may be followed without great difficulty. It is less immediately taxing than was the compact metaphorical vision of the sonnets, for instance, or than will be the rapid fire imagery of «Miss X» or of «Nadadora». Syntactical density, inseparable from the vocabulary of «cultismos», was readily accessible to the reader acquainted with Góngora. Alberti not only makes liberal use of the Gongoristic lexicon, but presents his own modern version of it, adding to the significance of new words by situating them in this unusual context. Together with «conchas», «cítaras», we find «transatlántico», «eléctrico», «eurítmicos».

---

[6] DÁMASO ALONSO points out that, contrary to tradition, it should be Don Luis de Argote y Góngora; see his Estudios y ensayos gongorinos, p. 540. Don Luis, however, chose Góngora as the name he preferred.
[7] DEHENNIN, op. cit., p. 170. See also D. ALONSO, op. cit., pp. 559-560.

Alberti's imagination unfolds with elegance the intricate curves of the Baroque sentence, strong with the substance of nouns that we confront, like blocks of invention, at each step:

> Tanto ajustar quisieron la sortija
> del ruedo a la enclavada
> del peregrino, fija,
> columna temerosa mal centrada,
> que, a una señal del viento, el áureo anillo,
> veloz, quebrado fue, ...
>
> *(Aguilar,* pp. 275-279)

In complete, organic collaboration, action, rhythm and language give cogent, almost palpable, consistency to this world of utter imagination. Alberti is still delineating a world that he sees clearly. Later will come the anguish in which alien forces invading this boldly drawn universe will transform his language and turn it, for a time, into an instrument for painful investigation.

The three short pieces of Part 5 in *Cal y canto* explore the bridging of distances in the journeys and messages of the twentieth century. The ticket in «Madrigal a un billete de tranvía» is invested with the symbolic meaning that flowers used to have. The same transformation is undergone by the airplane of «Atentado» bearing the beloved away: «Robada por un pez de acero y lona» *(Aguilar,* pp. 283-284); the machine is a new triton on a sea of stars and spotlights. In «Tren amor» the beloved's face, etched in the train window, is borne off, a rapidly disappearing photograph. She is already in another space, even before leaving the station: «Otra nación, sin sueño, no la mía, / de otro timbre y metal, goza y alumbra, / el perfil de la rápida penumbra / de tu fotografía». Inexorably, the train, drawing away, expands the distance between the two lovers as if the space within a picture were to grow until its elements lost all relation to one another: «Inútil claroscuro, inútil duelo, / roto por el espacio vengativo, / segador del enlace fugitivo / de tu anhelo y mi anhelo» *(Aguilar,* p. 284).

As counterpart to the mechanics of modern fables, the compositions of Part 6 present traditional poetic material in contemporary garb. Climbing through the heavens in «Venus en ascensor» («Cielos 1-7»), the twentieth-century love goddess traverses on each floor of heaven the setting for each moment of the amatory game, all in business-like terms, from the first floor:

> Abogado y notario de los males de amores.
>
> Eros, toga, monóculo y birrete,
>   clava a sus señorías
> en el arco voltaico de un billete
>   de cinco mil bujías.

—love's darts— to the seventh, the necessary, religious consecration, streamlined, artificial, too: «Séptimo: Bar azul del escándalo: Dios Padre y la Paloma» *(Aguilar,* pp. 287-289). Other compositions treat in equally biting terms such «Romantic» themes as death, «Mi entierro» subtitled («Naturaleza muerta»); dreams and spirits in «El caballero sonámbulo»; fairy tales, «Asesinato y suicidio».

The tree compositions of Part 7 celebrate contemporaneous heroes, the butterfly-like transience of the lost «flapper» in «Miss X», a channel swimmer in «Nadadora»[8] and «Platko», the famous Hungarian goalkeeper of the Barcelona soccer team. In *La arboleda perdida* Alberti tells of seeing the match between San Sebastián and Barcelona, where Platko's heroic play (he was injured, but returned) won the day for the Catalan team.[9] The slightly Gongoristic reminiscences of the poem were to close this period of Alberti's poetry. In fact, he had already begun *Sobre los ángeles*.

«Carta abierta», the last part of *Cal y canto,* represents a look backward to poetic origins: «... Colegio sobre el mar. / Infancia ya en balandro o bicicleta», an embracing of present-day realities: «De lona y níquel, peces de las nubes, / bajan al mar periódicos y cartas» and a look forward to upcoming work: «Sabed de mí, que dije por teléfono / mi madrigal dinámico a los hombres» (*Aguilar,* pp. 307-309). It rounds out the experiments of *Cal y canto* on a note of hope and confidence, soon to be shattered by the spiritual upheaval in *Sobre los ángeles.* The poem is presented as a fragment with the first and last sheets missing, and its very title underlines the idea of incompleteness. It is a most appropriate conclusion to a collection highlighted by formal experimentation in the guise of both traditional and contemporary composition.

## III.   «Sobre los ángeles»

*Sobre los ángeles* is the most important collection written by Alberti before his exile; indeed, many critics consider it his highest poetic achievement, and Geoffrey Connell sees it as «the greatest poetic work of the twentieth century».[10] It is certainly an impressive series of poems, of great beauty and also of great difficulty. The compositions are not grammatically abstruse as are those of *Cal y canto,* nor does the imagery present the same character of intricacy. For Alberti is not now engaged in a poeticization of daily experience, but in trying to identify suddenly unchained, antagonistic and destructive forces that flail his inner being. This upheaval distorts his perception and undermines the supports of his reality; in defining the enemy, as if to name his nature were an exorcism, a new vocabulary must be forged out of the ruins of a crumbling world.

*Sobre los ángeles* appeared in 1929, the same year as *Cal y canto,* and the great difference between these two works confirmed many critics in the opinion that the poet's development answered the mood of the

---

[8] This poem is somewhat reminiscent of APOLLINAIRE's «Zone». It is not certain, however, that Alberti knew of the French poet's work.

[9] *La arboleda perdida,* pp. 266-267.

[10] CONNELL, *op. cit.,* p. 17.

moment. Alberti's subsequent work has not dispelled this belief.[11] Nevertheless, there is a perfectly coherent evolution in the poet's work until now, a preference for the same basic themes, an ever renewed and yet ever recognizable style of metaphor. And as for the new conditions evinced by *Sobre los ángeles,* while they express a deeply personal struggle in an unmistakably Albertian manner, they are a poetic moment through which other poets of his generation, notably Cernuda and Lorca, also passed. All three, in descending to previously unexplored regions of their minds, used a language akin to that of Surrealism, though they did not embrace its doctrines wholeheartedly.

Alberti, in the throes of the deepest emotional turmoil, wrote, he says, «... a tientas, sin encender la luz, a cualquier hora de la noche, con un automatismo no buscado, un empuje espontáneo, tembloroso, febril, que hacía que los versos se taparan los unos a los otrs, siéndome a veces imposible descifrarlos en el día» (*A.p.,* p. 265). And yet, especially in the first two parts of *Sobre los ángeles,* his poems have a polished coherence that André Breton's «automatisme psychique» does not allow for.[12] There *is* an impact of Surrealism recognizable in this poetry, particularly in the third part of the collection. But by and large, Alberti worked well within the demands of form.

The evidence of careful composition is manifest not only in individual poems of *Sobre los ángeles,* but in the general organization of the book. It is divided into three parts, and an «Entrada» with one poem «Paraíso perdido», which serves as an introduction to the work. This poem captures its spirit and gives some idea of its intensity. Like *Sobre los ángeles* in its totality, «Paraíso perdido» is developed in three moments of increasing anguish arising from (1) the realization of a loss or an essential absence within and the questioning entailed by this awareness; «¿Adónde el Paraíso, / sombra, tú que has estado? / Pregunta con silencio»; (2) the further realization that the world surrounding the poet remains silent, that its most basic elements offer him no hold; there is no foundation to reality — «Diluidos, sin forma, / la verdad que en sí ocultan, / huyen de mí los cielos»; (3) the fear of being engulfed by the darkness around him, an appeal to the last resources of his mind, but his own angel («—Angel muerto, despierta») is unanswered, for the angel is dead. The lost paradise of earlier life remains unattainable and the poet contemplates an existence «... sin luz para siempre» (*Aguilar,* pp. 317-318).

In his excellent study on *Sobre los ángeles,* C. M. Bowra explains the three parts of the collection as 1) «the actual crisis immediately after it has happened (...) the sense of emptiness and meaninglessness which it

[11] CARLOS DE ONÍS, in his book *El surrealismo y cuatro poetas de la generación del 27* (Madrid, 1974), can still say: «... en Alberti parece que no puede hablarse, en general, de más unidad que la que resulta de su tendencia al cambio, a la movilidad, a intentar siempre lo más nuevo y del modo más extremado posible, a ensayar nuevos caminos, nuevos temas, nuevas fuentes de inspiración, sin detenerse mucho tiempo en lo que parecía un logro definitivo», p. 151.

[12] For a detailed account of the effect of Surrealism on the literary life of Spain in the late twenties and the thirties, see C. B. MORRIS, *Surrealism in Spain* (Cambridge, Univ. Press, 1972).

brings»; 2) «this sense of emptiness grows into something more anxious and more troubled, a conflict of light and darkness, and darkness triumphs»; 3) «Alberti slowly and laboriously picks up the broken pieces of himself and sees what remains after the catastrophe and what lessons he has learned from it».[13] While we would agree with this outline, some important qualifications bear on the specific intent of each part and of its components. Each section is entitled «Huésped de las nieblas» which suggests that, even though there is a progression in the book, it is not a progression towards discovery for the darkness remains throughout. Rather with the growth of the darkness there is a corresponding intensifying of the poet's will to survive. The final effort in «El ángel superviviente» is a sheer poetic act of will, where a lifeline is woven out of nothingness. In this sense the progression of the poems would be from a realization of inner chaos to a correlative vision of surrounding chaos, to a consequential return within the self, an attempt to reach deeper layers of the spirit, from which to begin a reconstruction. C. B. Morris bases his enlightening study of *Sobre los ángeles*[14] on the well-known statements of Alberti in the «Indice autobiográfico» of his *Poesía* in both the Losada and Aguilar editions: «1928. Amor. Ira. Cólera. Rabia. Fracaso. Desconcierto. *Sobre los ángeles*». Our emphasis will fall primarily on the poem's role in concretizing the unknown forces assailing the poet and on its function as a means of discovery. We shall also follow the collection's development in three parts and try to define those Surrealistic elements that actually appear.

What is the nature of Alberti's angelology? Any religious references are extremely problematical. True, there are in our traditions good and evil angels, and Alberti's, in this sense, should by and large be classed among the evil ones. According to some Christian and Islamic doctrines, the order of our cosmos is sustained by various hierarchies of angels. Alberti's angels have rejected this responsibility and exult, instead, in returning the cosmos to a primeval chaos. Actually, the poet's angels are a purely personal creation, embodiments of his struggle or the focus he gives to threatening compulsions within and around him: «... ángeles... como irresistibles fuerzas del espíritu, moldeables a los estados más turbios y secretos de mi naturaleza. Y los solté en bandadas por el mundo, ciegas reencarnaciones de todo lo cruento, lo desolado, lo agónico, lo terrible y a veces bueno que había en mí y me cercaba» (*A.p.*, p. 264).

«Huésped de las nieblas» (1)[15] consists of sixteen poems, of which the third, «El cuerpo deshabitado», is itself in eight parts. If we consider individually each of the poems of «El cuerpo deshabitado», we notice that «Huésped de las nieblas» (1) divides almost evenly into two sections, each concluded by compositions bearing the same title of «El ángel bueno». There are eleven pieces in the first half and twelve in the second.

---

[13] C. M. BOWRA, *The Creative Experiment* (London, 1949), pp. 224-225.
[14] C. B. MORRIS, *Rafael Alberti's 'Sobre los ángeles': Four Major Themes* (Hull, 1966).
[15] We shall use the numeration 1, 2, 3 for clarity in referring to the three segments of the book although Alberti leaves them unnumbered.

This division is not accidental. Critics, concerned with assigning Surrealistic or Nonsurrealistic characteristics to the collection as a whole, taking literally Alberti's assertions as to the intellectual and emotional turmoil that attended its writing, have not sought further than the individual unity of the poems,[16] or, as did Bowra, the general progression of its parts. But there is a careful development noticeable in each section. In this instance, the first half of «Huésped de las nieblas» (1) recalls elements that had been the support of the «Paraíso perdido», that earlier illusory world, and have now fled, leaving an abyss of emptiness behind. In «Desahucio» the forsaken condition of his soul is painfully realized by the speaker as, unexpectedly, new «guests» want to dwell in it:

> Te pregunto:
> ¿Cuándo abandonas la casa,
> dime,
> qué ángeles malos, crueles,
> quieren de nuevo alquilarla?
> Dímelo.
>
> *(Aguilar, p. 321)*

The void within, a humid torture chamber, becomes despairingly evident with the arrival of the new inhabitants: «Humedad. Cadenas. Gritos. / Ráfagas» (*Aguilar,* p. 321).

The eight pieces of «El cuerpo deshabitado» recall moments of the separation of the speaker's inner being from its previously valued supports, expelled because they become inimical or lost because undefended. The first of these is identified as a feminine presence, perhaps a traitorous love, «El amor imposible, el golpeado y traicionado en las mejores horas de entrega y confianza» (*A.p.,* p. 264). The speaker rejected the evil spirit that this love had now become: «Yo te arrojé de mi cuerpo, / yo, con un carbón ardiendo» (*Aguilar,* p. 322). Here it is he who assumes the role of the avenging angel, expelling the sinner from Eden. Ironically, what is left behind is an equally hostile world: «¿Quién sacude en mi almohada / reinados de yel y sangre, / cielos de azufre, / mares de vinagre?» Destruction reigns, earlier defenses fall: «... se derrumban las torres, / las empinadas / centinelas de mi sueño» (*Aguilar,* p. 324). Poem 4 of this sequence situates the disillusionment already at an early moment of apparent communion:

> Tú. Yo. (Luna.) Al estanque.
> Brazos verdes y sombras
> te apretaban el talle.
> Recuerdo. No recuerdo.
> ¡Ah, sí! Pasaba un traje
> deshabitado, hueco,
> cal muerta, entre los árboles.

---

[16] There has been little attempt to define the organizing principle of Alberti's collections as completed wholes.

Yo seguía... Dos voces
me dijeron que a nadie.

(*Aguilar*, pp. 324-325)

The sham of this love is objectified as an empty suit passing by. The idea of separation, initiated from the first line where every element stands alone, is confirmed by the multiple disjunction of the last two lines. Poems 6 (I) and 7 (II)[17] return to the idea of a lost paradise as a lost city. But whereas before the speaker had taken the initiative and expelled an evil presence, now, because of his inability to defend the inner city, he is left at the mercy of invading, destructive forces: «Llevaba una ciudad dentro. / Y la perdió sin combate. / Y le perdieron». Other shadows contemplate the loss and point an accusing finger; all that is left is a dark empty husk, easy prey for the destructive angelic host: «Y ángeles turbios, coléricos, / carbonizaron tu alma, / tu cuerpo» (*Aguilar*, pp. 326-327). «Visita», Poem 8, the last composition of «El cuerpo deshabitado» is a final glimpse of the departing soul, an empty ghost.

«El ángel bueno» provides a pause but is set in the past tense. Thus, the liberating quality of its reminiscence is muted and turns into the memory of yet another bereavement. The good angel brought renewed awareness for a moment; again, the world became visible, defined in space, time and light. The angel beckoned to an awaiting presence still capable of eliciting desire. The poet's soul, immobile until now, felt a potential ripple: «—¡Oh anhelo, fijo mármol, / fija luz, fijas aguas / movibles de mi alma!» (*Aguilar*, p. 328). This moment of reprieve anticipates that later one offered by the second «El ángel bueno», but it remains a mere flicker, a too sudden illumination through the dark moments of defeat. The predominance in this opening sequence of past experience represents a last effort to capture elements of a disintegrating personality by reestablishing the rudiments of memory, its main support.

The eleven poems —not counting «El ángel bueno» (II)— that complete «Huésped de las nieblas» (1) are an exploration of the chaos that the poet's inner being has become. They express mostly a struggle with, and an awareness of, the dark forces now reigning. Present tenses predominate, as befits the surveying of an actual condition, or at times there is a movement in the poem from a past event to a present realization, the latter remaining as the final state of things. Of past emotions only reflex action is left, meaningless but still moving the mind along worn paths, as a moth towards the light, such as the heart of «Madrigal sin remedio»: «viene solo al asalto / de esas luces, espejos de ceniza, / llevadoras a un muerto sur de muertes» (*Aguilar*, p. 328). The uncomprehending «I» of «Los ángeles bélicos» is buffeted by the winds of violence. Unloosed by a disintegrating memory, past actions, resentments, rush upon one another, swirling around the impotent observer privileged only to see:

---

[17] Alberti's own numbering within «Huésped de las nieblas (1)».

53

Gentío de mar y tierra,
nombres, preguntas, recuerdos,
frente a frente.
Balumbas de frío encono,
cuerpo a cuerpo.

Yo, torre sin mando, en medio...

(*Aguilar*, p. 330)

Another basic component of the mind, logic, crumbles also in «El ángel de los números». The angel that appears in this poem is not a destructive force, but a true guardian, though a helpless one. He and the «vírgenes» have custody over angles and numbers in the ideal firmament of reason:

Vírgenes con escuadras
y compases, velando
las celestes pizarras.

Y el ángel de los números,
pensativo, volando
del 1 al 2, del 2
al 3, del 3 al 4.

Impeccable clarity of lines is the responsibility of the virgins, necessary sequence that of the angel. This condition of clear certainty is suddenly destroyed by anonymous negating forces — «Tizas frías esponjas / rayaban y borraban / la luz de los espacios». The most secure truths known since childhood («las celestes pizarras») have been cancelled; light, the laws of the cosmos and those of nature equally abolished. Only formless fogs remain. The angel of numbers lies dead on his obliterated domain: «Y en las muertas pizarras, / el ángel de los números, / sin vida, amortajado» (*Aguilar*, pp. 330-331).

In the darkness of the spirit, only negatives serve to describe. Reason once destroyed, luck, its playful counterpart, no longer has meaning, and the «ángel sin suerte» becomes a guide through a world of total contingency («Canción del ángel sin suerte»). When reason and fortune are impossible, all hope likewise disappears; nothing worthwhile awaits («El ángel desengañado»): «—Me duermo. / No me espera nadie» (*Aguilar*, (p. 332). In the next three poems there reigns a suffocating ambience, a quiet and deadly darkness allowed by the death of all that is reasonable, hopeful or even aleatory. The mind is muffled by deceit («El ángel mentiroso»), obscurantism («Invitación al aire»), and bitter hypocrisy («Los ángeles mohosos»). But now, in a movement corresponding to that of «Los ángeles bélicos», forces of a more actively destructive, violent nature find their turn. «El ángel ceniciento» amplifies to a cosmic level the conflict of his warlike brothers. The laws of nature are overturned, the bonds holding matter together, fire, water, air, and earth are broken. As a rudderless vessel, the world tumbles through nothingness: «Dando bandazos el mundo, / por la nada rodó, muerto. / No se enteraron los hombres. / Sólo tú y yo, Ceniciento» (*Aguilar*, p. 334). The ashenfaced fury of this angel, witnessed by the poet alone, is one of the most awe-some visions in the entire collection. Of equal, though less inclusive, impact is the consuming anger of «El ángel rabioso».

The second poem entitled «El ángel bueno» concludes «Huésped de las nieblas» (1). The good angel is a messenger reestablishing contact with the world of order (heaven). This new evidence of communication is enough to release previously unbearable tensions: «Dentro del pecho se abren / corredores anchos, largos, / que sorben todas las mares». Light is regained and floods earlier dark passages: «Vidrieras, / que alumbran todas las calles»; sight once more identifies the world: «Miradores, / que acercan todas las torres». Human life, interrupted, teems again and renewal is possible after the storm: «Naufragios antiguos flotan. / La luz moja el pie en el agua». There is the excitement of days to come in a world free of threat, newly innocent:

> ... ... ... ... ... ... ... ... ... ... ...
> El mundo, con ser el mundo,
> en la mano de una niña
> cabe.
>
> ¡Campanas!
> Una carta del cielo bajó un ángel.
>
> (*Aguilar,* pp. 335-336)

Because the destructiveness of the forces that assailed the poet's mind in the second part of this section was much greater, the corresponding pause, if it was to be a pause at all, had to be more pervasive. While the first «ángel bueno» adumbrated the possibility of desire for the poet, this last one reassembles the components of life itself.

The tone of «Huésped de las nieblas» (2) is set by its first poem, «Los dos ángeles». Here the conflict between light and darkness is waged, but it is a nugatory battle, for darkness is not lifted. The speaker calls upon the «ángel de luz», his ancient companion, to descend upon him and burn the dark angel who has now taken possession of his being: «Angel de luz, ardiendo, / ¡oh, ven!, y con tu espada / incendia los abismos donde yace / mi subterráneo ángel de las nieblas». Through this spiritual cauterization, the poet hopes to find relief from his anguish, though no actual deliverance. The fallen angel has become so entrenched within his soul that existence is seen as a dark symbiosis, and the flaming sword must burn his spirit to reach its indweller: «¡Oh espadazo en las sombras! / Chispas múltiples, / clavándose en mi cuerpo». The speaker identifies himself totally with the parasitic presence within, but his voice, his call for help, rises as a third force. Suffering, burning, is preferable to engulfing darkness, it is at least a kind of life. In the next strophe is expressed the hope that the enemy may yet flee:

> Vuela ya de mí, oscuro
> Luzbel de las canteras sin auroras,
> de los pozos sin agua,
> de las simas sin sueño,
> ya carbón del espíritu...

This central part of the poem defines the dark angel's domain in negative terms: «canteras sin auroras» timelessness; «pozos sin agua» limitlessness and sterility; «simas sin sueño» formlessness and ever-denied repose; «carbón del espíritu» previous light consumed into its residue. In this suffocating, anguished emptiness, the burning angel's stab brings the desirable relief of sharp pain: «Me duelen los cabellos / y las ansias. ¡Oh, quémame!» Ultimately, he knows that his existence is wedded to that of the angel of darkness: «¡Quémalo, ángel de luz, / quémame y huye!» (*Aguilar,* pp. 339-340). He can only hope that the burning angel may flee and not be engulfed also by cold mists. The speaker has resigned himself to his domination.

The poems that follow —except for another fleeting visit by «El ángel bueno»— are efforts to give form to the multifaceted violence of his evil angel. The outside world, whose asperities might tear the veil of darkness, is now unattainable. In «5», the five senses are muted, one by one, drowned. And to prevent the possibility of making any true contact with a world outside, the poet is impelled aimlessly through it by «Los ángeles de la prisa».

These poems define the conditions of the poet's soul with respect to reality without. It is lost in a world of indeterminate, smothering darkness; it can establish no communication with reality, receive no renewing of experience, since the senses are unreliable; it rushes headlong on the surface of things, breathless and unstoppable. The spirit is then closed in upon itself and visited only by torturing shades. We saw earlier how Alberti described some of these moments. To conceive clearly and to respond to this condition, we must bear in mind the poet's highly physical relationship with his environment, his need for close sensuous contact with the concreteness of things. Now anguished bewilderment bends his sensitivity inward. The inner space which he had broadened and populated with sea and mountain memories, legend and written song, has been invaded by unrelenting, formless enemies. That is why his effort here is one of concretization, for him the first moment of understanding.

In its vulnerable isolation, the soul is torn by multiple and magnified guilts, actual, anticipated or remembered. Thus in «Los ángeles crueles» a childhood moment of brutality[18] palls over all those Andalusian years. The past has retained the cruelty of recently shattered, still palpitating bodies: «En tus manos, / aún calientes, de aquel tiempo, / alas y hojas difuntas» (*Aguilar,* p. 343). Other previously cool, ice-clear memories («Rosa-Fría, patinadora de la luna»), memories of beauty set to words, are soiled and repelling, as in «El ángel de carbón». An evil love has muddied all its earlier occasions, left a darkening stain, slowly spreading: «Amor, pulpo de sombra, / malo» (*Aguilar,* p. 345).

---

[18] In a short autobiographical sketch, dated 1929, written for *La Gaceta Literaria,* Alberti recalls how, as a child, he hunted and killed small birds. See *Prosas encontradas* (edited and compiled by Robert Marrast, Madrid, 1973), p. 28. Also quoted by CONNELL, *Concerning the Angels,* p. 12.

Several of the poems that conclude Part 2 of the collection begin to move away from earlier forms and into a more nebulous, more suffocatingly solipsistic region. They represent a first descent into depths yet unplumbed in *Sobre los ángeles*. The very questions whose answers the poet needs are uncertain, mysterious, as in «El ángel del misterio» where apparent certainty dissolves quickly into anxious querying. But it is in «Ascensión» that the imagery of descent is most clearly expressed: «Azotando, hiriendo las paredes, las humedades, / se oyeron silbar cuerdas, / alargadas preguntas entre los musgos y la oscuridad colgante». The movement of the poem reflects the very opposite of what its title suggests —there is in it a bitterly ironic religious connotation— for the only ascending depicted in it takes place in the last lines, an escape rather than a rising:

> Ecos de alma hundida en un sueño moribundo,
> de alma que ya no tiene que perder tierras ni mares,
> cuatro ecos, arriba, escapándose.
>
> A la luz,
> a los cielos,
> a los aires.
>
> (*Aguilar,* p. 351)

The imagery indicates imprisonment and torture. The poet's soul is at the very bottom of a dank dungeon. At the pit's bottom, the soul's residence has been long and forgotten («tumba rota»), and it must be sought as under the cold water of abandoned mine shafts. There lie the last remnants of a past life, mere echoes, but of these, too, the soul must be stripped and then flee «a los aires».

The last poem of this section («Los ángeles sonámbulos») avows a fall from previous exaltation and an admission of defeat. The poet pictures himself, or his soul, as a defeated king, beleaguered now by endless inquiry and holding no more secrets:

> Ojos invisibles, grandes, atacan.
> Púas incandescentes se hunden en los tabiques.
> Ruedan pupilas muertas,
> sábanas.
>
> Un rey es un erizo de pestañas.

The king, the innermost spirit, is as an empty house under attack. On the poem's first part, cruel, with daggerlike lashes, questing eyes rush against the defenseless soul: «Un rey es un erizo de pestañas». The poet's deposed spirit contains nothing of value, merely ruins and a dead, incoherent past. The poet can offer nothing more: «Lo sabéis, lo sabéis. ¡Dejadme!» But listening ears insist and penetrate to the very heart: «a los sótanos lentos de la sangre, / a los tubos de los huesos. // Un rey es un erizo sin secreto» (*Aguilar,* pp. 355-356). Nothing is left, not even the illusion of dissimulation.

«Huésped de las nieblas» (2) concludes on a note of despair as harsh as that which began it. The last shreds of self-esteem have been torn away from the speaker, his dismantled being left to decay as at the bottom of a prison cell. With «Huésped de las nieblas» (3) is undertaken an arduous probing; it is an effort to reach the deepest source of conflict and confusion in order to understand. In this sense the poems of this sequence are closer, in spirit, to Surrealism. In effect, the Surrealists also saw poetry as a means of investigation. Eluard in *La vie immédiate* maintains that «Surrealism, which is an instrument for gaining knowledge and for that reason as much an instrument of conquest as of defense, works for the uncovering of the profound consciousness of man».[19] Here, at this deepest level, Breton situates that «point of the spirit» in which all oppositions, all contradictions disappear.[20] Perhaps from this field of undifferentiated potential, Alberti's last angel, «El ángel superviviente» may climb from the field of battle: «Todos los ángeles perdieron la vida. / Menos uno, herido, alicortado» (*Aguilar*, p. 378).

Insofar, then, as Surrealism exalts the role of poetry as a means of discovery, as a verbal ladder, so to speak, with which to reach that profound coalescing source within the poet, Alberti, as did Cernuda, practiced it. In the final phase of *Sobre los ángeles*, such an impulse is indeed recognizable, accompanied by certain systematic distortions of the poetic vision, distortions that allow language to find unaccustomed affinities. In his earlier poetry, Alberti had expanded his inner space and given it temporal coordinates determined by a personal and an artistic tradition. This carefully elaborated panorama came under unexpected and unrelenting attack by the chaotic forces which «Huésped de las nieblas» (1 and 2) try to concretize, perhaps contain; but, at this point in the battle the poet finds himself destroyed and bewildered, all defenses spent: «Un rey es un erizo sin secreto». It is now time in «Huésped de las nieblas» (3) to try to discover the fountainhead of discord. To this end, language must be given freer rein; the artistic consciousness, which has so far served to perceive or circumscribe dark forces, must now take greater risks. Still, it retains visible, though more covert, control. There is now a more drastic turning away than heretofore from the usual strictures of space, of time, and from the normal logic of discourse.

The search for a source must begin in time. In correspondence to Poem 1 of the collection («Paraíso perdido») defining the extent of the poet's loss, the first composition of this third section, «Tres recuerdos del cielo», delves into the past, towards the origins of poetic time for it marks also a new beginning and a final effort. The poem consists of a «Prólogo» and three «Recuerdos».[21] The «Prólogo» provides the pretemporal and prespatial setting in which the meeting with and loss of the primigenial, distant beloved took place. It also presents the transition from comparatively sedate metaphor (for Alberti) to more alogical, demanding imagery:

[19] Quoted by J. H. MATTHEWS, *Surrealist Poetry in France* (Syracuse, 1969), p. 113. My translation.
[20] ANDRÉ BRETON, *Manifetes du surréalisme* (Paris, 1970), pp. 76-77. My translation.
[21] Subtitled «Homenaje a G. A. Bécquer».

No habían cumplido años ni la rosa ni el arcángel.
Todo, anterior al balido y al llanto.
Cuando la luz ignoraba todavía
si el mar nacería niño o niña.
Cuando el viento soñaba melenas que peinar,
y claveles el fuego que encender, y mejillas,
y el agua unos labios parados donde beber.
Todo, anterior al cuerpo, al nombre y al tiempo.

Entonces, yo recuerdo que, una vez, en el cielo...

*(Aguilar, p. 359)*

The pre-lapsarian conditions depicted in the first four lines are still readily accessible. This past is composed of potentialities. All the elements contribute to the idea of a world pristine in its innocence, in which attributes are interchangeable, and differentiation does not yet exist; knowledge plays no role and therefore time is not yet. The concept of the four elements which is developed more fully in lines 5-8 is introduced first in symbolic terms: «rosa» earthbound; «arcángel» spirit of the air; «luz» fire; «mar» water. It is also possible to read these lines from a specifically edenic point of view in which case «rosa» would suggest the garden and «arcángel» the later bearer of the flaming sword. But at this early moment, neither one has «cumplido años» —here the surprising contrast between this most matter of fact, quotidian manner of marking time and its present referents («rose», «arcángel») join the concrete with the ethereal in a manner that prepares for later, more drastic conjunctions— the garden is in its primeval flowering. Muted erotic undertones linked to the concept of beginnings are also present in the same context —the sin was one of knowledge but bore carnal connotations in that it meant the loss of innocence— the «rosa» is a love token and the «arcángel» will later punish. Also knowledge and birth are joined in the image of the light's ignorance of the sea's future gender. Lines 5 to 8 explicitly picture the four elements as active, eroticized forces, but with an undifferentiated eroticism, love itself being as yet merely an impetus without object. While at first one may be puzzled by the objects to which the four elements are drawn —human features— the last line provides a possible context wherein they belong. In it the poet visualizes cosmic time and space in terms of his own life («yo recuerdo...») and the pregenetic condition that it recreates refers to his own existence before the fall into love. The attribution of human desire to the cosmic forces is thus a perfectly coherent and not particularly Surrealistic poetic vision.

As we read the three «Recuerdos», we realize that their supposed successiveness («Primer», «Segundo», «Tercer») may be one of remembrance, but does not refer to that of the «events» recalled. «Primer recuerdo» concludes with the beloved dead and remote. «Segundo recuerdo» recalls the first meeting and «Tercer recuerdo» the first moment of love. But in cosmic time, or pre-lapsarian time, eternity reigns, and the characteristic of things eternal is not that they have no end, but that they have no beginning. In cosmic time successiveness does not exist. The poet separates his visions from his fallen, temporal condition.

The poems themselves pursue the cosmic theme. In the first one, the beloved is described in earthbound imagery, full of potential though still virginal; in her, action has not yet begun: «Paseaba con un dejo de azucena que piensa, / casi de pájaro que sabe ha de nacer». Her being is in a constant state of total receptivity to her surroundings. «Blanca alumna del aire, / temblaba con las estrellas, con la flor y los árboles. / Su tallo, su verde talle». The active element in the poem belongs to the lover: «por cavar dos lagunas en sus ojos / la ahogaron en dos mares». Here the contact is seen as a destructive force. The lover could not resist eliciting a response from the «Blanca alumna», but the response is fatal. The suggestion of an earth-sky interaction is maintained («anterior (...) a la lluvia y a las palabras», i.e., before the separation of land and water). The serene calm of the female presence, her existence in a state of total osmosis with her environment is shattered. Out of this violence grows differentiation, isolation and death as the sharply caesured final line suggests: «Nada más: muerta, alejarse» (*Aguilar,* pp. 359-360).

«Segundo recuerdo» and «Tercer recuerdo» retrace the history of the «courtship» of mutual damnation — from a «not yet» position, that is, viewing subsequent ill-fated events in terms of the pristine state that preceded them. «Segundo recuerdo» contains the greatest number of specific references to those events that preceded the advent of man, the rebellion of Lucifer and his angels:

> También antes,
> mucho antes de la rebelión de las sombras,
> de que al mundo cayeran plumas incendiadas
> y un pájaro pudiera ser muerto por un lirio.

The lines that follow refer to various moments of differentiation, that is, of decay or descent:

> Antes, antes que tú me preguntaras
> el número y el sitio de mi cuerpo.
> Mucho antes del cuerpo.
> En la época del alma.
> Cuando tú abriste en la frente sin corona, del cielo,
> la primera dinastía del sueño.
> Cuando tú, al mirarme en la nada,
> inventaste la primera palabra.
>
> Entonces, nuestro encuentro.
>
> (*Aguilar,* p. 360)

In this poem, it is the beloved who takes the active part in a movement that echoes the lover's in «Primer recuerdo». But events here antedate the fall into history. The beloved's action has a creative effect; it is at the origin of language. The poet continues to envision himself as the sky upon which «earth» traces her dreams. «Tercer recuerdo» remembers moments of conjunction or mutual interaction. The poem becomes clearer if we assign the male role, or that of the poet, to elements from above or verticality, and the female role to earthbound images.

Examined in this light, the first four poems of this «Surrealistic» portion of *Sobre los ángeles* conform to formal principles that seem to negate some of the premises of the movement. Symbolic or imagistic patterns, though perhaps more hermetic than heretofore, are not arbitrary. Nor do they develop haphazardly according to free association. As a unit, they are structured in terms of the intuition to be communicated. The «Prólogo» gives the pre-temporal setting of that first encounter; it begins with potential and ends in destruction. In the second «remembrance» the poet or lover is seen in terms of the beloved's effect on him, the results of her questioning; it begins with destruction —fallen angels— and ends with potential — the first word. The final piece presents, as we saw, wedded instants «... nuestra luna primera».

The poems that follow move towards indefinite levels of the mind, exploring them with more extreme, jagged, discordant imagery. Nevertheless, it is possible to discern a pattern of organization for the sequence as a whole. Following the «Recuerdos» and «El ángel de arena» which pursue the love remembrance, two poems of a transitional nature introduce the theme of betrayal or deceit central to later developments. «El alba denominadora» suggests a feminine betrayal. «El mal minuto» indicates betrayal by undefined forces around the poet. The next four poems explore a somber, shackled childhood. The darkness and sterility now threatening poetic invention is the central concern of the three poems that follow, and the next five delve into the poet's fallen condition and his attendant punishment. The final poem «El ángel superviviente» represents the first painful step out of the dungeon.

In «El alba denominadora» the woman-muse no longer has the power to inspire the poet; the names that her dreamed presence suggests are negations: «Sueño equivocado, Angel sin salida, Mentira de lluvia en bosque» or images devoid of their former fruitfulness: «¿Vertida estrella, Confusa luz en llanto, Cristal sin voces?» The poet cuts through his own indecision with a sharp denial: «No. / Error de nieve en agua, tu nombre» (*Aguilar,* p. 362). In «El mal minuto» the laws of time and space are abrogated in Surrealistic fashion: «alguien me enyesó el pecho y la sombra, / traicionándome». This occurred in the full height of his innocent enthusiasm «Cuando para mí eran los trigos viviendas de astros y de dioses». The mysterious event pinned him down, cinerary white, in the high noon of hope. Even his shadow's quick elusive dusk was permanently encrusted in the same deadly substance. His sentiments («el pecho») and his freedom («la sombra») became petrified. It was thus that he lost his poetic joy and was chained to the minute «el del secuestro, por el mar, de los hombres que quisieron ser pájaros» (*Aguilar,* p. 362). Forces and elements by nature propitious become devious; even the sea, that expansive, generous «Great Mother» seems now morose and mean-spirited.

Both pieces depict a betrayal that affected, in particular, the poet's mainspring of inspiration, turning it away from joy and towards despair. In the ensuing poems on childhood, Alberti explores those early instances of constriction and deceit which he now sees as preludes to his present

61

condition. In these poems of exploration, language struggles to capture early, cataclysmic moments, not merely as remembrances, but as recreations and exorcisms. Alberti situates the origins of his poetic disposition in those childhood days, but from the vantage point of his present despairing condition, this disposition is seen negatively, as a species of sacrifice, an unequal exchange. It is now necessary to seek the remote source of reverberations, those distortions of early innocence that were poetically fated, and they must be re-created with the only language able to do so: a more thoroughly liberated, near-chaotic expression at the very edge of intelligibility. As Aragon has said, this type of poetic utterance is «... at each step reinvention of the language. Which implies breaking the molds of language, the rules of grammar, the laws of discourse».[22]

However, Alberti has again stopped short of surrendering his artistic consciousness. The poems are enthymemically structured, though sufficiently unconstrained to communicate with immediate power the intensity of the emotional vortex that tugs at the poet. In «El ángel de las bodegas», he draws a parallel between the betraying of the «flor del vino» and that of the sap and essence of his family history. Wine must be seen in terms of its visionary, liberating potential. The poet discovers his first awakening to poetic good and evil, the suffering and the potential of his spirit, as he recalls the loss of the «flor»: «Fue cuando la flor del vino se moría en penumbra / ... / Y comprobé que un alma oculta frío y escaleras». While, together with the wine, an entire world of possibilities is lost to the poet-child in the empty cellar where darkness is invading the last sources of light («cera») and life («aceite») —«Las penumbras se beben el aceite y un ángel la cera»— their renewed possibility remains: «Guardadme el secreto, aceitunas, abejas» (*Aguilar*, pp. 363-364).

The long poem «Muerte y juicio» recreates the child's death to childhood, his premature loss of innocence. The first part «Muerte» considers the conditions after the loss in imagery where a light-darkness contrast predominates: «A un niño, a un solo niño que iba para piedra nocturna, / para ángel indiferente de una escala sin cielo...» Darkness acquires a positive value as unburdened oblivion («piedra nocturna») or indifference towards the absolute («una escala sin cielo»). But the tranquility, the waning flame of innocence, was killed and replaced by the demands of persevering light:

>  ......... él mismo, sin vida.
>  No aliento de farol moribundo
>  ni jadeada amarillez de noche agonizante,
>  sino dos fósforos fijos de pesadilla eléctrica,
>  clavados sobre su tierra en polvo, juzgándola.
>  Él, resplandor sin salida, lividez sin escape, yacente, juzgándose.

For, with the power of sight, comes the responsibility and destiny to use it, therefore, the burden of judging. Part 2 «Juicio» recreates the events that led to this forced commitment in terms still of light and darkness

---

[22] Louis Aragon, *Les Yeux d'Elsa* (Paris, 1959), «Préface», p. 14. My translation.

first, then of knowledge and ignorance. Birth is seen as violent conflict: «Bambolea el viento un vientre de gritos anteriores al mundo»; school is life-denying tedium or confusion («Perdido entre ecuaciones, triángulos, fórmulas y precipitados azules»). The child was deprived of innocence and enthusiasm, his only free possessions: «... no creíste ni en Venus que nacía en el compás abierto de tus brazos / ni en la escala de plumas que tiende el sueño de Jacob al de Julio Verne. / Niño. // Para ir al infierno no hace falta cambiar de sitio ni postura» (*Aguilar*, pp. 365-366).

To this group of poems that explore remote and lasting disillusionment also belongs «Expedición». It is the most Surrealistic in tone and imagery, and we quote it in full:

> Porque resbalaron hacia el frío los ángeles y las casas,
> el ánade y el abeto durmieron nostálgicos aquella noche.
> Se sabía que el humo viajaba sin fuego,
> que por cada tres osos la luna había perdido seis guardabosques.
>
> Desde lejos, desde muy lejos,
> mi alma desempañaba los cristales del tranvía
> para hundirse en la niebla movible de los faroles.
> La guitarra en la nieve sepultaba a una rosa.
> La herradura, a una hoja seca.
> Un sereno es un desierto.
>
> Se ignora el paradero de la Virgen y las ocas,
> la guarida de la escarcha y la habitación de los vientos.
> No se sabe si el Sur emigró al Norte o al Oeste,
> 10.000 dólares de oro a quien se case con la nieve.
>
> Pero he aquí a Eva Gúndersen.

(Aguilar, pp. 366-367)

Here Alberti has dislocated the normal structures of language in a manner very close to Surrealism. Logic is abolished and causal connectives are used with complete arbitrariness as in lines 1 and 2. Verbs are given an alien field of activity, and matter acquires volition (lines 3 and 4). Rigorous, arithmetical references are incongruously invoked (line 4). Spatial coordinates no longer apply (lines 5, 6), and disparate elements are joined on the same plane (throughout). But this incoherence is merely apparent; it converges to generate a sense of disjunction, of scission, whose impact is powerful though we may not perceive clearly its specific source. The speaker's soul, torn away from its familiar surroundings close to nature —or at least its nature— now finds no true light but cloudy reflections and faint, iterated, blurry glows in a manufactured setting. This world is one of increasing sterility, as lines 9 to 11 starkly suggest with growing schematization in their contrastive designs:[23] «guitarra-rosa» becomes «herradura-hoja seca», which becomes in turn «sereno-desierto» («sereno» = the design of his circulation through empty streets). There is an almost exact inverse correspondence between lines 11-12 and 3-4 (according to suggestive pairings: «luna-osos»; «virgen-

[23] Alberti's painterly eye has caught here a beautiful multiplication of lines.

ocas»; «guarida de la escarcha»-«habitación de los vientos»; «humo-fue-go»); while in lines 1-2 and 13-14 are echoes of one another in the more general sense of separation and desire for union. The last line allows the poem not to end on a negative note with the evocation of a Northern Eve, perhaps the objective of the «Expedición». All these sunderings have their cause or origin in Northern latitudes as if a powerful magnet tore away portions of warmer regions to scatter them pell mell on the snow. In this sense Eva Gundersen may be this force and could provide a new focus of union. The poet's presence at the center of the poem as in a moveable glass cage («mi alma... faroles») is the center of the vision or the dream.

The technique of highlighting the heretofore unseen qualities of certain objects by pairing them in unaccustomed relationships («ánade-abe-to»); «virgen-ocas»; «sereno-desierto», and so on) is not peculiar to Surrealism (in English and American poetry the Imagists also used it) nor is it new to Alberti, who has practiced it since *Marinero en tierra*. Here, however, its effects acquire new evocative power. There is a fairy-tale ambience to the images —intended to set the departure from the South as an Arctic explorer's adventure— that seems to situate it with the other inroads into the world of childhood attempted in this group of poems.

The three pieces that follow these memories of the past examine the denial of former poetic possibilities. The cool, desirable figure of early poetry —«Malva-Luna»,[24] «Rosa-Fría»— is now the center of deceit («No-vela», «Nieve viva»); the abode of inspiration has become a haunted house «adonde todo un siglo es un arpa en abandono» (*Aguilar*, p. 370).

The poems that conclude *Sobre los ángeles* from «Luna enemiga» to «Los ángeles feos» —excepting «El ángel superviviente»— are efforts to seize at their starkest the torments assailing the poet's spirit. He is as in deepest hell, and the language needed to plumb such darkness turns extremely harsh. Unexpected proximities and juxtapositions throw words into striking relief, the substance of names breaks down, again verbs extend their action to unaccustomed spheres. The poet's intensity is given at times seemingly unchecked rein, sequences of imagery are barely gathered in at the end to support the essentials of form. In «Luna ene-miga» the poet's soul is directionless «Y es que mi alma ha olvidado las reglas». This conclusion is necessitated by the phenomena that the poem tries to trace. The speaker's sense of identity, his inner «rules» have been lost, and he is at the mercy of external forces: «Como al chocar los astros contra mi pecho no veía, / fui hundiéndome de espaldas en los cielos pasados». Of these, only the most basic, gravitation, is perceived; it orders both space and time: «Diez reyes del otoño contra mí se rebelaron. / Angeles y traiciones siempre aceleran las caídas. / Una hoja, un hombre. / En tu órbita se quemaba mi sangre, luna enemiga». The poet's control over his past («Diez reyes del otoño») has been lost; it rushes back over his dispersed, dead being («Una hoja, un hombre»).

---

[24] Cf. *Marinero en tierra*.

In drastic contrast to the techtonic energies that now batter him, he has been deprived of his own «inner» force of gravity: «Salvadme de los años en estado de nebulosa» (*Aguilar*, p. 370). While in this poem unbending external necessity was contrasted to the aimlessness of the poet's sense of self, in «Castigos» common expectations are denied; the downfall into the soul's hell is projected in terms of outside realities; as a consequence the most basic facts of experience become unreliable. Time, space and matter are subverted: «Es cuando golfos y bahías de sangre, / coagulados de astros difuntos y vengativos, / inundan los sueños. / ... / Oídme». All anticipations that make existence bearable, from the most common to the most necessary, are false: «Yo no sabía que las puertas cambiaban de sitio, / que las almas podían ruborizarse de sus cuerpos, / ni que al final de un túnel la luz traía la muerte». Neither sleep, nor death, nor endings offer the least glimmer of certainty: «Porque siempre hay un último posterior... / ... / a los derrumbos de la muerte sobre el esqueleto de la nada» (*Aguilar*, p. 372).

In this poem and those that follow, the poet assumes a minatory stance, anticipating for a moment *Sermones y moradas,* a returned voyager from desolate lands that may be reserved for us all as conceivable transmigrations: «No os soltéis de las manos» is his injunction in «El ángel falso». The betraying guardian angel has been totally successful in precipitating the speaker's soul into the depths, but there remains to the condemned the consolation that such malevolence was exercised in vain, for he was already dead: «Todo ha terminado. / Puedes envanecerte, / ... / de que mataste a un muerto, / ... / de que asfixiaste el estertor de las capas atmosféricas» (*Aguilar*, pp. 373-373). A similar notion of final chaos is conveyed in «Los ángeles de las ruinas» and «Los ángeles muertos». The disarray in the poet's soul communicates itself to matter, its disorientation to measurable time. If the speaker feels any privilege —which he communicates as «poète voyant»,[25] but fated to a starkly negative vision— it is that of having experienced those extremes, lived with them. The dead angels are around us, in constant sowing of death and decay:

> Buscad, buscadlos:
> en el insomnio de las cañerías olvidadas,
> en los cauces interrumpidos por el silencio de las basuras.
> ... ... ... ... ... ... ... ... ... ... ... ... ... ... ... ... ... ... ...
> Porque yo los he visto:
> en esos escombros momentáneos que aparecen en las neblinas.
> Porque yo los he tocado:

Alberti proceeds through a transposition of elements and properties, but whereas transpositions of this sort generally involve an animation of the inert, here matter gains merely the awareness of deprivation or of death («los charcos incapaces de guardar una nube»; «una estrella pisoteada»; «el destierro de un ladrillo difunto»; and so on). At the end a suicide's

---

[25] Cf. *Rimbaud.*

steps leave clues towards the multiplication of futile death amid the refuse of civilization: «Cerca del casco perdido de una botella, / de una suela extraviada en la nieve, / de una navaja de afeitar abandonada al borde de un precipicio» (*Aguilar,* pp. 375-376).

*Sobre los ángeles* concludes in two moments. The first is «Los ángeles feos», which attempts a summary, a final rendering of accounts and a specific accusation: «Vosotros habéis sido». In «El ángel superviviente» there is the battered seed of possible renewal. Alberti concentrates his final attack on the ugly angels because ugliness is most alien to poetry, and because his struggle has consisted in the ever reiterated attempt to understand through his poetry the ugliness into which he was precipitated. It was as a poet that he felt the onslaught of evil forces; they endangered and may have permanently crippled his poetic inner being. Thus, they are the summary of his pain. The imagery used here grows from areas normally most alien to poetry, and we see objects common to poetic inspiration under attack from elements that belong to this alien realm: «La luna cae mordida por el ácido nítrico / en las charcas donde el amoníaco aprieta la codicia de los alacranes». The final undoing is a respite: «Al fin ya vamos a hundirnos» (*Aguilar,* pp. 376-377). This defeat, however, is outlasted. «El ángel superviviente» recalls an end of the universal nightmare in a confusion of cold, fire and hypocrisy: «Acordaos. / La nieve traía gotas de lacre, de plomo derretido / y disimulos de niña que ha dado muerte a un cisne». From the holocaust, an angel remains: «Todos los ángeles perdieron la vida. / Menos uno, herido, alicortado» (*Aguilar,* pp. 377-378). He is the counterpart of the previous «good angels» but now the debacle has been so total, the zones of antagonism encountered so unrelenting, that only the barest modicum of hope is left.

The last part of «Huésped de las nieblas» (3) with its exploration of the abysmal and most convulsive regions of the speaker's personal hell represents the final stage on the unswerving self-examination which, in comparison, began merely at its portal. Correspondingly, Alberti's verse moved consistently farther away from any forms and images that recalled his earlier work and into a realm of language as trenchant and unfamiliar as the experiences it sought to seize upon. And yet, while some techniques reminiscent of Surrealism are undoubtedly present, such as the discarding of temporal, logical and spatial laws, or the transposition of the properties of objects, there was never a surrender to structural or even metaphorical incoherency. In fact, even the last and most exigent part of *Sobre los ángeles* conformed to principles of organization which, though obeying the inner stresses of emotional ordeal, rather than any external aesthetic pressures, show that Alberti never entirely submitted to mere association. The downward spiral of his interrogation becomes all the more powerful through this liberation of form from all circumscribing constraints. It is this contained intensity that gives the collection its overwhelming impact and affirms it as one of the peaks of contemporary Spanish poetry.

## IV. Conclusion: «Yo era un tonto y lo que he visto me ha hecho dos tontos»

The poems of *Yo era un tonto...* were written in the same period as *Sobre los ángeles*. Although they are meant to be comical, their humor is melancholy. In picturing the great «fools» of the silent cinema vainly struggling against a hostile world, Alberti is projecting into reality around him the inner experience of his battle against the angels. Alberti's concern for the «fool» is not new. It surfaced first in «El tonto de Rafael» from *El alba del alhelí* (last poem of «El negro alhelí»), where the poet represents himself as incapable of dealing with the necessities of life (material goods, a career), surviving through his own innocence or the help of friends. In «El ángel tonto» the character of foolishness has changed somewhat in response to the more self-accusatory, intransigent tone of *Sobre los ángeles* as a whole and appears as a kind of witless indifference or suspiciousness on the part of the angel. Two basic aspects remain: the clash between the foolish angel and his surroundings, and the poet's self-identification with the fool.

The thirteen poems of *Yo era un tonto...* try to capture that conflict with reality so marvelously portrayed by the silent comics.[26] The poems are best read as verbal manifestations of the pratfalls, anecdotal nonsequiturs, gratuitous violence, and sentimentalism that were mainstays of the silent cinema. The «fool» as victim, sometimes uncannily perceptive, almost a visionary in our pragmatic world, was indeed a poet. Alberti's adventure at the «Lyceum Club femenino», which took place at this time, attests to his identification as poet with a world of absurdity and suggests also that this absurdity has for him clearly useful shock values. In all this poetry there remains a strong undercurrent of despair. The fool does not understand what is happening, but his emotional response intuits the inimical nature of these events and our misguided pride in pragmatic achievement: «y mi alma científicamente preocupada sabe que la elaboración del cacao a vapor adelanta muy poco con llorar» (*Aguilar*, pp. 427-428).

The comics' encounter with the modern world is intended to point out this world's encroachment and its deadly weight on man. Likewise, linguistically, the automatic sequence generated by certain sentences reminds us of the deadweight of facts and logic that language conveys and of the nonsense it hides. But these poetic fools, though often anguished by oppressive reality, also find their escape by overturning apparent evidence:

---

[26] According to Professor MARCIA WELLES, in her paper «Lorca, Alberti and 'los tontos del cine mudo'», in *At Home and Beyond: New Essays of Spanish Poets of the Twenties,* edited by S. Jiménez-Fajardo and John Wilcox (Lincoln: 1983), Alberti wrote these poems as impressions of the comic films presented at the Madrid Cine Club.

poca importancia agua.
Un kilo tiene 10 metros.
Un metro vale 20 litros.
... ... ... ... ... ... ... ..
Mecánica.
Amor.
Poesía.
¡Oh!

(*Aguilar*, pp. 431-432)

After the estheticist experiments of *Cal y canto,* Alberti's bout with his band of angels was an essential, tempering undertaking. It elaborated new links with his inner world, broadened considerably his realm of imagery and hardened the contours of his language. The demands placed on his expression by the forces that sought form in *Sobre los ángeles* liberated it of any previous limiting constraints. The «avant la lettre» absurdist explosion of *Yo era un tonto...,* striking in its own way as *Sobre los ángeles* was, and in itself a surprising anticipation of later literary tendencies, is a clear manifestation of this impetus.

## CHAPTER 4

ENTRE EL CLAVEL Y LA ESPADA: SEA TO SEA

## I. Introduction

The publications of *Verte y no verte*, 1935, *Entre el clavel y la espada,* 1941, and *Pleamar,* 1944, encompass the nine most turbulent years of Alberti's life, years whose vicissitudes for the poet seem a delayed existential echo of the spiritual agitation of *Sobre los ángeles.* Alberti's political commitment is now clearly Leftist —he published *Octubre,* a Communist review, with his wife, María Teresa León— and much of his poetic output reflects this commitment. Since 1931 when Margarita Xirgu presented his play, *El hombre deshabitado,* his interest in the theater had grown; it is as a dramatist that he received funds from the Republic to study the European stage and to travel extensively (1932). He continued to travel in a variety of cultural endeavors throughout Europe, to Russia and to America. In 1940, from Marseilles, he departed for Argentina (he will not return to Spain until April, 1977). With much energy devoted to these activities, a considerable portion of his writing, whether for the stage or as poetry, is politically motivated. While his geographical and existential horizons become wider — ideologically, his Communist allegiance may seem a somewhat restrictive posture, but it does not appear to have narrowed his views to a noticeable extent — there is no significant corresponding expansion in his lyrical work. The limits of poetic experience and technique achieved in *Sobre los ángeles* remain stable during this period, but the poet's sustained technical brilliance cannot overcome an occasional weakening of his voice. *Entre el clavel y la espada* is still a strong book. But in *Pleamar* we begin to notice moments of uncertainty. Here Alberti is learning to live with new angers and an overpowering nostalgia for Spain. His full vigor will not reappear until *A la pintura* with its extraordinary renewal of concept and form, and *Retornos de lo vivo lejano,* when he successfully turns his exile into poetic material.

From the Black Sea, where Alberti found himself when Ignacio Sánchez Mejías was killed, to the Mar de Plata, his home in exile, the poet's itinerary was one of tragic loss. The birth of his daughter Aitana in Argentina is the only net gain in these unsettled years. This is not to say that his poetry is unrelievedly unhappy. There are moments of joy in creation, happy poetic transformations of the world around him, songs to eroticism and life, especially in *Entre el clavel y la espada.* But on the whole a vast sadness penetrates his work and is not shaken off until *A la pintura,* only to reassert itself in *Retornos de lo vivo lejano,* though here in a different, more contemplative tone. Until reaching this new maturity, Alberti is at his best in moments of intensity: intense joys of discovery, as in his early poetry, intense anger or pain as in *Sobre los ángeles.* When emotion loses its specific supports, becomes diffuse, his work suffers; thus, the unevenness of *Pleamar.*

## II. «*Entre el clavel y la espada*»: Sea Changes

Alberti began to write *Entre el clavel y la espada* in 1939 in France. Although the tragic chaos of the Civil War is over, there is still much disquiet in his situation. Nevertheless, he feels that this hiatus —he did not think he would remain in France— is the proper moment for a reflective pause and for renewal. It is time to take stock, after exhausting his voice and his spirit for a lost cause, to reacquaint himself with language and the reality that it renews, thus to reinvigorate his creative impulse. Such is the sense of the first prolog to *Entre el clavel y la espada:* «Después de este desorden impuesto, de esta prisa, / de esta urgente gramática necesaria en que vivo, / vuelva a mí toda virgen la palabra precisa, / virgen el verbo exacto con el justo adjetivo» (*Aguilar,* p. 453). Language must fulfill the double task of affirming, inventing the world anew and communicating to the poet the desire to create in its pristine form. It will again build a bridge between the poet and his reality, as well as between the two antagonistic realms within him: the carnation or poetry, beauty, and the sword or violence, death. The impetus and significance of these forces together with the intercessive role of the poetic word are set forth in the second prolog: «Si yo no viniera de donde vengo; si aquel reaparecido, / pálido, yerto horror no me hubiera empujado a estos / nuevos kilómetros todavía sin lágrimas; / ... / ... tú, libro que ahora vas a abrirte, lo harías solamente bajo un signo / de flor, lejos de él la fija espada que lo alerta» (*Aguilar,* p. 453).

The crisis had been long and violent. A singular correspondence seemed to develop in recent years between Alberti's inner and outer worlds. As did the last one of his angels, the poet also rises «alicortado» and tries to go on. But his skies have changed, for now «... sobre dos amantes embebidos puede bajar / la muerte silbadora desde esas mismas nubes en que / soñaran verse viajando, vapor de espuma por la es- / puma». Unexpectedly, the sword may fall at any moment: «Espada, espada, espada, espadas», but the carnation, the creative will, imagination, will always rise out of any destruction: «... mandando des- / mandada, aferrándose ansiosa, imperecedera, en lo / que deseáramos eterno por debajo de los escombros, / aplastado por las ruinas. / Clavel, clavel, clavel, claveles» (*Aguilar,* p. 454). The collection spans this void, between creation and death, love and fear. With his accustomed concern for an overall architecture, Alberti opens the book with a sequence on love of twelve «Sonetos corporales» and concludes it in «Como leales vasallos», a backward look to Spain, memories of the sword. The five, intermediate parts follow the gradations from love to death; the epilog «Final de Plata Amargo» is a reflection on exile and the sadness of a new beginning that is still too full of what has just ended.

«Sonetos corporales» traces first the transformations of the body —a woman's body because its birth seems more of a continuation, perhaps, than man's, in terms of its role as new «vessel» of life— from its entrance into the world to its fulfillment in love (Sonnet 6). The last six sonnets are the masculine echo to those preceding. The seventh depicts rekindled desire (after the lovemaking of sonnet 6), but the war and death importune the lover's thoughts until the last sonnet where passion is exhausted and seems a sterile dream.

Part II of the collection, «Diálogo entre Venus y Priapo», is an erotic scene, the act of lovemaking turned into a song of physical joy. It may be read as an expansion of sonnet 6, but by situating the action at a mythological level it anticipates the transformations of Part III, «Metamorfosis del clavel». In this sequence of eighteen poems, the recurring motif is the transforming power of love (its metamorphosis) as a modern resumption of Ovid and in proper contextual sequence to the preceding mythical dialog. But, as with Ovid, the ultimate metamorphosis is that of the poetic, fabulating word. In this, Alberti seems to approximate the thrust of Cernuda's poetry. In effect, Cernuda explicitly situated the source of his poetry at the erotic center of his being. Alberti has never specifically equated eroticism and poetic impulse, but he comes close to doing so in this particular group of poems.[1] He also returns here to some of his early techniques, such as the introduction of folkloric motifs, a playful view of reality, the quick, imaginative vignette, wordplay.

The first six poems involve changes in which the sea or water represent or contain the object of desire. At times, it is the cause of transformations in the desiring subject; other times the object becomes the sea or a part of it. In Poem 1 the speaker wants to become a horse and possess the sea (a reminiscence, perhaps, of Chiron possessing Aphrodite, born of the sea foam). In Poem 3 the woman is seen as a sea over which the male member, a carnation, travels. Erotic desire may not only change the appearance of things, but their very being; thus, in Poem 5, the woman's sex becomes conch, tree, leaves. Poem 4 also links the feminine presence to a sea shell (perhaps again an echo of Aphrodite). The changes or confusions wrought by love may affect not only the nature of things, but also the most basic tenets of nature in general, because it is itself the strongest of impulses. In Poem 8, «Se equivocó la paloma»,[2] the dove's innate sense of direction, her perception of reality, are mistaken: «Por ir al Norte, fue al Sur. / Creyó que el trigo era agua. / Se equivocaba». The speaker's error in seeking love where it is not is as fundamental an

---

[1] ALEIXANDRE also forges this link, particularly in *Espadas como labios*, whose title is curiously reminiscent of this collection of Alberti's.
[2] This poem also became a popular song. Maruja Mayoral provides an interesting explication of this piece in *Insula*, No. 282, pp. 3, 14.

error as the dove's. In such a world where the laws of nature no longer obtain, all is possible: «(Ella se durmió en la orilla. / Tú, en la cumbre de una rama)» (*Aguilar*, pp. 482-483).

Many of the metamorphoses are an erotic affirmation. They may involve the coincidence in desire of two apparently disparate beings, human and animal. The animal, impelled by amorous instinct, yearns for and achieves union with woman or man (Poems 6, 9, 10, 11, 18). Earlier we saw how desire leads man (or woman) to seek a different form in order to participate in a species of cosmic love play (Poems 1, 3, 4, and 5). But it is in Poem 17 that the unifying power of Eros manifests itself with greatest force. In this singular piece all elements in the realm of nature and of man are fused in a chaotic Surrealistic point of origin: «Toros que desollados son vacas de jazmines / y alborotadas tetas flotantes de sandía» (*Aguilar*, pp. 488-489). Syntax is broken, to deny it its compartmentalizing function; language tends towards a kind of pre-logical agglutinative state. Female beings are described in terms of masculine symbols and vice versa: «vacas de jazmines», «arcos abiertos de delfines», «Toros que (...) son (...) tetas flotantes». In the vortex of this dynamic commotion, knowledge and will —as discriminating forces— are inoperative, negated. Curiously, to express in its frenzy the transforming power of love, Alberti returned to a near Surrealistic style as still best able to render the cosmic, undifferentiated fountainhead from which Eros rises and to which it seeks to draw us back.

## III. *Entre el clavel y la espada:* The Wake of the Sword

In the swing away from the carnation, Section 4, «Toro en el mar», begins the domination of the sword. The chapter is a memory of its victory, a further elaboration of the myth of the bull, like Spain, torn and bloodied, adrift on its seas. All of its twenty-nine poems are reflections on the triumph of death and violence in Spain, on the poet's loss of his land, the inevitability as well as the suddenness of the cataclysm. The deep bereavement that Alberti feels for his country is expressed in a fragmented elegy. The entire sequence is subtitled «Elegía sobre un mapa perdido». The protagonist is Spain, but seen from three different perspectives: as a geographical and historical entity, as represented by a soldier in the conflict, dead, dying or about to die, as mourned by the poet in exile. In various guises the image of the bull recurs as symbol of perennial Spain, joined almost immediately to that of the soldier, today's victim.

The first poem is low key, almost colloquial:

A aquel país se lo venían diciendo
desde hace tanto tiempo.
Mírate y lo verás.
Tienes forma de toro,
de piel de toro abierto,
tendido sobre el mar.

(De verde toro muerto.)

(*Aguilar*, p. 493.)

The first two lines present several concepts in the tone of an «I told you so». The country is shown as a single entity, preparing us for the transformation into or symbolization by the bull. Spain has been warned for a long time by outsiders more perceptive of her nature than she is: self-unawareness or blindness to her own nature is the reason for the warning: «Mírate...» Apparent objectivity is gained through the use of «aquel país» as if suggesting geographical and historical distance. The lack of awareness involves an ignorance of her own form, of her shape across the seas, and of all that this form contains or forewarns. The significance of this taurine form develops through an apparently straightforward description that actually stands for the country's inner contradictions: «forma de toro» is an image of power, «piel de toro abierto» is the tearing apart or sacrifice of this inherent power. But both the warning of the first lines and the «Tienes» that opens the last three also implies a circumstance that befalls the country or the bull: there is nothing to be done about this fact except to be aware of it — but there was no such awareness. The last line restates the previous three in concentrated form: «verde» = life = sea = hope; «verde toro» is a vigorous, hopeful, living animal, but it is «toro muerto», dead hope. The sacrifice of the bull in the *corrida* was then a ritual sacrifice of the country and anticipated the final, latest self-destructiveness of the Civil War. The bull's life is a constant self-immolation.

Poem 4 introduces in the soldier the second protagonist in the sequence as an element in the bull's tragedy. This soldier's blood is but another component of its fodder of suffering. In a context of powerlessness and of betrayed ignorance or innocence, the deadly diet is contrasted to the vastness of the bull's previous abode and aspirations: «... este toro a quien la mar y el cielo / eran aún pequeños como establo!» (*Aguilar*, p. 494). Poems 5 to 10 are moments of the soldier's death. In Poem 5 the land's response to this death encompasses all its realms, all the forms of life that it pours forth:

> Sobre un campo de anémonas,
> cayó muerto el soldado.
> Las anémonas blancas,
> de grana lo lloraron.
> De los montes vinieron jabalíes
> y un río se llenó de muslos blancos.

> (*Aguilar*, p. 494)

The soldier's immobility in death elicits increasing movement or life: changes in the flowers, the presence of the countryside's wildest, most secret dwellers («jabalíes» — alive in power and speed),[3] an echo from the earth's lifeblood, the river. The image of «muslos blancos», a turbulence of waters or perhaps fish in the form of women's thighs, suggests the reproach of denied potential, denied love.

Each vision of the soldier's death recreates a cosmic echo: the earth

---

[3] The boar is also, traditionally, a phallic symbol.

into which he is sinking (Poem 6), the sea mourning like a bride over his portrait (Poem 7), the moon bursting in blood (Poem 8). In Poem 9 the soldier's inner monolog on the gifts he will present to the woman who waits for him only reaches her as a terrified scream that wilts even the trees.

Poem 19, bearing as an epigraph «Muelle del Reloj», opens with the poet's melancholy gaze over the flowing waters of the Seine but soon becomes a meditation on exile and defeat:

> A través de una niebla caporal[4] de tabaco
> miro al río de Francia
> moviendo escombros tristes, arrastrando ruinas
> por el pesado verde ricino de sus aguas.
> Mis ventanas
> ya no dan a los álamos y los ríos de España.

Again, Alberti's image for Spain (bull) plays here a central role, joined to the traditional one of life as a river going to sea (a metaphor given particular resonance by Jorge Manrique's «Coplas»): «Miro una lenta piel de toro desollado, / sola, descuartizada, /.../ ... hacia el mar...» The piece develops in a pattern of gradual internalization, also in the tradition of meditative poetry. The opening stanza contains the greatest number of concrete elements: «Escombros tristes», «ruinas», «el pesado verde ricino de sus aguas». These elements are already considerably dematerialized: (1) emotionally charged qualifiers penetrate their concreteness; (2) they are given in a generalizing plural — except for the color of water, in itself an anticipating metaphor of the later «cloacas», and the river proper; (3) they are seen only in vaguest outline, through the smoky haze. Contrasted to this restricted, too dismal a reality, the last two lines seem to offer light and amplitude («ventanas», «ríos», «álamos»), but they recall an irretrievable condition forever lost in the despairing «ya no dan a los álamos y los ríos de España» (*Aguilar,* pp. 500-501). Slow but inexorable, the present participles, as frozen fragments of time, drag the debris of history to the empty sea.

Part 5, «De los álamos y los sauces, en recuerdo de Antonio Machado», centers almost exclusively on the nostalgia of exile, the condition of the poet displaced. The dedication to Machado —who died in France— sets the tone of the sequence, and the poplar is now the symbol of the poet's nostalgia. The harshness and despair that characterized many of the poems of «Toro en el mar» is becoming mitigated. Time is passing, slowly; the distance from the homeland is great.

The sequence opens on a note of deep sorrow. The early poems establish the willows and poplars as correlative supports of the speaker's memories and of his sadness. In Poem 2 the trees are crushing memories, a burden almost too heavy:

---

[4] «Caporal» used to be a popular brand of French cigarettes.

No puede, como es pequeño,
con tantos árboles grandes.

Sólo con la yerbabuena,
la flor del aire.

Alamo, me pesas mucho;
me doblas los hombros, sauce.

Se sentó. Y aunque era río,
no vino el agua a ayudarle.

*(Aguilar, p. 511)*

The last stanza is made to sustain the weight of the entire poem, as a metaphor to the second degree, in that *its* metaphor clarifies the meaning of the preceding lines. The first two lines merely present the contrast between a large burden and its oversmall conveyer. Also, the weight is multiple, the conveyer alone. The initial lack of definition of this being («No puede») reduces further his capacity. The second stanza, by implication, defines him as not very substantial, even delicate, since his nature can only bear the weight of «la yerbabuena, / la flor del aire». The nature of this being reveals itself through his complaint in stanza three; he is a man bowing under the weight of trees. But in the last stanza he is a river; and this metaphoric clarification then reflects back upon the rest of the poem to elucidate the nature of the being in question: man and river, i.e., weeping man.

We note here (as in Poem 19 on the Seine of the preceding sequence), a double metaphor in which the basic equation, trees = memories and sorrows, is merely implied. As we progress towards the revelation of the last stanza, the nature of the trees themselves is specified: poplars and willows. On one side, the man, an absence identified only in terms of his reduced capacity to support the heavy burden; on the other, the burden itself, trees first, then poplars and willows. At the center, the only element through which the man reveals himself, the river, which at the same time justifies the vision of the trees as a burden:

| Es pequeño | | |
|---|---|---|
| yerbabuena | | árboles |
| flor del aire | —río— | Alamo |
| hombros | | sauce |

In Poem 3 Alberti recalls some of the thoughts of his prolog to *Entre el clavel y la espada,* reaffirming his will to sing, regardless of circumstance («Y cantaré más alto»). He still feels a stranger in this land. That is why he will throw no roots into the new soil: «Y echaré mis raíces / de manera que crezcan hacia el aire» (*Aguilar,* p. 512). Most of the pieces in the sequence, however, do not accompany this challenging tone. They are somber in mood; the pendulum is in its backswing towards the sword.

Section 6, «Del pensamiento en un jardín», is dedicated to José Bergamín, then in Mexico, and is preceded by a thematic prolog. The sequence is one long poem in a variety of meters. The garden invites reflection:

75

«Trepe el mío [pensamiento], regado y verdeante, / por el sol del destierro y de la espera» (*Aguilar*, p. 523). There are numerous reminiscences, in form and imagery, of Alberti's earliest manner (from *Marinero en tierra* and *La amante*), as, for instance, in the very first lines; Alberti urges on his thought: «Calce, al subir, lo primero, / la espuela de caballero». Immediately, however, the contemporary dark note is sounded: «Galopar ensangrentado. / Potro de muerte. Dolor» (*Aguilar*, p. 523). Thereafter, the composition becomes a meditation, where the flowers and plants of the garden suggest only memories of the poet's past dead, and of his own exile, with repeated efforts to shake off this darkness and reaffirm the will to continue.

The seventh section, «Como leales vasallos», is presented as a poetic commentary on selected lines from *Cantar de Mio Cid*. The reverberations of the commentary and its subject include Machado, in whose «Orillas del Duero» the Cid is recalled as he went to his exile, the themes of exile proper, war and Spain, so indissolubly linked through history, and Alberti's own present exile. Through this evocation, Alberti wants to express the poignancy of his ever present homeland, as a wound which one keeps testing. Poem 6 is a gloss on the famous section in the *Cantar...* where, by order of the king, all assistance is to be refused the Cid and his companions: «... que nadi nol diessen posada...» It is now the new exiles whose existence must be decried: «¿Quiénes son los que así marchan? / Cerrad las puertas de casa». The refusal is sounded between each stanza: «—Ni pan, ni silla, ni agua /.../ —Ni hoz, ni pico, ni azada /.../ —Ni tierra para su alma». However, the last strophe suggests a ray of future hope: «Están cerrados los mapas. / En un huracán de sangre, / rueda una llave de plata» (*Aguilar*, pp. 535-536). This possibility of a return is sounded also in the last composition, Poem 8, where the sea will be a new bridge, «Se volverá el mar de tierra» (*Aguilar*, p. 537), in response to the line from the *Cantar...* «... tornaremos a Castiella». The impulse of hope that concludes Chapter 7 of *Entre el clavel y la espada* is somewhat mitigated by the final composition of the collection, «Amparo». This («Amparo») is the name given by the poet to the land that has received him (Argentina). Alberti invokes the country as a woman whose beckoning he has answered, though his mind is still full of another woman, the land he has just left. The new home can only be seen in terms of the lost one:

> Tu mar dulce tenía
> sabor de plata amargo,
> ... ... ... ... ... ... ... ... ... ... ...
>
> Amparo.
> Vine a tu mar de trigos y caballos.
> (Adonde tú querías.)
>
> (*Aguilar*, pp. 541-542)

The poet has surrendered his will to necessity.

The oscillation from the carnation to the sword, from the power of love to that of war, has been accompanied by a shift in technique that reflects the manifestations of these two forces. The sections under the sign of the flower are clear expressions of the poetic will, as befits compositions whose subject, being love, resides at the very center of the creative activity. They are either classical in form («Sonetos corporales») or in inspiration («Diálogo entre Venus y Priapo») or in the power assigned to the poetic word — also in Ovidian reminiscence («Metamorfosis...»). «Toro en el mar», the elegy to Spain, begins the sweep towards the empire of the sword. If we consider «Amparo» as an epilog (justifiable to some extent because it is a single composition which, while maintaining the nostalgia for the homeland, looks towards a new residence), «Toro en el mar» is the central section. It forms a link between the two parts of the book in that it uses a classical image, Spain as the bull, and contains likewise as a clear symbolic presence the soldier that stands for the people of Spain. It is also a sequence of love poems, the love of things lost, and this emotion is still the transforming energy that infuses new metamorphoses. (Bull = Spain, unknown soldier = Everyman.) Sections 5, 6 and 7, although they contain moments of hope, continue decidedly under the sign of the sword.

## IV. Conclusion: «Pleamar»

In the short prolog to this book of poems (Aguilar), Alberti insists on the central concern, already expressed in the previous collection, to which almost all of his poetry will return henceforward: «... continúa agudizándose la nostalgia insufrible de la patria...» As he tries to adapt himself to his new home, Alberti will also seek new modes of expression in an effort to elaborate a renovated basis for his poetry. In Pleamar he writes for the first time aphoristic poetry and tries his hand at evoking other forms of art through language («Versos sueltos para una exposición» and «Invitación a un viaje sonoro»). The very short sixth part, «Versos sueltos para una exposición», represents the poet's first effort in what is to become a major aspect of his work henceforward: the merging of poetry and painting or rather the attempt to turn painting into poetry. Alberti tries to capture movement and form in nine out of the ten short pieces of the sequence. This attention to compositional elements, joined to an enthusiastic profusion of color will contribute later to the brilliance of A la pintura.

In Part 8, «Invitación a un viaje sonoro», Alberti once more finds inspiration in another art form, music. The second poem «España», subtitled «Fantasía», uses the poet's feeling for the old Spanish ballad to construct a new one recalling the Reconquista in which the principal character is the perennial water that sustains the land: «El agua siempre es la misma, / pura, lejana, sin nombre, / agua de cabello antiguo, / voz de nunca...» (Aguilar, pp. 661-662). He captures with a light touch the movement of the Zarabanda (in «Croft. Zarabanda»); the musical interweaving becomes an interweaving of words, the metamorphosis of one object into many and back again:

Pasa
de rumor solo a ser agua.
De dos, a ser una sola.
De nardo,
al amarillo más pálido.
No soy lluvia
ni soy verano.

(*Aguilar*, pp. 668-669)

In other pieces there are frequent quotations from popular songs, as in a *Jota* by Falla, a *muiñeira* by Aguilar. On the whole, a different mood seems to pervade this last section of *Pleamar*. The tone is playful, and at times we have the impression of reading the Alberti of the earliest poetry.

It is best to consider *Pleamar* as a transitional collection for Alberti, one in which he tries to reexamine some of his poetic constants, and seeks new strength in memories and his new environment. Alberti's poetry, from *Entre el clavel y la espada* to *Pleamar*, reflects the difficulties of this period in his life. He has been uprooted from the soil and ambience that created the background to his work, his ideological and human hopes have been destroyed, and he is thrust into an unwanted journey to distant lands. It is not until he finds a new world of imagery and feeling that his expression will fully regain its earlier power, as happens with his renewed interest in pictorial art and the poetry of *A la pintura*.

CHAPTER 5

FROM THE CANVAS TO THE SCENE

I. *Introduction*

Much of the poetry examined in the previous chapter represents a period in the poet's work (1934-1944), when emotional adjustments had to be made. All that Spain represented for Alberti as a mainspring of poetry was no longer available. Nature offered new forms, and the social climate in which the poet moved was suddenly the restrictive one of the political exile. In the later poems of *Pleamar,* other arts captured his attention. Yet neither painting nor music are unaccustomed sources of poetry in Alberti, whose artistic career began with painting, and who sought much of his initial inspiration in Barbieri's *Cancionero.* Now, in *A la pintura,* he focuses exclusively on pictorial art and finds in it not only a vigorous means of renewal for his own expression, but also an occasion to reassert both his classical and his experimental modes. Most of this chapter will be devoted to a reading of this collection. *Poemas diversos* follows *A la pintura* and, as the title suggests, consists of varied pieces, many of a circumstantial nature. A similar theme is pursued here, however, in that a large proportion of these poems celebrates painters, musicians, and other artists of the poet's acquaintance. We shall conclude this chapter with a review of *Poemas de Punta del Este,* in which several prose «journals» alternate with songs and short poems. Alberti recalls those days as «... quizá felices, cuando Aitana aún era como un duende que desaparecía en los pinares» (*Aguilar,* p. 847). Many of these compositions are landscape impressions in which still vivid images of another countryside, that of Spain, are superimposed on the contours of the new land. Here again as to a large degree in *A la pintura,* the past beckons. Alberti's poetry is now born of a tension between present and past, whose lines of force are visual, esthetic and emotional reminiscences.

II. *A la pintura* («*Poema del color y la línea*»): Prelude

The body of this collection consists of forty-nine poems —twenty sonnets on instruments and elements of painting, twenty-nine poems on individual painters— and six series of poetic aphorisms on various colors.

Three poems of an autobiographical nature serve as introduction to the work and nine poems devoted to painters known to Alberti at the time of composition in Argentina and Uruguay conclude it, for a total of sixty-three pieces in its final collected form. The first edition appeared in 1948 with Losada. Subsequently, the Losada *Poesía completa* (1962) gives 1945-1952 as dates of composition, whereas the *Aguilar* edition has 1945-1967. There is one addition in the Aguilar text, Poem 46 on Miró, probably written after 1952, perhaps as late as 1967. We have noted no other changes.

There is no doubt that this collection is one of the peaks of Alberti's post-Civil War work —the other would be *Retornos de lo vivo lejano*— and of all his poetry. Its achievement is comparable to that of *Sobre los ángeles* if in another key. The backward look to Spain and the past is still an important component of these poems. Most of them recreate the first impression left on Alberti as a fledgling painter by the great masters, though this initial awareness is subsequently redefined by the esthetically more mature poet. But such is the weight of remembrance in the sequence that Ricardo Gullón, for instance, does not hesitate to call it Alberti's «primer libro total de la nostalgia».[1] As we suggested earlier, underlying many of these poems is the tension generated by remembrance, the effort to recreate through language not only another artistic medium, but the memory of previous encounters with it. When it does appear, this not uncommon structural pattern of tension tending toward resolution, so frequent in literature generally as to have almost become a cliché, manifests itself with such multilayered effectiveness that it seems to recreate the concept anew.

The idea of both contrast and complementarity is present in the very subtitle of the book, *Poema del color y la línea*. For instance, color and line can be mutually strengthening, or they can be set almost as antagonists in the painting. Or line may suggest direction, organization, containment, while color seems a more direct expressive force, instinct, imagination, and so on. Yet again, in some instances, these roles may be reversed. Connotations do not, of course, remain unalterable, they are born of the entire poem, of the entire collection. Another equally significant pairing, in opposition or in conjunction, would be form and freedom, a facet of the color/line couple. Also, within the same context, but now specifically in the realm of poetic technique, are the sonnet and free verse forms.

Under the general title of «1917», the three introductory poems seek to bridge a double distance: (a) the actual gap left by time and events between the Alberti of that year in Spain and today's Alberti on the Río de la Plata; (b) the spiritual break, that, the poet now feels, occurred when he abandoned painting altogether in favor of poetry. Today's writing on past, though perennial, paintings may bridge both distances, if the poet can only recover that pristine, reckless enthusiasm: «Diérame ahora

---

[1] RICARDO GULLÓN, «Alegrías y sombras de Rafael Alberti (Segundo momento)», first published in *Asomante*, XXI, Nos. 1 and 2, 1965. Subsequently in MANUEL DURÁN, *Rafael Alberti*, p. 250.

la locura / que en aquel tiempo me tenía, / para pintar la Poesía / con el pincel de la Pintura» (*Aguilar,* p. 690).

Those moments are recalled as initiations to color (Poem 1), to form (Poem 2) —of nine and eight *redondillas*[2] respectively— and to the Prado Museum (Poem 3), in more stately alexandrine distichs. Poems 1 and 2 present the youth as apprentice while the third, longer piece is devoted to his early impression of the great masters in the museum. Poem 1 from the quickly sketched setting of the first stanza —date, biographical detail («mi adolescencia»), essential tools of the painter: «... una caja de pintura, / un lienzo en blanco, un caballete»— penetrates gradually into an Impressionistic landscape of color. The second stanza joins the apprentice's joyful feelings to the open potential of form: «... la imprevista / lección abierta del paisaje». The third stanza contains a general statement on color followed by two forms, seen already exclusively in terms of hues, typical of the Impressionists: «... al árbol en violeta / y al tronco en sombra de morado». In the fourth stanza the transformation is complete: «Comas radiantes son las flores, / puntos las hojas, reticentes, / y el agua, discos transparentes / que juegan todos los colores». Thereafter only colors sing, with objects offering the barest support for their display. The last three stanzas move beyond the representative capacity of colors to suggest their sheer inventive power: «Llueve la luz, y sin aviso, / ya es una ninfa fugitiva / que el ojo busca clavar viva / sobre el espacio más preciso» (*Aguilar,* pp. 689-690). The conclusion envisions this power transmitted from the painter's to the poet's hand —we quoted it above— as it seeks to link that past enthusiasm to the present task.

In the second composition Alberti considers the «... academia necesaria» of copying the statues of the Casón.[3] These copies in black and white will train his hand to the certainty of lines and volumes; the poem recalls the birth of design learnt from the sensuous and classical form of Aphrodite: «Mi mano y Venus frente a frente». The progress in this poem parallels that of the previous one, though here it manifests the growing autonomy of line and shadows. The last three stanzas embrace the realm of motion, aptly evoked by the rising figure of the goddess, «Y el azabache submarino / ciñe a la hija de la espuma», leading once more to the latent birth of poetry: «Nada sabía del poema / que ya en mi lápiz apuntaba. / Venus tan sólo dibujaba / mi sueño pristino, suprema» (*Aguilar,* pp. 690-691).

The more expansive movement of Poem 3 follows the triumphant merging of color, form and history in the masterpieces of the Prado, dazzling to the youth's untutored eyes. The piece is carefully orchestrated with an intrada, several parts and a coda.[4] The first part focuses on nude

---

[2] Strophes of four octosyllables with consonant rhyme in *abab* or *abba*.
[3] Museum of reproductions in Madrid. Cf. *La arboleda perdida,* pp. 100-101.
[4] In the first Losada edition (1952), the third introductory poem is divided into five stanzas, the first three of sixteen lines, the fourth of twenty-two and the last of twenty. The Losada complete poetry has an initial stanza of four lines and further divisions at lines thirty-two and forty; for the rest, Aguilar and Losada follow the same stanzaic divisions.

81

forms — mainly feminine as recreated by the great sixteenth and seventeenth century masters. Myth, beauty of line and brilliant color elicited in him an ancestral spark of recognition: «Y —¡oh relámpago súbito!— sentí en la sangre mía / arder los litorales de la mitología, / abriéndome en los dioses que alumbró la Pintura / la Belleza su rosa, su clavel la Hermosura».

The poem concludes with a more strictly biographical sequence that allows again, as in Poems 1 and 2, the tools and techniques of painting to take center stage and to merge with the poet's own creative endeavor. Through the merging of both arts we plunge to the center of the present activity at its most technical level: the problem of turning form and color into language by trying to live backwards those moments when the poet remembers the joy «de buscar la Pintura y hallar la Poesía, /.../ de nacer un poeta por morirse un pintor, / hoy distantes me llevan, y en verso remordido, / a decirte, ¡oh Pintura!, mi amor interrumpido» (*Aguilar,* pp. 691-694).

All three poems of the introduction conclude with a consideration of the task at hand. They are personal reminiscences of Alberti's early awakening first to the principal elements of pictorial art, then to their most illustrious exemplifications in the Prado. The three components of the entire collection are thus anticipated: Poem 1, with its emphasis on color, finds its developed echo in the six sequences on individual colors; to Poem 2, on form, answers generally the sonnet sequence; the third part contains the germ of the poems on individual poets.

Beyond these rough correspondences, further aspects of the collection are intimated now: the strongly biographical note that remains as a background to this rediscovery of the art; a constant return to the demands of form; and the interplay between this never forgotten exigency and all the other elements of painting, such as color, light, representation; the confrontation between historically determined norms, the perennial values of painting, and the particular manner in which the masters achieve these lasting values. More specifically, a vocabulary is generated and a metaphorical context mapped out: Titian's «claridades corpóreas», Rubens' «ninfas aldeanas»; «oro... piadoso», «añil pensativo», «estancias» and «vergeles» for early painting; «violentas oquedades», «tracoma harapiento», but also, «justo azul», «nieve severa» for Spain; «aura», «céfiro», «brisa» in Velázquez; El Greco's «vida subterránea», «fantasmal verdiseco»; Bosch's «diablo ratoneril y tierno» and «airados escobones». And finally, to reassert his purpose throughout, Alberti deploys a virtuosity of cadence and sound, clear vowels for light, white or golden, dark vowels for darkness and harsh reality, whereby the basic accord of this celebration does become the interpenetration of language and remembered painting.

## III. *The Sonnets*

The central development of *A la pintura* opens with an unnumbered sonnet that bears the same title. It seems at first simply a thematic introduction, a summary of many of the technical or external elements of painting which will be individually treated by subsequent sonnets.[5] Immediately, we are struck by the vocative form of the poem, a form that will be adhered to in exact parallelism in all other compositions of this type. This apostrophic stance, though it is particularly striking in the sonnets, will reappear in several of the pieces on specific painters (e.g., Miguel Angel, Tiziano, Velázquez) and suggests some initial questions on interpretation. To Ana María Winkelmann —see note 5 above— this vocation «confiere un valor humanizante a los términos abstractos y establece la idea de un diálogo-monólogo».[6] It may be useful to develop further this notion within the context of Alberti's intention in remembering and, perhaps, comprehending anew the nature of painting through poetry. There is a sense in which poetic apostrophe acts as a «radical interiorización»[7] of the object or individual invoked. They are transformed into inner forces, abstracted from time and subjected to the power of poetic discourse — precisely what Alberti already undertakes to do in the three poems of the prelude. It is in this sense that the apostrophe becomes a dialog with the self. Thereby a somewhat didactic overtone is heard in Alberti's invocation of the painter within himself. This function of the apostrophe in the whole of *A la pintura* must remain as a background to any analysis.

The poem «A la pintura», then, introduces us not only to the topics that are to be treated by the other sonnets, but also to the latter's perspective —as developed apostrophes— and even to the inner pattern of contrast and tension which we suggested above is inherent to the whole sequence. We quote it in full:

A ti, lino en el campo. A ti, extendida
superficie, a los ojos, en espera.
A ti, imaginación, helor u hoguera,
diseño fiel o llama desceñida.

A ti, línea impensada o concebida.
A ti, pincel heroico, roca o cera,
obediente al estilo o la manera,
dócil a la medida o desmedida.

A ti, forma; color, sonoro empeño
porque la vida ya volumen hable,
sombra entre luz, luz entre sol, oscura.

---

[5] The introductory nature of this poem is further emphasized by its variant rhyme scheme: *abba abba cde cde,* as opposed to that of the other sonnets where the tercets are in *ccd eed.* Cf. ANA MARÍA WINKELMANN, «Pintura y poesía en Rafael Alberti», *Papeles de Son Armadans,* XXX, pp. 147-162.

[6] *Ibid.,* p. 152.

[7] Cf. JONATHAN CULLER, «Apostrophe», *Diacritics,* Dec. 1977, p. 66.

A ti, fingida realidad del sueño.
A ti, materia plástica palpable.
A ti, mano, pintor de la Pintura.

*(Aguilar, p. 695)*

In this first and the other sonnets, Alberti achieves again the excellence with which he evoked Góngora, demonstrating that he is one of the best practitioners of the form in the language. The demands of the sonnet are, of course, perfectly adjusted to the structural and technical aspects of painting that they seek to transmit. These formal elements are captured in a state of tension with the inner expressive force of conception or imagination. The carefully symmetrical disposition of the poem further leads us to notice not only connotative parallelisms, but also echoes of assonance and alliterations within and between individual lines.

The opening apostrophe, «A ti, lino en el campo», contains in potential the developments of the rest of the poem. We have, first, the flower («lino»), then the idea of a canvas (also in the sense of a sail) against a background of forms and life, and therefore, a potential field of representations. The flower is the form born of the seed, the seed also produces the oil that is used in painting, and the metaphor thereby contains the idea of painting. The rest of the quatrain develops this potential in terms of containment and possibility. «A los ojos» is the intermediate term, in the second line, between the surface and the expectation, as vision translates potential into form. In the third line the two appositions to «imaginación» express its control («helor») and its liberty («hoguera»). The last line summarizes these two ideas in perfect correspondence of sense: «hoguera»: «llama desceñida», «helor»: «diseño fiel». The sounds themselves reinforce the correspondence in that the final *a* of «hoguera» is repeated in the *a's* of «llama» and «desceñida»; the *el* of «helor» is reproduced in «fiel», and the sequence *e o* of the same word reappears in the *e o* of «diseño». There is also an echo of «diseño» in «desceñida», whereby a community of sound suggests the necessary interactions of design and freedom. The second quatrain continues the same pattern with respect to the brush and the line, equally parallelistic developments of initial elements through their potential for form and free inspiration:

«Línea» → «impensada», «concebida»; «Pincel» → «roca», «cera», gathered again in abstract terms in the last line, «medida»-«desmedida». The patterns of sound likewise echo one another («p*i*ncel» → «l*í*nea») and, in fact, a sequence is established that flows from the first line of the poem, «l*i*no» = «p*i*ncel», where the sounds link both terms and bring to mind further similarities, the brush as flower.

The tercets offer a complex web of correspondences through sound and sense, with alliteration, assonance, synesthesia, and oxymoron that bring all the principal elements of painting to a resolution. Their effect is to fill that potential canvas of the first quatrain, give meaning to the lines of the second with color, movement and light. As instances of sound correspondences (*o - u*) and inner rhyming, we quote the last lines of each tercet: «sombra entre luz, luz entre sol, oscura» (*o - u, u - o, o - a*);

«A ti, mano, pintor de la Pintura» (*a - o, i - o, i - a*). In this final line is the total realization of the very first one: «mano» recalls «lino» and «pincel», whose echo reappears in «pintor» and «Pintura» (the *p* was already in cam*p*o). The hand in form and potential is as the flower, it is the flower on the canvas, as the «lino en el campo». The tension between form and freedom is resolved in action. All of painting (capitalized to signify the entire art) is contained in the «hand». The «hand» in this final line and the «eyes» in line two circumscribe this abstract description within indispensable human concreteness.

We have stayed with this poem at some length because, as we indicated, it summarizes and anticipates the pattern of the other sonnets and because in its formal brilliance it is also an illustration of the quality that will characterize them all. Their sequence moves, as does the sonnet itself, from the general to the specific and from external to internal means. Other interrelated patterns contribute to give the collection its highly integrative character. We saw that the «eyes» and the «hand» were the two human elements that appeared in the opening sonnet. The first two sonnets of the sequence proper («A la Pintura» is unnumbered) are II, «A la retina» and IV, «A la mano». Then comes VI, «A la paleta», IX, «A la pintura mural», and XI, «Al lienzo», XIV, «Al pincel», and XVI, «A la línea». So far all these elements are specifically contained in the introductory sonnet: palette we saw as color; the canvas and mural painting appear as «extendida superficie», line and brush are also particularly mentioned. The rest of the sonnets generally deal with compositional aspects of the art. There is also another organization into which the sequence of sonnets falls and that links them to the specific artists treated in the other poems. Here the correspondence is not one to one, but certain tendencies or characteristics of these painters are often treated in the sonnet that appears next to their poem, e.g., XXI, «Al claroscuro», XXII, «Rembrandt», XXIII, «A la composición», XXIV, «Poussin», XXX, «A la luz»; XXXI, «Velázquez»; XXXVI, «Al movimiento»; XXXVII, «Delacroix».

All these sonnets (beginning with II) follow the same invocative pattern in their detail. Each quatrain begins with «A ti» as does the first tercet and the very last line. The last line in traditional sonnet fashion will generally concentrate the imagery of the poem in one final metaphor which is also the specific apex of the final tercet. This emphasis on the repeated pattern, the decision to submit to the strictest formal demands, which, as we suggested, answers to the topics that these sonnets treat, might seem to tip the balance slightly in favor of form as the most highly prized value of the art for Alberti. Angel Crespo, in his perceptive article on Pythagoreanism in *A la pintura* makes a strong case for this preference.[8] Nevertheless, a careful reading repeatedly suggests a sustained equilibrium between passion and form, imagination and containment, bearing out the vigor that arises from the tension between these forces. There is a clear

---

[8] ANGEL CRESPO, «Realismo y pitagorismo en el libro de Alberti *A la pintura*», *Papeles de Son Armadans*, XXX, pp. 93-126.

distinction between those elements of painting that are its structural supports, and those that are the expresson of its inner power. The tension remains: the hand is «alma del jardín de la Pintura»; color is «gloria y pasión»; shadow is «claro Luzbel», and so on. And in his acute analysis of «Al ropaje», Ricardo Gullón suggests as one of its intents «revelar la ambigüedad del ropaje que cubre y descubre, vela y desvela, da formas o las borra».[9] Notwithstanding the concern with form that has always been a strong component of Alberti's work in individual poems as well as in entire collections —and *A la pintura* is an outstandingly clear example of it— he is at his best when imagination deploys its energy in equal battle with the demands of discipline.

It is in the very last sonnet of the sequence (XLVII) that the Apollonian —or Pythagorean— seems to triumph. «A la divina proporción» develops in stately progression the delights of compassed, harmonious beauty, but the idea of tension, though muted, is present still, if only through the suggestion of willed limitation. For while proportion is seen as «maravillosa disciplina», it is still a discipline: «A ti, maravillosa disciplina, / media, extrema razón de la hermosura / que claramente ataca la clausura / viva en la malla de tu ley divina». As before, the duality is present, a moving interpenetration of beauty and form, beauty because of form. Still, this movement progresses through a contrast of forces: «maravillosa disciplina» becomes «extrema razón», and the verb phrase of the first quatrain is «acata la clausura»; this «clausura» is «viva en la malla». The key to the poem's composition lies in this concept of discipline, «cárcel feliz», as a source of beauty, but the initial tension must this time resolve itself. It does so in the final three lines by means of the perfect form and perfect resolution of movement in mystical tradition: the sphere. This last tercet offers the abstract source and goal of proportion in the Pythagorean harmony: «Luces por alas un compás ardiente. / Tu canto es una esfera transparente. / A ti, divina proporción de oro»[10] (*Aguilar*, p. 793).

A general progression of the sonnets is towards abstraction, that is to say, from external and instrumental aspects of the art towards internal and compositional ones. The sequence of the poems on individual painters is roughly historical with a clear predominance of Renaissance and Classical artists, but as it concludes with Miró and Picasso —Miró as a later addition— it would be tempting to define its direction also as towards abstraction. Actually, there are few painters from the Modern Age. If there is a preference, it seems to be the one suggested by Angel Crespo: «... Alberti es un amante del arte figurativo y que, dentro de él, prefiere a los pintores que se expresan mediante la representación de figuras humanas».[11]

---

[9] RICARDO GULLÓN, *op. cit.*, p. 254.
[10] ANGEL CRESPO, *op. cit.*, p. 106.
[11] Alberti's play *Noche de guerra en el Museo del Prado* joins his memories of Goya's paintings to those of the Civil War.

## IV.  *The Artists and their Colors*

Alberti begins his historical retrospective in the fourteenth century with Giotto. The poem reproduces the essence of Giotto's art through repetitions and parallelisms, seeking to capture its solemn, serene development, and the self-reflexive dedication of the activity and the painter to the supreme artist, God. Its structure follows the art of painting a mural, from means to representation and back to the artist as God's chosen instrument. Each of the seven stanzas invokes God's praise of various elements in the art, starting with the brush: «Laude, Señor Dios mío, / al hermano pincel» and includes the wall and line for the fresco (stanza 2), pencil, pen and outline (stanza 3), the human figure (stanza 4), colors (stanza 5), movement, landscape, angel, clothing (stanza 6), and the painter (stanza 7). Once the basic means of painting have been enumerated in unhurried calm, the figure of man rises in the central stanza: «Laude, Señor Dios mío, / a la humana figura, / ardiente paralela, recta hermana / de la infinita hermana arquitectura»; he is presented in symmetrical proportion to his environment, at the heart of God's «infinita arquitectura», as lines directed heavenward. Although central, the human figure is significant only because it partakes of the surrounding universe, both divine creations: only four lines are devoted to man. This and the first stanza («al pincel») are the shortest. Around the human figure the colors come to life: «Laude, Señor Dios mío / al hermano color, a los colores». The painter's humble praise rises with heavenly blue to crown the expanse of calm, unmixed values:

> al verde, al blanco, al rojo, al amarillo,
> al negro, al oro, al rosa
> y al que es lengua pintando tus loores
> cuando se eleva airosa
> a humilde, a pobrecillo
> pájaro fiel mi mano:
> el claro azul, el buen añil hermano.

Each color separated by a comma appears in all its solid integrity; the qualifying attention paid to blue, doubly present at the end of the stanza, elevates it to the heavens it paints. The very movement of the lines seems to raise it as on a stately three-runged ladder: from «y al que» to «humilde», color and speech combine in the praise; from «mano» to «pájaro», to the act of painting it —the hand as a Franciscan brotherly bird— the last line is the sky's blue triumph in focused intensity.

Under this sky and around the human figure, forms and landscapes expand: «al pausado, solemne movimiento / al hierático mar y rígido paisaje». In its midst hovers the ingenuous, floating figure of an angel, central in the stanza in a longer line that suggests its movement, a reminder of God's benevolent attention to his ordered creation: «Laude al ángel que boga sin el hermano viento, / al simétrico orden sin hastío / y al salmo rectilíneo del ropaje». In the final stanza the painter speaks through the poet's lips to suggest the triple concurrence of creation:

87

God, the painter, the poet; as we began, we return to the act of the artist:

> Laude, Señor Dios mío,
> porque me armaste dulce, cariñoso,
> y en una edad oscura
> me concediste el hábito glorioso
> del hermano mayor de la Pintura.
>
> (*Aguilar*, pp. 695-697)

While Giotto's painting envisions man and his universe in direct relationship with the Creator, Piero della Francesca's, in Poem 3, moves the heavenly harmonies earthward. The composition in ten heptasyllable *redondillas* is an exact formal counterpart in movement and rhythm to the calm, composed advance of lines and volumes expressive of cosmic design. Each *redondilla* ends with a period and contains at most two sentences. The very disposition of elements in the poem answers to a desire for lucid, unhurried demonstration: the line (stanza 1), volume (stanza 2), form (stanza 3), construction (stanza 4). The two central stanzas, 5 and 6, situate man also at the center as with «Giotto», but now only as an intelligence:

> Arco puro la frente,
> y basamento erguido
> el cuello, sostenido
> melancólicamente.
>
> ¿De dónde la mirada
> redonda que origina
> la impávida retina
> sin eco, concentrada?
>
> (*Aguilar*, pp. 698-699)

The head, and the eyes as portals of the soul, are sufficient emblems. Here, in the eyes, is the only possible source of mystery, reflected by the interrogative that stands out in the otherwise unbroken flow of the poem. And the mystery is at best contained by the eyes' circularity, analogous to the greater cosmic orb. As if to submit further this muted mystery, the next stanza reiterates the earthly solidity of all forms, in connotative echo to the «basamento erguido» of stanza 5 —the neck as column— «Aquí la forma aferra / sus plantas en la tierra / como si fuera el cielo». All movement, susceptible of uncertainty, is resolved into an echo of the great pervasive harmony: «Lo que el viento conmueve / y con su ala suscita / es solo una infinita / música de relieve». The last four stanzas resolve motion into representation: stanza 7, earthbound form, and stanza 8, movement as harmony; stanza 9, struggle and calm expounded in mural serenity; stanza 10, design contained in number and proportion: «Místico del diseño / y del número, santo. / Tu aritmética es canto; / tu perspectiva, sueño» (*Aguilar*, pp. 698-699). Earthly forms are compactly disposed; Piero's painting uncovers their ideal components in rigorous perspective.

Poem 7, «Leonardo», is composed in two parts: the first in two stanzas of unrhymed hendecasyllables, twelve and eight lines respectively, the second in nine shorter stanzas of five lines (the first and fifth) and four lines for the rest, also hendecasyllabic. Alberti sees in Leonardo the epitome of intelligence, of the Apollonian, the analytical eye. His coming-to-be is a second creation out of light (stanza 1): «Al fin la Luz se decidió a ser ángel». In gradual descent toward our realm, following light, wisdom, grace and beauty unite as the four elements that constitute Leonardo's being. The movement of the verse seems halting, as in flashes of insight, except for the central part of this first stanza where wisdom finds its seat in the artist's mind: «... —He aquí mi frente, / mi nueva casa para el pensamiento, / dos bellos ojos dulces reposados / para el mar de la pura inteligencia». In stanza 2 once the Ideas have descended from their Heaven, this union in «... el lecho impecable de las bodas» is the source of Painting as «Bodas de los colores con la ciencia».

The second part of the poem first follows the application of such reasoned and precise artistry to the world of objects. The brush becomes an instrument of meditative analysis, the art a means of reascending to the firmament that was its source. In stanza 6 the poet plunges into the painter's agonized investigation of this world's imprisoning web:

Yo lo siento llorar, enfurecido,
dulce y severo, enmarañado y solo,
como una matemática radiante
y elíptico en la araña de su vista.

(*Aguilar*, pp. 702-704)

The duel between the dissecting, abstracting eye and the solid presence of reality is the axis of this second part of the poem. Leonardo is an angel of light or reason, seeking the transparency of things. The work he has left is testimony to this mission and its author's time transcending cosmic vision:

Pero es el Ojo Universal quien vive,
es la inmortal Retina quien perdura,
escrutando el perfil de las edades,
rayándolo en las láminas del tiempo.

(*Aguilar*, pp. 702-704)

The first aphoristic sequence on colors follows the poem on Leonardo and is dedicated to *Azul*. Alberti's treatment of this color establishes a general pattern that will also be followed for the others: its manifestations are sought in the tradition of painting, principally, or in aspects of reality (to a much lesser degree); but even when describing objects not specifically in paintings, blue is seen in terms of its painted values, and its hues become also objects in the world: «¿Cuántos azules dio el Mediterráneo? /.../ /.../ Los azules de Italia, / los azules de España, / los azules de Francia...» Each tradition gives a new aura to the color that expresses the period's character («El azul Edad Media delicado») while the color also captures the essence of individual artists: «Venecia del azul Tiziano en oro», «En la paleta de Velázquez tengo / otro nombre: me llamo Guadarrama». In some instances the poet introduces a purely personal vision in which blue is filled with his own subjective symbolism: «El mar invade a veces la paleta / del pintor y le pone / un cielo azul que solo da en secreto». The blue series concludes with the color's own discovery of its newest universal value: «Dijo el azul un día: / —Hoy tengo un nuevo nombre. Se me llama: / Azul Pablo Ruiz Azul Picasso» (*Aguilar*, pp. 704-708).

With *Rojo* Alberti's vision becomes more exclusively personal. Red, a dominant color in earthy hues and passing blooms, is from the outset linked with time: «Soy el primer color de la mañana / y el último del día», and fewer painted instances of it are cited. It is the color of feeling, of bodily activity: «Me llamo excitación, cólera, rabia, / estallido del día de la ira», and a peculiarly Spanish tint: «rojo español redondo de las plazas». Although often subdued into pink, red remains for Alberti an expression of strong emotions and of the solidity of things: «Mas me calman las tierras, el sentirme / de sus hondas umbrías penetrado» (*Aguilar*, pp. 721-725). In contrast to the assertive connotations of red —and we speak of a tendency, not an invariable reference— *Amarillo* displays a versatility that approaches that of white. In its first definition, it is linked with light: «Acciono con la luz, soy un activo / cómplice de la luz contra la sombra». It has qualities of airiness and transparency, but is also an essential component in painting the human body, nude or clothed. It glows in medieval gold and gives to painting the light of reason: «Un ordenado esférico amarillo / naturaleza muerta» (*Aguilar*, pp. 734-738).

*Negro* and *Blanco* offer some of the most striking possibilities, black in its own right, not merely as contrast to its opposite, and white because it is part of all the other colors and contains them all. The effort to define the semantic variations of black suggests to Alberti some remarkable images: «Negro Rembrandt, punzado / negro en la frente limpia del acero», «Un negro como flor de la alegría» (*Aguilar*, pp. 765-770). *Blanco* suggests to Alberti a series of precise personal reminiscences, both poetic and circumstantial: «Yo vi —Rafael Alberti— / la luz entre los blancos populares». Here the word game that his own name suggests (*alb*) leads him to equate part of his being with the color and brings to mind his *Cal y canto* period. The last two statements recall, by means of the color, the central contention in much of the volume; life and representation, composition and spontaneous beauty: «Blanco puro, total, mas prisionero / en un cuadrado, un círculo, un triángulo»; «Recordad que también yo soy la rosa» (*Aguilar*, pp. 780-784).

Alberti has focused on individual painters (e.g., Giotto, Piero della Francesca, Leonardo) as instances of a predominance of form or a tendency to idealization, to abstraction. With the next sequence of Italian painters, we enter a world of more palpable, concrete, naked shapes; though they be gods and goddesses —or the near titanic presence of early Biblical personages— such rich mythologies are seen in what they represent that is purely human. This realm of human and divine interac-

tion is heralded by the poem on Michelangelo, where the painter appears
the unwilling Prometheus upon whom an intransigent God thrusts the
power of painting as a torch to rekindle man's recalcitrant, lukewarm
faith:

> Clamó por ti el Señor,
> te llamó por tu nombre allá en las cimas
> en donde, extraviado, antiguo y loco,
> habla consigo mismo,
> mordiéndose en voz baja su secreto.
> —Miguel Angel —te dijo. Y en tu mano,
> cerrándola, lo puso.
>                         Y tú la abriste.
>
>                         (*Aguilar,* pp. 709-715)

«Miguel Angel», the longest poem devoted to one painter, consists of
twelve segments of varying length and prosody, the shortest being three
lines (10) and the longest (11) a concluding piece that extends over seventy lines in uneven stanzas. Alberti subtitled this poem «Fragmentos»
admitting from the outset the impossibiliy of capturing in one single
vision the totality of Michelangelo's work. Alberti wants to establish,
from the beginning, a clear distinction: the difference in quality of inspiration between that other Renaissance giant, Leonardo, and Michelangelo.
The former, as we saw, had knowledge and vision descend upon him in
concert, Light, Wisdom, Grace, Beauty, as Graces all. In contradistinction,
Michelangelo's birth was attended by stormy violence: «No las Gracias,
las Furias, las frenéticas, / desesperadas Furias / te acunaron de niño.
Fueron ellas / el Angel de la Guarda de tu sueño». The next stanza
(quoted above) is the call, God's peremptory, arbitrary demand. The
Lear-like image of God as a superannuated wanderer above reaches down
to Michelangelo as to another self («habla consigo mismo»), for him to
reaccomplish creation for heedless and forgetful mankind. The next two
stanzas show a Michelangelo lost on earth and a stranger in it, in a
loneliness that parallels that of his Lord:

> Mirad aquí al violento,
> al desnudo, al hambriento
> de Eternidad.
> ... ... ... ... ... ... ... ... ... ... ... ... ... ...
> Mirad aquí al amado del rayo y la tormenta,
> al pobre solitario de las olas.
>
>                         (*Aguilar,* pp. 709-710)

In these four sections Alberti uses the vocative with special effectiveness. For God's dialog with the painter is an auto-dialog, and the poet's
invocation is in its turn an auto-dialog in creation. This impression
emerges with particular force through the quality of the language, strongly reminiscent of Alberti's previous auto-dialog in *Sobre los ángeles,* and
pursued throughout the Michelangelo poem. In stanzas 5 and 6 humanity
weeps through the painter:

Llora el hombre.
… … … … … … … … … .
Los cabellos se me empapan
de sombras y estoy desnudo
en las sombras.
… … … … … … … … … .
Son las sombras las que lloran
en las sombras.

(*Aguilar*, p. 711)

The fall of man is relived in all its intensity and with the further weight of sinning centuries, by the artist who sees himself and us as shadows of our first luminous existence.

At the poem's center, Section 7 situates the painter's brush as middle term between the artist and God, the artist and the world, God and the world:

Pincel en soledad, pincel hundido
en lo oscuro, llenando
de ráfagas de luz y de temblores
de tierra todo el cielo.
Solo por ti la cara desvelada de Dios,
pincel movido al soplo de trompetas finales,
pudo ser descubierta entre las nubes.

(*Aguilar*, pp. 711-712)

The brush is the very personification of Michelangelo's lonely task, in a re-Creation, a re-inauguration of man's world and of its Armageddon. There is an upward movement in the first four lines from the dark depths to the firmament. The brush is alone with the elements it re-establishes, in a creation that moves from earth to heaven («… llenando / de ráfagas de luz y de temblores / de tierra todo el cielo») in opposite direction from that of its original instance. The last three lines reveal to us God at our last moments anticipating our history's conclusion. To the «ráfagas / de luz y de temblores / de tierra» of line 3 corresponds «soplo de trompetas finales» in line 6: «ráfaga» — «soplo»; «de luz y de temblores de tierra» — «trompetas finales» («trompetas» conveying the idea of light, sound and vibration).

Sections 8 to 10 attend to the forms and images of Michelangelo's painting with special connotative references in Section 8 to moments from the Fall of Man in the Sistine Chapel. There is an immediate parallelism between 8 and 7, in that the first part of 8 is a direct rewriting in different terms of the beginning of 7: «Pincel en soledad, pincel hundido / en lo oscuro…»; 8: «Cabellera agitada en la noche…» Mankind's concrete suffering is relived by the poet in echoing interior duplications. The senses are painted and rekindled by language, first hearing (stanza 1): «escucho como barres, melancólica escoba / esta tierra de muertos»; then sight: «miro cómo buscáis, descaminados ojos, / ya en la nada, un refugio» — again we recall here the imagery of *Sobre los ángeles*. The

92

sense of touch appears in a more generalized manner in the final stanza: «Llueve sobre los hombres... [...] La Humanidad perdida, sin vestido sin alma, / va flotando errabunda». The poet joins his voice to the artist's own which he hears and sees in his paintings. Sections 9, 10 and 11, treat more particular elements of Michelangelo's painting, bodies, clothing, the welter of human forms amidst a chaotic nature, all immediately expressive of man's anguish in his banishment: «¡Qué confusión de brazos / y piernas baja y sube! / La noche abre su mano / y el sueño brama y cruje».

Section 12, the last part of the poem, is its complex recapitulation set in terms of the artist's life as an anguished, headlong pursuit of God's semblance on earth, an effort to capture movement, imprison it, seizing the Creator's features in his Creation. In the contrast between immobility and movement, Alberti expresses Michelangelo's effort to contain time itself. The painter appears first as a displaced, ancient Titan in the modern world of Rome: «... eco de trueno antiguo / casi extinguido ya, solo...» Only the sea may perhaps be vast enough to support the truth that he bears: «Tal vez la mar, oh Dios, pero montaña, / no de espumas y olas, sí de cumbres / congeladas, de mármol... /.../ Y galopa». Alberti pictures Michelangelo's creation as a cyclopean rearrangement of forms that may show forth God's evidence:

> ¡Oh Dios, oh Dios, oh Dios! Va a abrir la mano,
> va a arrancarle de cuajo las pupilas
> a la luz, va por fin a revelarte
> su última luz, dejándote a Ti ciego.
> ¡Al mar, al mar! Tal vez allí...
> Y galopa.

(*Aguilar*, pp. 709-715)

God's lonely wandering above (Section 2) is retraced on earth by the artist, and God's initial gesture, closing the artist's hand around the secret («... Y en tu mano, / ... lo puso») is repeated in the poem's conclusion as Michelangelo, now true Prometheus, steals the light with which to reveal to the Maker his own Creation.

As we have seen, Alberti has organized these «Fragmentos» in a closely-knit pattern. Section 7 on the brush appears as the hinge that articulates the two main parts of the poem and that reflects them: its first four lines are as an activation of light upon darkness and the last three are the revelation of God's features to the brass of final trumpets. In similar fashion the entire poem moves from the dark birth of its beginning to the stolen light of its final stanza. And the last section in echo to the Biblical reference, «God's face moved upon the waters» (images of the sea as marmorean features), ends with renewed, revealing light. Within the poem, through its invocative patterns and inferences to the poet's own creating anguish, a play of mirrors, of repeated images of creation, arises in powerful reverberations.

The last two Italian painters treated by Alberti are Tintoretto and Veronese. From the former, he highlights the turbulent movement of his scenes, the compelling violence that attracts him like a maelstrom: «No te miro, me anego / en ti, mar agitado, / pincel arrebatado / en un carro de fuego». Seven stanzas of uneven length press forth in short, restless lines: «Todo se cae, rueda. / Todo se precipita...» (*Aguilar,* pp. 725-726). In contrast, Poem 15, «Veronés», suggests the calmer outlines of statuesque forms. It centers on the painting indicated by the subtitle «Alegoría de la Primavera» and flows slowly in free verse and long meandering sentences that follow the ample lines of Veronese's figures:

> Si los ríos, Amor, Gracia fuerte, anchurosa,
> de dilatadas ansias y caderas;
> si los ríos, los jóvenes, más anhelados ríos
> se alzaran, se doblaran,
> un amanecer largo, y sólo fueran hombros,
> pechos altos, abiertos y muslos extendidos...
> Si pudiera tocarlos,

The poet's desire grows as he traces the painting's deep, rhythmical forms and concludes with an eager call to lovemaking: «ven ya a gritar, luchar, morir conmigo, / en la despeinadora, / naciente y plena luna saludable!» (*Aguilar,* pp. 727-728).

Between the painters of Italy and those of Spain, Alberti situates artists from the Northern School, German and Flemish, and, as a geographically transitional figure perhaps, between those colder regions and the Peninsula, the Classical Poussin, master of composition. After the Elysian serenity of Veronese's «Alegoría de la Primavera», we descend with «Bosco» to a vertiginous, tumultuous vision of deathbound life. In one of the most extraordinary poems in the collection, Alberti transposes Bosch's delirious universe into frenzied language. The devil, in endless spiraling metamorphosis, leads the feverish dance of mankind into hell: «El diablo hocicudo, / ojipelambrudo, / cornicapricudo»; «diablo palitroque»; «diablo garavijo»; «El diablo liebre».

> Barrigas, narices,
> lagartos, lombrices,
> delfines volantes,
> orejas rodantes,
> ojos boquiabiertos,
> escobas perdidas,
> barcas aturdidas,
> vómitos, heridas,
> muertos.
>
> (*Aguilar,* pp. 729-732)

The poem's disposition emphasizes the dizzying movement of the dance, as does its language in topsy-turvy accumulations and verbal invention, fantastic as the images of the painter's fevered imagination. The sounds are harsh, mostly strong consonants and occasional tongue-twisters («sipilipitiebre, sipilipitriva»).[12] In the concluding stanza the poet stands back

---

[12] As many other nonsense words (yet perfectly clear in the context) and puns in the poem, this is practically untranslatable.

and cuts off the circular dance with a stroke in swift, vertical imagery that encompasses the realm of the artist's creation: «Pintor en desvelo: / tu paleta vuela al cielo, / y en un cuerno, / tu pincel baja al infierno» (*Aguilar,* pp. 729-732). At the same time, the painter's instruments re-establish the distance between the artist and his work, between us and the poem as artifice.

The movement of withdrawal, very marked in this poem, is a frequent technique of Alberti's, when he feels that the painted world and its verbal rendition must be securely framed as re-presentations («Giotto», «Piero della Francesca», «Leonardo»). He uses it also in «Rembrandt»:

> ¡Oh pintor empapado de espectros, oh dolido
> pincel, oh dolorida mano extraña
> rompiendo los tabiques de las sombras,
> nimbada para siempre
> por la brecha de luz del infinito!

> (*Aguilar,* pp. 741-742)

These final lines join the torment of creation to the struggle of light and darkness, in order to concentrate on the means of the painter the tripartite tension that has structured the entire piece: «A la luz se le abrió, se le dio entrada / en los más hondos sótanos»; «Un latido, un murmullo, / un quejido creciente / de color subterráneo que se expande»; «¡Oh fúlgido espadazo repentino! / Noche rasgada, impunemente herida.» Rembrandt's hand, «nimbada para siempre / por la brecha de luz del infinito!», becomes the communicating element between universal creation and his reproduction of it.

In his introductory poem on the Museum of El Prado, Alberti envisions Spanish painting as closely linked to our earthbound existence and yet permeated in its detail by an exaltation of form, to such an extent that reality is true only because it seeks to transcend itself, to unrealize itself, as it were. In «El Greco» this tendency becomes a thrust toward the mystical: «Aquí, el barro ascendiendo a vértice de llama, / la luz hecha salmuera, / la lava del espíritu candente». The equation: («barro», «llama») = («luz», «salmuera») = («lava», «espíritu»), which we can render also as «barro» + «luz» («llama») = «lava», suggests the general development of the poem and anticipates its imagistic movement: man and earthly elements tortured by their upwards compulsion. In terms of a specifically poetic technique, the real appears from the outset almost exclusively through its metaphorical transformation, that is to say, it is abstracted from its substance. To transmit best the ceaseless movement of El Greco's art, Alberti uses blank verse whose extreme variations in length and uneven stops also suggest the halting surge of upward aspiration. To this rising thrust from below corresponds a downward collapse, from firmament to hell:

> Aquí,
> la tiza delirante de los cielos
> polvoreados de cortadas nubes,
> sobre las que se vuelcan

en remolinos o de las que penden,
agarrados de un pie, del pico de un cabello,
o del cañón de un ala,
ángeles de narices alcuzas y ojos bizcos,
trastornados de azufre,
prendidos por un fósforo traído en un zigzag del aire.

*(Aguilar,* pp. 752-754)

«Nubes» to «azufre», the lines follow the angels' downfall, their appearance foreboding their ultimate destination: alliteration in «z» and harsh consonants prepare the realm of «azufre». Similar sounds open and close this descent: «tiza delirante», «zigzag del aire» and further inner correspondences of sound imbue the image in synesthesia of yellow light and broken movement: «trastornados de azufre», «fósforo traído en un zigzag». Compositional parallelisms are also present in «*pico* de un cabello» — «narices *alcuzas*».

Abstraction is further accomplished by the disappearance of elements into their color, as in «Una gloria con trenos de ictericia, / un biliar canto derramado» where sound and image are resolved into greenish-yellow hues. Or in the overexpansion of metaphor at the expense of its origins, all this contained in the long-drawn, rising interrogative inflection:

De dónde, aquí, hacia dónde
el lagrimal torcido
de coagulada lágrima casi en gota de lacre,
el devorado manto,
el tiritante traje tenebroso,
tinto de un vino tinto de la tierra,
abrasando los cuerpos
en invasión contra los deslumbrados
rostros o desceñidas manos frías en puntas
aspirantes a alas?

*(Aguilar,* pp. 752-754)

Here «manto», «traje», even though its presence is reinforced by the alliteration («tinto... tinto... tierra»), is overcome by its qualifying burden and ultimately disappears through the contrasted whiteness of winglike hands. Also «puntas / aspirantes a *alas*» recalls «coagu*la*da *lá*grima» and earlier «... cabello / o del cañón de un *ala*». The poem concludes with a reference to the artist's technique as a direct reflection of, a participation in the tortured universe of his creation; the effort to wed diametrically opposed elements is rendered through baroque oxymorons: «Oh purgatorio del color, ... /.../ ... etérea / cueva de misteriosos bellos feos, / de horribles hermosísimos...» *(Aguilar, pp.* 752-754).

There could hardly be a more striking contrast in painting than that between El Greco and Zurbarán. Where the former was turmoil, concentration, spiritualization, the latter is serenity and sensible evidence. Passion has given way to thought. Alberti has chosen a stately composition in eight stanzas of six hendecasyllables (ababcc) to communicate the calm precision of the Extremaduran painter. Expression and thought, in bonds as intimate as they are certain, proceed through unhurried exposition to their conceptual culmination in ideal harmony: «Gire en tu eternidad la disciplina / de una circunferencia cristalina». Zurbarán's painting deals with absolute values in a perfectly Apollonian world where light, thought and painting are equal. The first stanza conveys that pervasive tendency of the artist's work as a work of considered, light (reason)-imbued definition

> Ni el humo, ni el vapor, ni la neblina.
> Lejos de aquí ese aliento que destruye.
> Una luz en los huesos determina
> y con la sombra cómplice construye.
> Pensativa sustancia la pintura,
> paraliza de luz la arquitectura.
>
> (*Aguilar*, pp. 755-756)

Three strong statements follow the growth of forms through a rejection of vagueness, by means of the glow of an inner light, to vagueness's opposite, thought and light-frozen form («arquitectura»). To overwhelm the «destruye» of the second line, already ineffectual in its agent («aliento») and thrust away, the rest of the stanza opposes: «determina», «construye», «paraliza de luz». To «humo», «vapor», «neblina», «aliento» are contrasted «luz en los huesos», «sombra cómplice» (i.e., shadow as accomplice of light, as its defining counterpart), «Pensativa sustancia», «arquitectura».

Stanza 2 establishes the «Pensativa sustancia» of things, infused with reason by the painter's mind:

> Meditación del sueño,
> ... ... ... ... ... ... ... ... ... ... ... ...
> severo cielo, tierra razonable
> de pan cortado, vino y estameña.
> El pincel, la paleta, todo es frente,
> medula todo, pensativamente.
>
> (*Aguilar*, pp. 755-756)

Between the meditation and its instruments («el pincel», «la paleta»), themselves seen as pure thought, stand the elements of the representation, individual forms and textures become universals. In stanza 3, the thought that has penetrated the objects on the canvas shines forth through them, expressing the divine order that permeates all: «Piensa el tabique, piensa el pergamino / del volumen que alumbra la madera». The reasonable presence of reality becomes, in stanzas 4 and 5, a disposition to prayer and evidence of the world above: «Ora el plato, y la jarra, de sencilla, / humildemente persevera muda, /.../ La nube es un soporte, es una baja / plataforma celeste suspendida». But the ethereal, no matter how compelling, can be achieved only through its patterned appearance below: «Mas lo que muestra es siempre un andamiaje / para enganchar en pliegues el ropaje». The last three stanzas center on the painter himself rather than his work, on the very art of painting («Rudo amante

97

del lienzo, recia llama»), the earth-bound mysticism that he imparts to his representations («Fe que da el barro, mística terrena») expands into the compulsion of form («Pintor de Extremadura, en ti se extrema, / dura y fatal, la lidia por la forma») (*Aguilar,* pp. 255-756). We are on earth, but earth contains the divine.

The essence of life in all its manifestations, the nobility of sheer existence, are what Alberti sees in Velázquez, himself a great admirer of Zurbarán. As he did for Michelangelo, Alberti chooses to render the scope of Velázquez's painting by means of fragmented impressions. From the first «fragment», we contemplate the exact rendition of life:

> Se apareció la Vida una mañana
> y le suplicó:
> —Píntame, retrátame
> como soy realmente o como tú
> quisieras realmente que yo fuese.
> Mírame, aquí, modelo sometido,
> sobre un punto, esperando que me fijes.
> Soy un espejo en busca de otro espejo.
>
> (*Aguilar,* pp. 757-763)

Painting as reality is stressed through clear repetition («Píntame», «retrátame»; «realmente», «realmente»). Life has found its master representer, at last, and wishes for its final form at his hands («modelo sometido»; «esperando que me fijes»); the last line of the section introduces the movement of interior duplication that is frequent in Velázquez («Las Meninas», «Venus in the Mirror», «Arachne», etc.) and captures the depth of existence, reaching out to the viewer. The second fragment sets forth the power of Velázquez's painting as a zenith of achievement and light: «Mediodía sereno, / descansado / de la Pintura. Pleno / presente Mediodía, sin pasado». In this art, not only life, but painting, reach their fullest realization.

For Alberti, a visit to the Prado was a leisurely stroll through the world of Velázquez: «... y entraba por la puerta de tus cuadros». Paintings, as open doors, portions of space through which air and light circulate, sounds, movements, backgrounds that live and give life to the figures they frame. There are in all six fragments (numbers 3 to 8) that recall Alberti's personal impressions. The rest of the poem treats: aspects of technique (9 through 15); subjects (16 through 25); general qualities (26 through 32).

> Más vida, sí, más vida,
> y tu pintura,
> pintor, de haber vivido,
> más que real pintura hubiera sido
> pintura sugerida,
> leve mancha, almo cuerpo diluido.
>
> (*Aguilar,* pp. 757-763)

The cycle is thus closed by a return to the beginning, with an emphasis on art as artifice, where life («vida», «vida», «vivido») equals painting («pintura», «pintor», «pintura», «pintura»), and painting is the light blush and spirit of living matter («leve», «mancha», «almo cuerpo diluido») (*Aguilar*, pp. 757-763).

The poem on Goya is strongly reminiscent of that on Bosch; though somewhat less frenzied in movement, it is just as fantastic, but with a fantasy that is the unperceived madness of the daily life we choose not to think about. The hell that Bosch painted was Medieval and carnival-esque with flashes of rotund humour amid the frantic dance, laughter and dread cheek by jowl. Goya, true heir of Bosch in Spain's disastrous eighteenth century, paints a terrifying, but not unfamiliar, world, where monsters lurk in our own selves and sometimes come to life, leering also behind the careless dancers:

> La dulzura, el estupro,
> la risa, la violencia,
> la sonrisa, la sangre,
> el cadalso, la feria.
> Hay un diablo demente persiguiendo
> a cuchillo la luz y las tinieblas.
>
> (*Aguilar*, pp. 770-773)

Hell has floated up to our surface and resides with us. Reason and madness, vice and virtue, all are equally flayed into manic revolutions by savage blind forces. All the structures of society manifest themselves through violence and crime, as if the most brutal energies of history had been unleashed. Goya painted both the appearance of the world and its demonic substructure and gave them equal representational value; his compelling force imbued dreams with such evidence that they overshadow their objective supports, while the actual world he pictures was itself nightmarish. He was the first artist who dared to show us the darkest, lurking recesses of our being and the fragility of the social convenant that holds us in check. But even reversed values can be turned into great art: «Pintor: / En tu inmortalidad llore la Gracia / y sonría el Horror» (*Aguilar*, pp. 770-773).

Inevitably, Alberti's recreation of Goya's real and imaginary nightmares sharpened in his mind equally turbulent scenes of his own recent past and of the Civil War,[13] and it may be as an attempt to hold such memories at bay that he now turns to the calm groves of Corot. In the poem dedicated to the French «paysagiste», the summoning forth of this painter's serene world is so strong as to suggest almost an effort of will on the poet's part, through the deliberate re-creation of Corot's soothing and ordered panoramas. In this poem Alberti begins immediately with an evocation of the painter's spirit seen through his art, reversing the movement of the majority of his other pieces where a consideration of the painter's work would lead to concluding comments on his craft: «Tú, alma evaporada, / tú, dulce luz de sol desvanecida, / álamo de cintura más

---

[13] Alberti's play *Noche de guerra en el museo del Prado* joins his memories of Goya's paintings to those of the Civil War.

delgada / que la paleta que en tu mano anida». The poem's development takes us from this initial «Tú» to the concluding: «Dame tu gracia, tu infantil dulzura, / el amor que no tiene el tiempo en que he nacido; / dame la más humilde rama de tu pintura, / y no me des la pena de tu olvido». The painter's spirit is brought down into his creation, giving temporal substance to the «tree». Stanza 1 establishes the equation: «alma» = «álamo + paleta», and stanza 2 reverses it as «brush» = «living tree»:

> Hojas a tu pincel en cada aurora
> le nacen. Brisas juegan
> con sus verdes cabellos florecidos.
> Tu pincel a la hora
> en que los sonrosados de la tarde navegan
> se te duerme de pájaros dormidos.
>
> (*Aguilar*, pp. 773-774)

Through the development in this stanza of some of the elements of stanza 1 (e.g., «álamo» → «hojas»; «anida» → «pájaros»), the anthropomorphic «álamo de cintura más delgada» is paralleled by «verdes cabellos». The painter's spirit is sought and discovered, fully alive within the ideal portion of time captured by his work, and ever repeated with every contemplation. The next stanza develops the other major element of Corot's painting, water, an element implicit in the very first line —«evaporada»— as was the tree: «alma»-«álamo». But the water, become mirror, also provides a means of direct entry for the poet who wants to see a portion of his own past, or of his soul, in the painter as painting, as mirror of water: «Espejo desvelado / de aguas que cantan quietamente quedas, / déjame que me sueñe ensimismado / por tus estremecidas y húmedas alamedas». Now the poet's idealized past becomes one with the painter's as an ancient myth revivified, and the evocation of the artist occasions the poet's sharpened nostalgia: «viera yo por los ojos tranquilos de tus puentes / el fluir encantado de la vida, / viera desde tus montes y valles inocentes / mi arboleda perdida» (*Aguilar*, pp. 773-774). The poem is the instrument of the poet's remembrance; the latter now resides in it as the artist's spirit does in his landscape, in his tree as brush and his soul as time-keeper.

Other painters of the nineteenth century to which Alberti dedicates a composition are Delacroix, Cézanne, Renoir, Gauguin, and Van Gogh. The last three painters of the collection are Spanish and belong to the twentieth century: Gutiérrez Solana, Miró and Picasso. To contain the brilliant turmoil of Delacroix' painting, Alberti selects traditional heptasyllabic *redondillas*. The romantic's painting seems pure impetus where anecdote and craft are inseparable: «El color como drama. / Como luz, la vehemencia. / Como línea, la urgencia / del rapto y de la llama» (*Aguilar*, p. 775). But with Cézanne we enter an altogether different world of simplicity. It is the morning of modern painting; the artist and his craft are born together to the new evidence of elementary forms: «La plástica, diaria, muda vida / es una interminable, trabajosa mañana, / una cosa cualquiera, definida: / la manzana, el reloj, la damajuana». Alberti's gaze alternates between the man and his work, the tenacious craftsman and his compact surroundings. All is subjected to the necessities of definition; blue, the only color mentioned, serves as background to simple shapes: «Te conoce el azul, te reconoce / el nuevo tema: / la forma, el pleno goce / de la forma, color pleno en esquema». With «Cézanne» we return to the most basic truths of painting where «todo se determina / por el cubo, el cilindro y por la esfera» (*Aguilar*, pp. 776-778).

Renoir's painting bursts in an efflorescence of pink flesh. Colors come to life and rush towards a common source in roseated hues, imbuing all forms with intense sonority:

> El rosa canta junto al mar,
> el ancho rosa nalga por el río,
> el rosa espalda puesto a espejear
> al sol y a resonar
> rosa talón por el rocío.
>
> (*Aguilar*, pp. 778-779)

From the poem's first lines: «Los colores soñaban. Cuánto tiempo, / oh, cuánto tiempo hacía!» to its conclusion: «ya todos son ramos de flores. / Y rosa», a cascade of color tumbles out of, or into, pink. In this verbal painting, language creates potential pinks even in those hues at the other end of the chromatic scale:

> El amarillo, cabellera.
> La cabellera, rosas amarillas.
> ... ... ... ... ... ... ... ...
> El plata, ser olivo
> y vino de clavel el rojo vivo.
>
> (*Aguilar*, pp. 778-779)

Here, sound correspondences seem to stain «olivo» with some of the «vino» in «clavel» while «rojo vivo» and «plata» also produce pink. All is a synesthetic harmony of sound, color and movement.

In his poem on Gauguin, Alberti wants to evoke an atmosphere of dreamlike, exotic mystery. Forms and landscapes that remain almost inpenetrable to the Western eye suggest by their presence the mystery of existence —man's and nature's— of lush life born of the sea. There is only one verb in the entire poem, in stanza 1, serving merely to hint at transformations, intermediary stages in which the painter captures the symbiotic relationships that prevail in his primeval world between all its elements:

> El color,
> de viaje,
> se hizo aroma de flor,
> perfume de paisaje,
> isla, amor.
>
> (*Aguilar*, pp. 784-785)

101

In gradual transformations «El color / de viaje» becomes «isla, amor»: «flor» → «paisaje» → «isla»; «aroma» → «perfume» → «amor». Later relationships are established both by sound and meaning as, for instance in the development of the possible colors of the sea:

> Mar, mar, mar,
> poesía
> misteriosa,
> verde, amarillo, rosa.
>
> Melancolía
> quieta.
> Alegoría
> carmín, morado, violeta.
>
> Esmeralda
> palmar,
> orilla gualda.
>
> (*Aguilar*, pp. 784-785)

«Mar... verde» → «Esmeralda»; «mar... amarillo» → «orilla gualda»; «palmar» reinstates the sea phonetically at the center of meaning. Alberti ends with an inner echo of sound and meaning and a return to the first stanza, in circular conclusion:

> Pintor:
> pura,
> al sol de mirada segura,
> sueño real,
> flor
> irreal,
> tu pintura.
>
> (*Aguilar,* pp. 778-779)

Between «Pintor: / pura» and «tu pintura» mediate light, the dream and the colored form (*Aguilar*, pp. 784-785).

Surprisingly, Picasso suggests to Alberti a rather straightforward treatment. A variety of verse lengths is restrained by assonance and frequent rhyme. The painter is seen as a Spanish bull: «De azul se arrancó el toro del toril, / de azul el toro del chiquero». This central image is then followed through the early «periods» of painting, blue and pink, then cubism: «Entre el ayer y el hoy se desgaja / lo que más se asemeja a un cataclismo». Finally, painting can become political action: «Guernica. / Dolor al rojo vivo. /.../ ... Y aquí el juego del arte comienza a ser un juego explosivo». Although out of Spain, Picasso's bull is ever reliving its anguish.

The central, unitary development of *A la pintura* ends with this poem on Picasso. The static, quiet shores of Giotto's sea have become a window on Picasso's unpredictable re-creations:

> ¿Quién sabrá de la suerte de la línea,
> de la aventura del color?
> ... ... ... ... ... ... ... ... ... ... ... ...

Y se descubre esa ventana
que se entreabre al mediodía
de otro nuevo planeta
desnudo y con rigor de geometría.

(*Aguilar*, pp. 794-797)

But the basic elements remain: light, color, line, composition. Here, Alberti's poetry found new resources in his own earliest inspiration. It reached one of its peaks by looking back with nostalgia and anticipating also the pleasures of his reacquaintance with that first interest. Having thought that he could only become a poet by turning away from painting, he has come to realize some of his greatest poetry by returning to painting.

## V. *Conclusion: «Poemas de Punta del Este»*

The prose reflections and passing impressions that comprise «Diario de un día» —there are two such sequences— give us straightforward commentary on those activities and interests from which Alberti's poems spring. Always, his mind returns to his Spanish past or lingers on his present isolation, explicitly at times, other times indirectly:

Un gallo de voz enronquecida canta pegado al muro de mi cuarto. Silencio. Repetición. No hay vecino que le conteste. Del otro lado del mar, los gallos duermen su primer sueño todavía. (*Aguilar*, p. 853)

It takes no interpreting to see Alberti's own condition in that of this insistent, hoarse-voiced rooster, displaced and alone. The collection closes with an anguished iteration of this same thought in «¡Qué solo estoy!»: «¡Qué solo estoy a veces, oh qué solo, / y hasta qué pobre y triste y olvidado!» (*Aguilar*, p. 895).

Nevertheless, two ancient passions now possess the poet with newfound vigor: the sea, whose never-quite-abated fascination resurges strongly in several poems, and painting, whose demands he feels as strongly now as in his earliest youth: «Mi primera y avasalladora vocación me llama hoy, al cabo de casi treinta años de dormida, con una persistencia de la que ya comienzo a tener miedo» (*Aguilar*, p. 852). It is not without uneasiness that Alberti considers this turn in his creative path, although *A la pintura* offers ample proof of the happy marriage of the two arts. Still, as with the sea's presence, the attraction of painting for the poet is but one of the forms taken by his profound nostalgia for the homeland. His exploration of the world of colors is to him as a discovery of lost territories, and painting becomes a homeward voyage: «Mañana, antes aún que amanezca, me volveré a embarcar, cada vez con más ansia, hacia ese país de los colores...» (*Aguilar*, p. 857).

In the second «Diario de un día» Alberti is able to stand back and cast an appraising eye at his working methods and at some important characteristics of his poetry. Time has become all important. He rises with the dawn, writes his first words as the cock crows. His sense of pressing time approaches that of the great Baroque poets, Quevedo in particular, «el desvelado poeta de la muerte» (*Aguilar*, p. 862). And although he admits to the Baroque tendency of his verse, its design is ultimately bathed in Apollonian light: «Mas cada guía de esta difícil enredadera es clara, entramando un total de dibujo preciso que concreta lo oscuro, volviéndolo luminoso» (*Aguilar*, pp. 861-862).

Although *Poemas de Punta del Este* follows *A la pintura* in the usual sequence of Alberti's complete works, most of its compositions were contemporaneous with the great poems on painting. It was no diminution in his poetic powers, but rather a shift of focus, or the absence of a strong poetic object perhaps, that makes these poems at times take too a prosaic a turn. In some senses and despite the chronological evidence [*A la pintura*, 1945-1953 (1967 for Miró); *Poemas de Punta del Este*, 1945-1956], this book is transitional in the poet's work. He will find an energizing focus again when he allows nostalgia and the exile's voice to pour forth unchecked in *Retornos de lo vivo lejano*.

## CHAPTER 6

*RETORNOS DE LO VIVO LEJANO* TO *BALADAS Y CANCIONES DEL PARANÁ* (1948-1956): LONGING

The nostalgic backward glance to Spain, across the ocean and the years, a muted accompaniment in *A la Pintura* and explicitly entoned in *Poemas de Punta del Este,* reaches its most powerful orchestration in the collections that follow. *Retornos* develops to its fullest expression the poet's deep and unabating longing for Spain, times and regions past. And in *Baladas,* he seeks in the traditions and geography of a new land a mythical substratum of sufficient force to join the rich linguistic and folk history that underpinned his earliest Andalusian poetry. But, whether his remembrance is a deliberate focusing of emotion as in *Retornos,* or a conscious effort at mythmaking as in *Baladas,* Alberti's Spain leaves its profound and unmistakable imprint throughout.

As in *A la pintura,* also, many of these poems mark new peaks of excellence for Alberti, again concerned with restructuring a lyrical space and moved by overpowering emotions that seek and create tangible, vivid objects to people its confines. As always, Alberti is at his best when the poetic object, without losing its links to the concrete, is hypostatized in a moment of perfect fusion with the poet's spirit, with exact adequation of phonetic and semantic values that seem to give it renewed, lapidary form. The return of a myth implies a desire to abolish duration, and at the source of Alberti's poetry of this period there is an ever present tension between this desire and the realization that it contains its negation within himself. In more specific terms, the past is valued because it is past and yet still ours, because time has refined away its accidents and left to us the essential in each moment, if only we know to capture it. This is Alberti's overarching concern from *Retornos* to *Baladas;* to seize the past in its remoteness and its present vitality at once, objects and moments that are past and living: both collections are «retornos de lo vivo lejano». In our reading we shall focus on Alberti's effort to delineate what he finds of his personal history as singular myth in *Retornos* and what he finds in his new land as an effort to fuse both approaches into a personally and poetically valid tradition in *Baladas.*

## I. «Retornos de lo vivo lejano»

*Retornos* is composed in three parts of eleven, twenty and eleven poems, respectively. Frequently long lines, often of thirteen and fourteen syllables, in long, uneven stanzas, sustain the flow of memory along spacious banks. Although *Retornos* as a whole does not manifest as compact an ordering as did *A la pintura*, there is, besides the unity of tone and general intent that give the collection its sense of completeness, a more precise organization along temporal, circumstantial and emotional coordinates: the first part traces mainly early memories while following (a) the development of the poet's artistic consciousness, his feeling of separateness; (b) remembering as a poetic activity. The second part examines the meeting of love and poetry as a doubly creative conjunction. The third part recalls moments and conditions favorable or adverse to poetry. *Retornos,* thus, is as much an examination of the poetic endeavor as it is a remembrance. Again, poetry is an instrument of discovery as it was in *Sobre los ángeles,* where Alberti employed it to bring to light his deepest anxieties or in *A la pintura,* where he used it to reproduce the varieties of pictorial space; its realm is now living memory, the geography of his past.

The sequence's first composition, «Retornos de una tarde de lluvia», epitomizes the entire book: although it seems to be at first an attempt to recall certain very early moments of the poet's life, its true subject is the effort of language to transcend time. The poem is among the longest in this collection, consisting of three stanzas of sixteen, thirty-two and seventeen lines, respectively, predominantly of alexandrines and hendecasyllables. As the poem opens, the meditative gaze has turned inward and is now projected across the rain to the other shores:

> También estará ahora lloviendo, neblinando
> en aquellas bahías de mis muertes,
> de mis años aún vivos sin muertes.
> También por la neblina entre el pinar, lloviendo,
> lloviendo, y la tormenta también, los ya distantes
> truenos con gritos celebrados, últimos,
> el fustazo final del rayo por las torres.
> Te asomarías tú, vejez blanca, saliéndote
> de tus templadas sábanas de nietos y ojos dulces,
> y mi madre a los vidrios de colores
> del alto mirador que descorría
> una ciudad azul de níveas sombras
> con barandales verdes
> resonados de súbito a la tarde
> por los dedos que el mar secretamente
> y como por descuido abandona en la brisa.
>
> (*Aguilar,* pp. 903-905)

«También» subsumes the condition now existing out of which the poet wants to create a remote counterpart. Immediately we have a spatial duality here/there. This «también» transfers to the as yet nonexistent landscape all the substance of the here and now. The suspended action of two gerunds «lloviendo» and «neblinando» gathers the momentum of «también» —accented nasals suggest effort and insistence— to anchor solidly an identical, absent moment. But the second line begins immediately to undermine this design. The expanse of «bahías» contains a void, and «mis muertes» also, through its negation of time. A tentative equilibrium is reached in the third line, though all its elements are needed to counteract «mis muertes»; «mis años aún vivos» and «sin muertes». «Bahías» is left as an emptiness to be filled. The poem's task will be to give substance to this emptiness, but between the impulse (line 1) and the completion (line 3) stands destruction (line 2) as between the poet's present and his youth stand the years of death, war and exile.

The elaboration of «there» from «here» continues in line four with incantation-like repetitions of «también» and «lloviendo»; «Neblinando / en aquellas bahías» has become «por la neblina entre el pinar», gradually giving form and substance to that void, while soon (line 5) «lloviendo» itself acquires greater spatio-temporal definition; sounds («truenos con gritos celebrados») and distant lightning slash through the blurry screen of water. Having been rent by the concreteness of these two perceptions, in line 8 the gray background of mist and time begins to part. Above the horizon the distant past acquires form: the grandmother, only an abstraction, a ghost («vejez blanca», «templadas sábanas de nietos y ojos dulces»), glimmers forth to recall secular continuity; the mother is closer and more vivid («y mi madre a los vidrios de colores»); both are evoked by «asomarías», a conditional of potential, customary action. Below, the city draws the elements of its form from these two figures:

> «ojos dulces»        «vejez blanca... sábanas».[1]
> «una ciudad azul      de níveas sombras»
> «con barandales verdes»
> «vidrios de colores»

The omnipresence of water is once more felt in the last three lines where sight and sound join to give further life to the setting and reintroduce the link to the present and the shore, origin of the meditation. The return to this actual present («abandona») from the wished-for present of the first line —actually a future of probability («estará ahora lloviendo»)— has been insensibly accomplished by means of a careful gradation of verb tenses, from the first line: «estará... saliéndote» (line 9), «descorría» (line 11), «abandona» (line 16). This focusing forth is accompanied by a sequential development of sound and sight, imagery that is brought to bear on the stanza's last three lines to give it a particular clarity in contrast to the abstract tenor of the final metaphor. A comparison of the concluding lines to the first and the second major moments of the stanza would make this clear:

[1] While «ojos dulces» appears indefinite as to color, the transposed phonetic (a)zul — (d)ulces allows for the link. In fact, a close reading of these lines uncovers extensive phonetic echoes intimately linking the two visions.

1 $\left\{\begin{array}{l}\text{«truenos con gritos celebrados, últimos» — sound} \\ \text{«el fustazo final del rayo por las torres» — sight}\end{array}\right.$

2 $\left\{\begin{array}{l}\left.\begin{array}{l}\text{«... níveas sombras»} \\ \text{«con barandales verdes»}\end{array}\right\} \text{— sight} \\ \text{«resonados de súbito a la tarde» — sound}\end{array}\right.$

The similar syntactical disposition of these phrases further enhances the parallelism and suggests general movement towards the fusion of sight and sound effected in the very last lines:

| «truenos | con gritos | celebrados | últimos» |
|---|---|---|---|
| «níveas sombras | con barandales | resonados | de súbito a la tarde» |

Thus is the present of the last lines made possible, as well as their bright emergence from the storm.

The effort to fuse past and present conditions becomes more explicit in the second stanza, as does the turning inward of the poem. The first lines, for a fleeting moment, seem to bring about the desired communion:

> Saldría yo con Agustín, con José Ignacio[2]
> y con Paquillo, el hijo del cochero,
> a buscar caracoles por las tapias
> y entre los jaramagos de las tumbas,
> o por la enretamada arboleda perdida
> a lidiar becerrillos todavía con sustos
> de alegres colegiales sorprendidos de pronto.
>
> (*Aguilar*, pp. 903-905)

«Saldría» maintains the conditional mood that in the preceding stanza introduced the grandmother and the mother — that is, the only two *events*. There has been now a gain in specificity in that particular names are recalled. The storm has passed. The speaker and his friends go looking for snails. But after the storm is *now*. They seek through tombs and the «enretamada arboleda perdida»;[3] «todavía» in line 6 refers to the present, of course. The poet envisions himself in an hypostatized present/past reenacting his youthful games. The development is concluded with a construction («con... sorprendidos de pronto») that recalls those at the end of the two sentences in stanza 1. But the projection cannot be sustained, undermined as it is by the presence of death at its center — «mi muerte» of stanza 1, has remained in «tumbas» and «enretamada arboleda perdida», and it becomes introspection, chained to the present:

> (Estas perdidas ráfagas que vuelven sin aviso,
> estas precipitadas palabras de los bosques,
> diálogo interrumpido, confidencias
> del mar y las arenas empapadas.)
>
> (*Aguilar*, p. 903)

---

[2] Cf. *La arboleda perdida*, Ch. II; Agustín and José Ignacio are cousins of Alberti's.

[3] «Retama» (gorse) also connotes bitterness; one says «amargo como la retama».

Here, all that remains of the past is the manner of its return. These lines that heed the «perdidas ráfagas» of remote days are themselves a sudden gust interrupting the fragile edifice of invention. The act of remembrance itself will now become the focus of the poem. It had been adumbrated by the poetic presence which stood at the beginning behind «También»; the elaboration of past/present moments as creative activity, the weaving of tones of a musical and poetic instrument, moved towards the center of concern in the last three lines of that first stanza, with the sea itself as the artist: «resonados... / por los dedos que el mar... / ... abandona...» Now the poet takes center stage, though as yet as mere receptive presence.

However, the space-time transposition that had arisen so naturally before must now be forcibly elicited and defined: «Reclino la cabeza, / llevo el oído al hoyo de la mano». The man gives way to the poet, and if the picture that arises now belongs both to the past and the present, it is because it was then, as it is now, an idealized dream: «... Oigo un galope / fatigando la orilla de castillos, / de bañadas ruinas y escaleras / con los pies destrozados en el agua». This will be the last individualized scene. It is the final stage of the pattern of recovery of past/present moments and its concluding phrase is an echo of earlier ones: «... ruinas y escaleras / con los pies destrozados en el agua». The sequence of last words in this pattern clearly leads to the destructive triumph of temporality: «... gritos», «últimos», «resonados de súbito», «sorprendidos de pronto», «... pies destrozados en el agua». All temporal referents («últimos», «de súbito» and so on) have disintegrated into their eponymous image, water.

Here, at the middle point of the poem the interiorization that had interrupted the earlier scenic development affirms itself fully with the sudden surfacing of the poetic «I» and the poem's shortest sentence to this point: «Yo sé quien va, yo sé quien se desboca / cantando en ese potro negro de sal y espuma». The present tense, dominating since the parenthetical moment of introspection, will remain in force until the end of the stanza. The here and now is inescapable; «que se desboca...» is the same today as then, his goal now as distant as it was. It is the poet's younger self who rushes headlong:

> Quiere los arcos, busca los dinteles
> que dan a los difíciles poblados sin neblinas,
> armónicas comarcas, firmamentos precisos,
> cielos sin nebulosas,
> paraísos sin humo.
>
> (*Aguilar,* p. 904)

This region appears to him an accessible, clear future, this goal also the present poet's. He, however, has tried to reach it through his pen to give it substance out of time, believing it an attainable past. At the mutual crossing of their desires, the goal becomes the perennial essence of the poet's creative endeavor, threatened by the indefinite rain and mists of time on all sides.

The hold of the present is unshakable. The rain has not stopped, it hides the sea and the bridge to the other shore — geographical and meta-phorical. The avalanche of time, the curtain of death, of war and exile, falls across the stage: «Llueve sin mar, sin mar, sin mar. Borrada / la mar ha sido por la bruma...» Now, once time has breached the barrier into the present, it threatens also the future, and all vision:

> ... Pronto
> se llevará los bosques también, y ni estos troncos
> tan posibles, tan fáciles,
> cimbrearán de pie para decirme
> que han muerto, que se han muerto
> esta tarde de nieblas y de lluvia mis ojos.
>
> (*Aguilar*, p. 904)

In fact, the very enterprise of language is endangered, its differentiating capacity eroded: «¿Quién ve en lo oscuro, / quién pretende sombras, / quién concretar la noche sin estrellas?» There remains only a confused murmur in the dark. For the exiled poet, the distance from the homeland, his separation from ancestral sources, means a threat to the mainspring of poetry, the possible muting of his voice and darkening of his vision:

> ... Quedan
> ya sólo quedan, ¿oyes?,
> una conversación confusa, un errabundo
> coloquio sin palabras que entender, un temido,
> un invasor espanto
> a regresar sin ojos, a cerrarlos sin sueño.
>
> (*Aguilar*, pp. 903-905)

As we intimated at the beginning of our reading, the possibility of forging strong links to the far past, of erecting its moments with sustained clarity, depended on the poet's ability to penetrate the curtain of death and time (line 2). The ocean offered the bridge —an inspiration to Alberti, as always— but it also affirmed the distance. It linked both shores, present and past, but likewise affirmed the temporal gap. The idealized past, when viewed from the present, is undermined by present conditions. And the poet's effort to delimit with clarity, to give esthetic substance by means of language to those past moments, threatens the fragility of these moments by the creating self-awareness that imposes, once more, present dispositions. Thus, the endeavor contained the source of its dissolution within itself. That is why although the poem is written in three stanzas, it actually consists of two parts: a) The effort to create essential scenes of the past to which the present may be solidly anchored — already reflection on this very activity begins its undermining action in stanza 2: «Estas perdidas ráfagas... arenas empapadas»; b) The awareness that the younger self was also the younger poet («Yo sé...»), whose purposes were then as they are now — real circumstance now penetrates fully, and time invades all in a curtain of rain. The storm has not lifted. The two senses that contributed to the creation are deadened: sight first, «¿Quién ve en lo oscuro», then hearing, «ya solo quedan, ¿oyes? / una conversación confusa...»; then, sight again, «a regresar sin ojos...».

110

And yet, lest we see in the poem only an expression of the past's unattainable remoteness, we must remember the figure: «cantando en ese potro negro...» the poet's youthful counterpart. For in this vision, and in that of the dreams he rushes to, there is the seed of positive elements that are later to contribute strongly to the hopeful component of *Retornos* and all of Alberti's poetry of remembrance. As Carlos Feal Deibe has very acutely pointed out: «Alberti con frecuencia, al evocar el pasado, se imagina a sí mismo soñando, fantaseando; es decir, dedicado también en el pasado a la evocación de una realidad no presente. No es por tanto simplemente soñar que se está en otro sitio, sino soñar que se está en otro sitio del que, a su vez, sueña en evadirse».[4]

«Retornos de una tarde de lluvia» was constructed in a double pattern with one pivotal turn at about midpoint that divides it in two approximately equal parts and in three stanzas, with the central one —the movement towards poetic introspection— twice the length of the other two. Similarly, Part one of the book divides into two groups of poems; Poems 2 to 5 recalling specific past moments; Poems 7 to 11 focusing on the difficulties and significance of remembrance. Poem 6, «Retornos de una mañana de otoño», examines the effort to remember itself but in terms of fleeting images of the past and may be seen also as the composition that accomplishes the turn away from events toward their recording *per se*. Naturally, as in the introductory poem, the transfer from one mood to another is gradual, with elements from both present in the two to some degree, and we must keep in mind the limits inherent to such orderings.

It is the poetic component of his earlier personality that Alberti highlights in the next four compositions (2 to 6), seeing in it the source of his feeling of imprisonment and alienation. Each poem selects an important scene from this point of view. In «Retornos de los días colegiales», the poet sees his boyhood self going to school early in the morning, still half asleep, to meet the dead abstractions of textbooks. Away from concrete, palpitating life around him, the sea, the river, he is as «... un pobre remero castigado / que entre las paralelas rejas de los renglones / mira su barca y llora por asirse del aire» (*Aguilar,* pp. 905-906). The anger that had marked Alberti's previous recall of his useless years in school in *Sobre los ángeles,* for instance, has been replaced by sadness. The imposed servitude to what he sees as worthless instruction is now felt all the more keenly because he remembers the intensity of his youthful rebellions, his thirst for the immediacy of experience, as early indications of his artistic vocation and fully a part of the most valuable, most salutary constituent of his life.

«Retornos de un día de cumpleaños (J.R.J.)», while it seems to break with the rhythmical and stylistic mold of the collection, fits naturally within it in general and within this group of poems, in particular, because it is a scene recalling Alberti's *poetic* past, and its relationship to the present is an essential element of its lyrical structure. The capacious long

---

[4] CARLOS FEAL DEIBE, «Rafael Alberti, de la nostalgia a la esperanza», paper read at the MLA Conference, December, 1977.

line has been broken up into heptasyllables, with occasional hendecasyllables that allow for momentary expansion, as landings up a long stairway. The effect is one of tenseness with intermittent relaxations or ascending hopes. The alexandrine suited the mind's meandering, the delving backward of memory, leisurely plumbing time. But this event (the birthday) has remained unique and vividly present in Alberti's mind. There is no need to reconstruct it; its very emotional components are easily relived still, and it is this emotion that the short lines, rising uninterrupted by strophic divisions, transmit. Alberti once more climbs the steps to Juan Ramón Jiménez's apartment, bearing as an offering his first collection of poems:

> Subí yo aquella tarde
> con mis primeros versos
> a la sola azotea
> donde entre madreselvas y jazmines
> él en silencio ardía.
>
> (*Aguilar*, pp. 909-911)

The longer lines afford short seconds of rest on the way up, moments of descriptive amplification. The younger poet's verses were as water to a burning divinity, perhaps the meeting of sea and sun. He also bears in them the older poet's past, similar in many ways to his own; and when seen from the vantage point of the present, the poem becomes a double offering, for it brings to Alberti, now alone, though not by choice, fresh water from his own past:

> Él entonces tenía
> la misma edad que hoy,
> dieciséis de diciembre,
> tengo yo aquí, tan lejos
> de aquella tarde pura
> en que le subí el mar
> a su sola azotea.
>
> (*Aguilar,* pp. 909-911)

The emotion of remembering, the deliberate courting of the past is the axis of «Retornos de una mañana de otoño». From the beginning the «Retorno» is admittedly an escape: («ya es hora de gritar que estoy llorando, es hora / ya otra vez, nuevamente, de gritar que lo estoy»). The present remains a temporal referent through most of the composition, bathing the scene in aleatory light that is constantly threatened by dark incursions from the world of actual circumstance. Finally, a future unalleviated by the journey backward is anticipated: «Me encontrará la noche llorando en esta umbría» (*Aguilar,* pp. 911-912). The poem seems almost an admission of defeat in that the effort to recapture particular past moments in their full vigor appears impossible, or at least, what *can* be recuperated is not sufficient to lift the pall from the present. Henceforth, the very act of remembering will become the poet's principal concern, for: «sabes bien que el arroyo / que corre por tu voz nunca ha de repetirse, / que a tu imagen pasada no altera la presente». In this latter poem «Retornos de un día de retornos», Alberti imagines himself in the future, back in Spain, receiving a visit from his past exiled self, that is to say, remembering himself. The visitor is shown around various rooms and corners of this different and yet familiar house — aspects of the other self. But somehow there is no true encounter, no communion. The gap between one's different moments cannot be spanned. It is best to accept the condition of stranger: «... no tienes más ámbito que el de los esca-lones / que uno a uno descienden a las viejas aceras, / ni más dulce con-suelo que perderte invisible, / peregrino en tu patria, por sus vivos re-tornos» (*Aguilar*, pp. 912-914).

In «Retornos a través de los colores», a bridge across the years is thrown by the colors now surrounding him to their fertile counterpart of long ago. Again, however, the memory of these hues has faded; a species of triangulation between actual, imagined and remembered colors is needed in order for the latter to be recognized as the former's true, weaker image: «Aquí están. Tú los tocas. Son los mismos colores / que en tu corazón viven ya un poco despintados» (*Aguilar*, pp. 915-916). The loss is even greater in «Retornos de un museo deshabitado», where the poet's deliberate effort to people the empty frames of past galleries only return him ghosts. And with «Nuevos retornos del otoño», Section one of the collection concludes on a note of sadness, the poet admitting the unyielding effect that the present has on his spirit, when returning seasons give greater weight to endings than to beginning: «Perdonadme que hoy sienta pena y la diga. / No me culpéis. Ha sido / la vuelta del otoño» (*Aguilar*, p. 918).

Alberti quotes in full the first poem of «Retornos de amor» —second chapter of *Retornos*— as an epigraph to the last chapter of *La arboleda perdida* and says: «'Retornos del amor recién aparecido' se llama este poema. En él se rememora, después de más de veinte años, el estado de cueva en que vivía y la luz principal que echando sus cabellos en mis manos me hizo subir al sol y sentir que en el mundo la primavera no había muerto» (*A.p.*, p. 300). In this opening poem, love's appearance is then a saving revelation:

> Cuando tú apareciste,
> penaba yo en la entraña más profunda
> de una cueva sin aire y sin salida.
> Braceaba en lo oscuro, agonizando,
> oyendo un estertor que aleteaba
> como el latir de un ave imperceptible.
> Sobre mí derramaste tus cabellos
> y ascendí al sol y vi que eran la aurora
> cubriendo un alto mar en primavera.
> Fue como si llegara al más hermoso
> puerto del mediodía. Se anegaban
> en ti los más lucidos paisajes:
> claros, agudos, montes coronados

113

de nieve rosa, fuentes escondidas
en el rizado umbroso de los bosques.

*(Aguilar,* pp. 921-922)

In multifaceted imagery the beloved's hair is both a ladder of salvation
and the dawn's light, her body is the spring sea. The submarine muse has
been found again. She is at once the water that washes over the seascape
and the seascape itself. The contrast is of course all the sharper since the
poet sees himself then as near spiritual death —lines 2-5: «estertor»,
«cueva sin aire y sin salida», and so on. Underlying the development of
the first stanza[5] —and that of the second— is a proportional metaphor of
sight and water, unawareness and life.

The second stanza amplifies the image of the beloved as a newly
discovered country and concludes with a negation of the poem's opening:
an awakening from eternal night to the light of the sun:

Ya iba a dormir, ya a despertar sabiendo
que no penaba en una cueva oscura,
braceando sin aire y sin salida.

Porque habías al fin aparecido.

*(Aguilar,* pp. 921-922)

Alberti's remembrance gains strength under the powerful impetus of
love that seems to plunge at will into the past to recover scenes and
events permeated by emotion. Scenes are evoked only insofar as they
contain some facet of the poet's love; it is this sentiment that supports
them and gives them significance. Also, because of the lasting imprint of
love, fewer poems in this section turn inward towards the remembering
activity itself. In «Retornos del amor en un palco del teatro», Alberti
contrasts the grand gestures and agonized cries of a staged drama with
the quiet certainty of love from within a secluded box. The poet is still
entranced by the memory of an emotion that manifested itself always and
anywhere, and by contrast to its inner truth transformed external reality
into mere appearance:

¡Ah, gracia de los años, maravilla
de ofrecerle al amor cualquier penumbra,
la de un coche una esquina solitaria
o la de un palco de teatro mientras
puede, sin verla, hasta pasar la muerte!

*(Aguilar,* pp. 922-923)

Other times, the beloved figure lends reality to a setting, changes all
its elements into aspects of itself. «Retornos del amor tal como era» is
an intimate recasting of the birth of Venus:

Eras en aquel tiempo rubia y grande,
sólida espuma ardiente y levantada.

---

[5] There is no stanzaic division in *La arboleda perdida.*

> Parecías un cuerpo desprendido
> de los centros del sol, abandonado
> por un golpe de mar en las arenas.
>
> *(Aguilar,* p. 924)

The woman's attributes —sea foam and sunlight— are those of the goddess. But although she seems to belong to a supernatural realm, she is no mere apparition; there are at first elements of stability and duration in her form: «Eras .../ sólida espuma... levantada». The establishment of the image must struggle against time; it is the very fiery intensity radiating from the woman's figure that seems to burn up its spatial and temporal contexts. The lover himself is consumed by this pulsating exhalation of light. First the beloved seems a part of the sun's core fallen to earth. On the beach, she manifests the characteristics of her origins and, burning intensely, ignites all matter around her; here the emphasis is still on her surroundings:

> Todo era fuego en aquel tiempo. Ardía
> la playa en tu contorno. A rutilantes
> vidrios de luz quedaban reducidos
> las algas, los moluscos y las piedras
> que el oleaje contra ti mandaba.
>
> *(Aguilar,* p. 924)

In the last stanza the poem focuses on the woman's own being; she is pulsating fire —as the sun's core was— and burns time itself. Finally the poet, as another element in this sun's periphery, bathes in its radiance:

> Todo era fuego, exhalación, latido
> de onda caliente en ti. Si era una mano
> la atrevida o los labios, ciegas ascuas,
> voladoras, silbaban por el aire.
> Tiempo abrasado, sueño consumido.
>
> Yo me volqué en tu espuma en aquel tiempo.
>
> *(Aguilar,* p. 924)

To support the mythical-Platonic implications of the piece —the world below approaches truth, i.e., light, or is reduced to it through the intermediary light bearer, Venus-as-Sofía— which assert the beloved's perennial substance, Alberti contrasts her to her surroundings by means of verbs in the imperfect, which suggest duration in the past, joined to past participles that also give the sense of completion; the one verb in the preterite, contained within that duration, is «volqué» and describes the speaker's action. Another means of conveying this notion is the repetition of the temporal reference «en aquel tiempo» as if to anchor events securely. Likewise, the effect of the beloved's presence —fire— is repeated verbatim («todo era fuego»), twice, or by implication, through the use of words belonging to the same semantic complex, golden light or fire, e.g.: «rubia», «ardiente», «sol», «arenas», «ardía» —here the initial *ar* as well as the color links «arenas» and «ardía»— «rutilantes vidrios de luz».

115

The only comparably permanent element of the poem —water, the sea— is not explicitly mentioned, but appears through its proximate components, «playa», «oleaje», «algas», and so on. It too, however, finds its counterpart within the female figure and is therefore somehow modulated by her: «onda caliente en ti».

Turning back, the poet's erotic glance creates self-sufficient, necessary instances against a background of contingency. This may be accomplished, as we have just seen, by making its object a substantial idea in a quasi-Platonic sense; or through contrast against the passing of other things; or by elevating the moment actually and metaphorically above the surfaces on which we live. In «Retornos del amor en una azotea», such elevation creates for the couple's love a special locus in the cosmic order: «Lejos, las cumbres, soportando el peso / de las grandes estrellas, lo velaban» (*Aguilar*, pp. 824-925); and in «Retornos del amor ante las antiguas deidades», the beloved enjoys the same beauties as those of represented goddesses: «Tú eras lo mismo, amor. Todas las Gracias, / igual que tres veranos encendidos» (*Aguilar*, pp. 925-926).

Yet at times the erotic moment must be actively beckoned. Thus in several poems, such as «Retornos del amor en las dunas radiantes», or «Retornos del amor en la noche triste», the poet considers how vital to his present has become the memory of loving. In «Retornos de amor en las dunas radiantes», the recreated memory of «Retornos del amor tal como era» becomes itself the sought-for image: «¡Oh, vuelve, sí, retorna la de aquellas mañanas / radiantes de los médanos». This invention to the second degree must be anchored in the mind by the sea's swell that brought it ashore: «¡Oh, sí, vuelve, retorna como entonces, tendida, / con tus rubios cabellos de ángel entre los pechos!» But the same hypnotic rhythm brings the awareness of passing time and of the distance between then and now: «¡Oh, ser joven, ser joven, ser joven! No te vayas, / vuelve, vuelve, retorna, retorna a mí esta tarde» (*Aguilar*, pp. 926-927).

The last poems of «Retornos de amor» find the beloved in settings suggestive of fertility and eroticism. «Retornos del amor en las arenas» is again an early marine scene, immediate, full of the vigor imparted by the sea, the poet's other perennial source of youth. In counterpart to «Retornos del amor por los antiguos callejones», where the lovers become lost in cloistered walls whose superannuated liturgies were all that remained of once fervent adventures, «Retornos del amor entre las ruinas ilustres» hails the clear, unencumbered passions of mythical antiquity. There is no danger in treading these paths: «Vamos, amor, por calles que se fueron, / por claras geometrías que llevaban / al misterioso amor...» (*Aguilar*, pp. 936-937). The poet envisions a future for his love that may also lead others to such clarity.

It is with a similar desire to re-encounter a Mediterranean transparency that Part 3 of *Retornos* opens in «Retornos de un poniente en Ravello»: «Se asomaban los dioses, las inmóviles formas tutelares, / verdeados de umbría, a las barandas / del detenido ocaso». This fragile moment belongs still to the harmonious era of ancient gods. The instant is suspended in «... el sueño / de la diafanidad y la armonía, / de la paz ya sin fin, detenido el poniente» (*Aguilar*, pp. 943-944).

The majority of the poems of the last sequence of *Retornos* recalls moments of the poet's past more recent than those of the first part and not pertaining to his love experience. Their concerns are generally circumstantial, though frequently they become reflections on the poetic activity. Thus, in «Retornos de Yehuda Halevi,[6] el castellano», Alberti explores aspects of the medieval poet's life that echo his own. The introductory lines bring to bear a poetic tradition: «Te he conocido tarde, poeta, cuando ahora / en medio del camino de la vida, / oigo de entre mis manos resbalarse, / latido por latido, triste, el tiempo». Mediating between him and Halevi we read Dante and also Quevedo's famous «¡Cómo de entre mis manos te resbalas! / ¡Oh, cómo te deslizas, edad mía!» The second stanza imagines the easy, roving itinerary that could have joined both poets in the Spanish journeys: «... Te hubiera / ofrecido un limón de un patio de Sevilla, / una rama de olivas de Lucena». Alberti seeks to capture the joyful temper of the ancestor who could then, and still does in spirit, always roam as an exile, a species of pilgrim at home: «Yo también como tú siento en mi día / el misterioso llamamiento, el aura / invitadora al viaje...» The final two stanzas, with their muted return to the beginning, become a calling forth of Yehuda's spirit to sustain that of the present poet who will also pursue his task against the odds of exile and time. The implied circularity of the composition suggests the ever renewed possibilities of poetic response across the centuries: «Tu poderoso aroma que hoy me llega, / fuerte de siglos y de fe, me empuje, / fijos los ojos, sin temblor y puro, / Yehuda Halevi, poeta, el castellano» (*Aguilar*, pp. 944-945).

Two other poems[7] in the sequence attempt to resume a dialog with poet friends. In «Retornos de Paul Eluard», though this poet was a contemporary, his recent death rendered the spiritual dialog all the more urgent. With «Retornos de Vicente Aleixandre», it is geography and recent history that separate the former friends. This poem is the last one of the collection, and Alberti contemplates now the possibility of his exile's end:

> Que tus soles
> venideros no pasen y, altos, sigan
> penetrándote siempre
> de igual temblor para que en mi retorno
> tu misma luz de hoy pueda hablarme.
>
> (*Aguilar*, pp. 857-958)

In this respect, the heart of the sequence is «Retornos de la invariable poesía», «el *retorno* singular incomparable»,[8] according to Ricardo

---

[6] Poet and philosopher (ca. 1075-1141). Traveled through Christian and Muslim Spain. Died in Egypt seeking to return to Israel.

[7] Missing from the Aguilar edition (but extant in Losada) are «Retornos frente a los litorales españoles», «Retornos del pueblo español», «Retornos de Bertold Brecht», probably because of their political intent.

[8] RICARDO GULLÓN, *op. cit.*, p. 262.

Gullón. In his invocation of poetry, Alberti needs but to consider the evidence within himself so that the poem is less a «retorno» than the assertion of a permanence. The long searching line of other «Retornos» gives way to a strongly cadenced hendecasyllable, heightened at times by shorter lines of seven and eight syllables. The poem consists of seven stanzas of uneven length and occasional assonance. The final stanza becomes more expansive — to allow its powerful affirmation a wider rhythmical scope. As in a broadening river toward the sea, the slightly searching tones of the opening strophe are resolved into a deep, broad-banked surge.

The poem opens with a resolute apostrophe to lasting poetry and a dismissal of whatever questions the poet might ever have had on its certainties: «¡Oh poesía hermosa, fuerte y dulce, / mi solo mar al fin, que siempre vuelve! / ¿Cómo vas a dejarme, cómo un día / pude, ciego, pensar en tu abandono?» The contrast that is to remain as the axis of the piece, the disjunction to be resolved, is already apparent in these lines: there is first, at the very surface, the exclamative heralding of poetry and its constant presence; against it is set the question of the last two lines, its interrogative force undermined by the implied, negative answer which is, itself, another affirmation of faith. Lines 1 and 2 state, respectively, (a) the evident qualities of the art; (b) its unwavering allegiance to the poet; (c) lines 3 and 4, dismiss the poet's possible present and future lack of faith; (d) dismiss his past lack of faith. Thus, a and b assert poetry's perennial value and constancy; c and d, though dismissing it, imply the intermittence of the poet's belief. Poetry transcends time, of course, and remains as an almost Platonic Idea: one verb is sufficient for its action, which is eternal return («siempre vuelve»). The poet, as a man, is subject to history —four verbs are used in the last two lines to describe his possible waverings— «un día» is opposed by «siempre»; in his weakness, poetry will sustain him.

In stanzas 2 and 3, Alberti glances back at his poetic career. Stanza 2 is a general overview; again, there is a containment of historical change within the bonds of the art's equanimity. At the origin, the child opened to the grace that poetry shone upon him, a flower to the sun. Later, he was supported in familiar protective communion («de tu mano»). Stanza 3 is slightly more specific; the poet's early work, its risks and fancies, thrived under poetry's direction, flew on «her» wings: «... era / un soplo grácil quien me conducía». Stanza 4, central to the development, makes of poetry the poet's source of knowledge and joy in his greatest personal triumphs, his joining of painting and language, his love. And in both instances, as earlier, the glow of poetry is almost an existential evidence. Again, unity underpins development: a threefold question that receives but one answer: «¿Quién tocó con sus ojos los colores, / quién a las líneas contagió su aire, / y quién, cuando el amor...?»

The next stanza, 5, plunges into the terrors of history and destruction. It is poetry now that remembers forgotten deaths and bears the victims in a stronger flame than man's across war's turmoil. The beginning of stanza 6, the final one, in rhythms reminiscent of St. John of the Cross's

118

*liras,* is an exclamatory celebration of the art's quasimystical support: «ella» (poetry), too, joined the poet in his exile, a veteran of the struggle and a comrade:

> ¡Oh hermana de verdad, oh compañera,
> conmigo, desterrada,
> conmigo, golpeado y alabado,
> conmigo, perseguido;
> en la vacilación, firme, segura,
> en la firmeza, animadora, alegre,
> buena en el odio necesario, buena
> y hasta feliz en la melancolía!
>
> (*Aguilar,* pp. 954-955)

The tone is more intimate; the inner contrast, though still present —repetitions and echoed constructions maintain it— seems muted and in the interchange of past participles (lines 2, 3, 4), there is a hint of identification. The concluding lines, in broader rhythms, exalt poetry as life and poetry as creation. The contrast now is even quieter than before, because the poet's life is becoming one with the art and with it will transcend time: «Me matarán quizás y tú serás mi vida»; likewise the poet sees no distinction between himself and the world around him: «Porque por ti yo he sido, yo soy música, / ritmo veloz, cadencia lenta...» Between the art and the poet was the world and its history. Poetry has exalted the poet out of history, and he has exalted reality also out of its discontinuous state. The fusion is complete: «Porque por ti soy tú y seré por ti solo / lo que fuiste y serás para siempre en el tiempo» (*Aguilar,* pp. 954-955).

Here, the poet does for his entire enterprise what he has wanted to do throughout *Retornos* for those moments that were privileged in his memory, making of them no mere poetic remembrances but re-inventions, newly structured wholes that transcend their temporal origin. *Retornos* is the elaboration of a lasting myth, whose initial life-spark was a personal past, but whose completed forms are universal.

## II. «*Baladas y canciones del Paraná*»

Alberti's persistent need to establish a dialog with the concreteness of the world around him is one of the driving forces behind this long collection of short lyrics. The poet knows that he must come to terms with the land; that he must plumb the depths of his new landscape. These pieces represent his first concerted effort to do so. Accustomed to the more easily encompassed geography of Spain and of the Cádiz shores in particular, a region whose character had penetrated his entire being, the vast expanses of the new Continent seemed almost overwhelming in their alienism. Alberti's attention to the land's presence will consist first in an effort to possess what he considers its major constitutive aspects: Horses, the wind, the river, the flatlands. Gradually, they acquire symbolic, almost mythical, overtones, in particular in those ballads that recall the myste-

119

rious tragedy of the «Mayor loco». Inevitably, however, Spain imposes its outlines and blurs the confines of his new home. Nostalgia for other landscapes surges forth; the new land becomes transparent to the old. The feeling of being uprooted which is now a constant in Alberti's poetry becomes then especially acute. He begins to question the very possibility of the poetic enterprise.

Thus, in this effort by the poet to vitalize a forbidding poetic space, we can define three principal components: 1) the desire to give lyrical substance to his environment, to reestablish his poetic orientation; 2) instances of unrelenting longing for the past; 3) an inward turn of attention to his craft and a consideration of its possible course under the new conditions. It is the relation of these new conditions to those of his first efforts that, as Alberti tells us in the prose commentary to the collection, imposed upon him the same verse forms: «Vuelven de nuevo a mí, con tanta intensidad como en los más claros momentos de Marinero en tierra, las canciones de corte musical, de repetidos estribillos, pero de contenido diferente» (Aguilar, p. 997). The majority of the songs and ballads is predominantly in assonanted octosyllables. Alberti uses the most direct means of expression, selecting the simple concrete instance. His vocabulary is at its most spare: he prefers to expand the connotations of his language by repeating the same words in a variety of modulating contexts. The collection consists of three chapters: «Baladas y canciones de la Quinta del Mayor Loco»,[9] comprising seventeen consecutively numbered songs and seventeen titled ballads; «Canciones I», fifty-six numbered songs; «Canciones II», thirty-nine numbered songs.

Again, the first poem of the collection sets a mood that will prevail over many of the other compositions and, in particular, those in which Alberti tries to come to an understanding of his changed environment: «Canción 1» also epitomizes the form and strategy of a large proportion of these pieces — the pattern is iterative and circular, straightforward language suffices; the situation is reduced to its barest elements: «Bañado del Paraná! / Desde un balcón mira un hombre / el viento que viene y va». After the opening exclamation, its only alteration of tone, the poem flows in a minimally modulated development. This exclamation imposes the first, overpowering total vision of the landscape. Its heightened mode reflects the speaker's first impression while it stamps the perception as the permanent background of the wind's course. Actually, in spatial terms, there is an upward movement from the flatlands (line 1) to the observer (line 2) to the wind (line 3). The second stanza continues this movement into the depths of the wind: «Ve las barrancas movidas / del viento que viene y va».

In the next stanza the gaze has fallen downwards: «Los caballos, como

---

[9] I. R. WARNER, in a footnote to his article «Subjective Time and Space in Alberti's 'Baladas y canciones de la Quinta del Mayor Loco'», Bulletin of Hispanic Studies, Vol. L, 1973, points out that this section of the book first appeared in Ora marítima (Buenos Aires, 1953): «The title is taken from the name of a house, situated on an island formed by two branches or the Paraná, where Alberti spent his summer vacation during these years», p. 374.

piedras / del viento que viene y va». It continues in this direction in parallelistic development to delve on «Los pastos, como mar verde», «El río, como ancha cola», «Los barcos, como caminos», «El hombre, como la sombra», and «El cielo, como morada». «Del viento que viene y va» is the concluding refrain in each instance. The last stanza reaches into the inner depths of the observer, in correspondence to the upward depths of the wind at the beginning («barrancas»): «Ve lo que mira y mirando / ve sólo su soledad» (*Aguilar*, p. 1001). There are several interrelated developments of interest in the composition, all converging onto the final lines and involving the movement/immobility opposition. The refrain comprises two elements of uneven length: «del viento que viene...» is a descending movement toward the spectator. In correspondence to this longer interval, the gaze's descent encompassing the central fact of the poem, from the «barrancas» to «el hombre», and «y va», would be a departing movement, along which the eye rises up to «el cielo». It seems a sudden ascent but in view of the final stanza, it is metaphorical rather than actual: the external «morada» and internal «su soledad», are one and the same.

The gazer's inner being is as an empty «morada» also, for the wind to blow through, while his physical self is nailed down to this spot, to his lonely exile, crushed by the enormous expanse before him. The transference of the wind's abode is implicit in the homophony: «El h*ombre,* como la s*ombra* / del viento...» In this emptiness all movement comes to rest. The rhythm has prepared us for this. The first stanza flows uninterruptedly from «un hombre» to «va» and so does the second, from «ve» to «va», where we have situated the only real upward movement. Thereafter, a comma rends the first line of each stanza with caesura that with «como» acts as a mirror between the two halves («Los caballos, como piedras»). Besides the refrain itself, other repetitions contribute to the gradual stagnation of all movement; there are only four verbs (apart from «viene y va» in the refrain) in the entire poem. The first «ve» controls the seven central stanzas; it is elided in stanzas 3 to 8 while the man also disappears behind the static landscape — these are the strophes that follow a descending movement. The final stanza repeats the «mira» of stanza 1 and seizes it into «mirando»: «Ve lo que mira y mirando / ve sólo su soledad». «Ve» is also repeated and «sólo» becomes «soledad». All the preceding elements have been neutralized into «lo que», and all other words in this stanza are repetitions. The impression is of a vortex that draws the gaze inward to «sólo su soledad», whose homophony recalls the earlier instance of this effect («hombre — sombra»), also centered on the «o» sound, as a dark emptiness.

Movement has stopped, and with it, time also stretches as an uneventful desert. The objects whose arrest has communicated this condition were selected also in diminishing potential for movement: «caballos», epitome of speed and grace, are «piedras», unyielding and dead; «pastos» whose expanse and mutability draws the eye quickly to the horizon are a flat «mar verde» — an altogether different sea from that of *Marinero en tierra*. «Río», traditionally the symbol of time's passage, change and so on, is an «ancha cola», reduced to the role of wake of aftermath of a vaster body. «Los barcos», also symbols of voyage and adventure, have become mere potential movement, «caminos»; man, finally, whose field of possible activity is greatest, is merely the wind's «sombra».

To conclude, it is also possible to see here the permanent hypostatization of four elements important to the collection as a whole: the horse, the boat, the river, and the wind. All four are symbols of movement and poetically synonymous with one another. All the objects of the poem are linked to these components at several points. The horse is like a river, and now like the stones at its bottom, immobile. Other words linked to the horse are: «pastos», «ancha cola», «caminos». The river is a horse and has its «ancha cola»; it may also suggest «caminos» for «barcos». The boats on the river are as horses; they are linked specifically to «caballos» by means of «caminos» (and the latter's suggestion of stones, «piedras»). All these elements are defined in their static conditions by the wind, their metaphorical counterpart, sustaining and negating them at the same time. The central identification is that of the man with all of these correlatives in their ultimately unitary meaning, joined to them by the wind, his isolation and inertness projected on theirs.

Three of these components recur with similar functions in the «Balada de lo que el viento dijo», the third one of the first sequence. In this instance, the emphasis is on time, on its cessation:

> La eternidad bien pudiera
> ser un río solamente,
> ser un caballo olvidado
> y el zureo
> de una paloma perdida.
>
> (Aguilar, pp. 1003-1004)

The dove joins horse and river in a similar condition of futility. «Solamente» deprives the river of a background against which to flow, so that instead of duration or direction, we have mere presence; the horse, forgotten, is also deprived of its usefulness, fallen out of human purpose and time; the lost dove —Alberti treated this notion with a slightly different turn in «Se equivocó la paloma»— is not even seen, but merely heard. The wind is also present as before, an agent of distancing: «... viene el viento / que ya le dice otras cosas» (Aguilar, pp. 1003-1004). The poem concludes with a repetition of the first stanza, a closed circle. Eternity is a flat expanse without horizon, with no beginning.

The central group of poems in this first part of Baladas consists of five ballads on the «Mayor loco», the «genius loci», as I. R. Warner suggests. This English critic finds a link between the Major and the wind and sees in the mysterious figure also a focus of «feelings of oppressiveness and restriction».[10] The five ballads give us disjointed portions of a legend of «thwarted lust» and death. A sense of onerous mystery emanates from the tale whose main force also resides, as it does in legend generally, in

---

10 Ibid., p. 380.

its being ever repeated as if it were destined to happen ceaselessly — the Major's personification of the wind underlines the recurrence motif. The structure of these ballads is consistently cyclical, even where there seems to be a compact sequence of events, such as in the last one, «Balada oscura de la vuelta del Mayor loco»: A rider and his horse are shot; a window slams shut, the blood flows to the river; the house is empty and dark:

> Dos disparos en la tarde.
> Un caballo rueda herido,
> y un hombre, con el caballo,
> rueda herido.

> (*Aguilar*, pp. 1021-1022)

In this stanza, except for the first line, almost all else is repetition, and the only verb «rueda» twice describes repeated movement. The first line, which is the «given», so to speak, two shots of mysterious origin, prepares the rest of the poem. It is separated from the remainder of the stanza by a full stop, but attention to certain of its phonetic constituents reveals some initial merging with the ensuing double movement — two shots are also a repetition. The two hard «d's» in «Dos disparos» (supporting phonetically the semantic content) are moderated into the softer «d» of «tarde». This soft «d» reappears in «rueda herido» — words that are almost homophonic. Thus, the stanza's sound pattern partially bridges the break between the first line and the last three, effecting a participation of the former into the general repetitive pattern.

These poems represent Alberti's effort to seize his environment in some way, to render it susceptible of lyrical treatment. And if he returns to the same topics, it is because he needs to look on these familiar outlines now that he has begun to acquire them, finding new modulations to unchanging states. The majority of the pieces of «Canciones I» deal with matters of poetry, either directly or through celebrations of other poets, and remembrances of Alberti's own past work. There are times when the memory of lost friends has a calming effect on the poet's spirit and may even lead to almost joyful contemplation. «Canción 16», in memory of Machado, discovers that in tranquillity the real becomes more familiar:

> Un río que no se mueve,
> pero que nos da la mano,
> susurrando nuestro nombre.
> Un caballo que levanta,
> al vernos pasar, la frente,
> queriéndonos decir algo.

> (*Aguilar*, p. 1040)

Alberti invites the old master to gaze at a serene, humanized landscape. Precisely those elements in it that previously concretized for Alberti the feeling of distance and discontinuity are now, more than receptive, eager to establish a dialog with man. The older poet's melancholy spirit seems to have softened all asperities and to have enabled Alberti to discover, for a moment, a soothing intimacy in his present environment.

Although deep longing and an oppressive sense of isolation maintain in the first two-thirds of the collection a pervasively dark mood, there are occasional moments of resigned peacefulness, as in «Canción 16», or «Canción 24» (also in «Canciones I») on the passing of Pedro Salinas, as bereavement is tempered by the serene joy of acceptance and the hope of joining the brother poet, though in death, in the homeland. Also, in «Canciones II», the coming of autumn, the last exuberance of nature, affects the poet's mood and elicits in him at the outset a few jubilant poems. Songs 1, 2, 4 seem to promise a new outlook: «En el otoño —¡viva el sol!—, / en el otoño, amor» (*Aguilar*, «Canción 2», p. 1067). But the mood is ephemeral. Soon the season brings to mind the autumns of Spain, and with them memories of other songs. In «Canción 28», Alberti recalls the gaiety of his first poetry and looks forward to its future possibilities: «... Y, sin embargo, ¡qué alegre, / qué alegre y feliz ha sido / —y volverá a ser— mi canto!» (The ellipsis links this piece with the preceding one, and a particular dark sequence of «Canciones», 21 to 25, whose central theme is forgetfulness and death.) The halting rhythm of these introductory lines is an injunction to take heart. Those that follow ponder the deep source of that happiness, a source that has not yet run dry and awaits more propitious times: «Allí están mis marineros / aguardando.» Alberti uses the images that once peopled his poetry («salinas», «pueblos blancos»), and they represent the vital forces of Spain, «aunque clavados ahora / con tres clavos...» This «aunque» is an echo of the «y, sin embargo» of the first line, linking the poet's present state and that of his work to the state of Spain under Franco's dictatorship. But the three nails are plainly insufficient to hold down indefinitely all that vigorous joy (one and one-half lines out of twenty-four) which «saltará de nuevo al viento, / cantando, / alegre y feliz, cantando» (*Aguilar*, p. 1082). This and other poems with similar implications, poems in which there is evidence of a refusal to remain resigned, in which Alberti recalls the past to find strength, allow the last part of *Baladas* to counterbalance its first chapters.

There has also been a poetic gain, a coming to terms by the poet with the new spaces around him, so that the past and the present may join their respective energies in creating a strong sustaining hope towards the future. This conjunction is clear in «Canción 39», the last of «Canciones II»: «Sol de esta tierra, yo llevo, / de otra tierra, un sol adentro. // Aquí está el tuyo, aquí el mío, / frente a frente, pero idénticos» (*Aguilar*, p. 1089).

*Retornos* and *Baladas* were written concurrently; in fact, the dates for *Retornos* (1948-1956) contain both collections. It was a time of difficult adaptation, when the temptation of the past was almost insurmountable, and the poet had to exert all his strength in order to bridge the chasm between his two worlds so that the new one may also become a source of poetry. From the vantage point of 1967, when the words that follow were written, there remains no disjunction: «porque yo no podré cantar ya nunca dividiendo en dos partes el correr de mi vida: aquí, de este lado, lo sereno, luminoso, optimista, y de este otro, lo dramático, oscuro, triste, todo lo señalado por los signos crueles de mi tiempo. Por esta causa son así, no de otro modo» (*Aguilar,* p. 997).

CHAPTER 7

ABIERTO A TODAS HORAS TO CANCIONES DEL ALTO VALLE
DEL ANIENE:  RECOVERED SPACES

I. Introduction

These two titles encompass the last collection of Alberti's lyrical work. From the first compositions of A la pintura to the last ones of Retornos stretches a span of eleven years (1945-1956) during which, surprisingly, the poet's fecundity reached a peak with seven books of poetry. Some occasional pieces in Poemas diversos take us to 1959, but they are of minor importance. So that, on the whole, there is a four-year gap separating this period of intense activity from the publication of Abierto a todas horas, 1960, initiating the latest group of works which comprise also: El matador, 1961-65, Poemas con nombre, 1965-66, Roma, peligro para caminantes, 1964-67, Canciones del alto valle del Aniene, 1967-71, and Otros versos, 1968-72.

Much of this poetry consists of poèmes de circonstance and suffers from the weaknesses common to the type: a certain lack of spontaneity and occasional prosaism. Although Alberti's demanding sense of composition is evident even now, it functions more often than not as an enclosing frame and seems not to respond to the poem's inner necessity. For this reason we shall emphasize principally the poetry of Abierto a todas horas, Roma, peligro para caminantes and Canciones del alto valle del Aniene,[1] in which Alberti pursues most effectively his clearest poetic concerns.

Alberti's attention to the temporal, his desire to recapture the past or his tendency to see his present condition in terms of the past, reached a peak of intensity in Retornos and in Baladas. In this latter book, however, we noted a determined attention to and interest in his immediate circumstance, as he tried to give intrinsic poetic meaning to a landscape initially transparent to previous ones or simply overwhelming in its strangeness. He sought to find legendary and metaphorical resonances: the «Mayor loco», the «caballo», the «viento», the «río», and so on. Space was beginning to recover its preeminence at the expense of time, recalling thus the importance it had in his earliest work and which it began to lose while the poet was still in Spain, gradually in Sobre los ángeles, decisively

---

[1] These last two titles will appear hereafter as Roma and Canciones.

in *Verte y no verte*... Of course, even in those early collections there were occasional, nostalgic memories of childhood, so that the glance outward, what we termed the definition of a poetic space, was never an exclusive disposition. Now, beginning with *Abierto a todas horas,* though in a very muted manner, Alberti again seems to cast an outward glance, watching at times —especially in *Canciones*— for the pure pleasure of noting the presence of things. Temporal considerations enter frequently in these lyrical descriptions; the weight of years and experience, still his condition of exile, cannot but exert their pressure. This is particularly the case in the early portions of *Abierto a todas horas,* where the poet is moving out of one moment and into another, and a longing for the past is still of primary importance. But the poem does not veer immediately to these considerations. More often, the picture is given for itself, though it bears with it a burden of time.

## II. «*Abierto a todas horas*»: Transition towards Things

This collection open with «El otoño otra vez», a chapter of thirty-two, generally short, poems in the aphoristic manner. Alberti considers the season from its first to last phrases, and although all its connotations affect his perceptions —time passing, the sense of the end of things, an occasional look backward— he attends to objects as they are and prefers to let the present overlay the past or the future. The opening two notations bracket the field of attention left to explore. The first one envisions the last wafts of summer heat as «su espada enfebrecida / en el cuerpo naciente del otoño», and the second announces the arrival of the «mejor música de las cuatro estaciones». As a time of transition, the fall is an ending and a beginning. But the poet will be concerned, precisely because of its initially dual nature, to draw a clear profile of the world around him. His first test will be to resist the temptation of the nebulous, the indefinite, the blurring of things contrived by autumn mists. That is why in the third composition this temptation is surrendered to only in the conditional: «Saldría con mi perro a la neblina» (*Aguilar,* p. 1107).

The drizzle erasing spatial coordinates can also be a correlative of the indefinite attraction of other spaces, an attraction still felt at times quite strongly. At this time, however, Spain elicits the poet's longing as a personal, immediate need, not a past condition of things. In fact, he looks forward to a future reintegration to his native soil, as in Poem 14:

> Otoño silencioso de este bosque,
> ¿me estoy desvinculando de la patria,
> alejando, perdiéndome?
> Haz que tus hojas, que se lleva el viento,
> me arrastren hacia ella nuevamente
> y caiga en su caminos
> y me pisen y crujan
> mis huesos confundiéndose
> para siempre en su tierra.

> (*Aguilar,* p. 1110)

As in most patterns of apostrophe, the poet's question is addressed to his own self, and the personified autumn is likewise his own state of mind. Against the voiceless immobile background, the question follows the progressive separation of the speaker from his origins in three verbs that suggest gradually more distance and disorientation: «estoy des-vinculando», «alejando», «perdiéndome»; the gerund implies arrested movement, as if each successive state were seized separately, in discontinuity.

After the appeal of line 4 which, with its sharp caesura, belongs still to the moment of quest —the rhythmical pattern of the four first lines, especially 2 to 4, suggests a halting uncertainty— the last five lines rush forth uninterrupted, driven by a powerful surge of yearning towards, again, the restrained movement of a gerund, «confundiéndose», and the site of ultimate rest «en su tierra». In contrast to the first lines, the verbs that would bear the speaker from his displacement denote concrete action: «me arrastren», «caiga», «pisen», «crujan»; also, besides «crujan» itself, their action conveys a harshness of sound that seems to cut through the previous deadening silence. Through implicit metaphor, the poet could be as a leaf, and thus could reintegrate the very soil of his country.

Several levels of meaning join to give the short poem its compact force and multilayered effect: 1) movement from the abstract to the concrete as we have just pointed out; a further correlative of this movement is the shift from the first person pronoun «me» («me estoy desvinculando») to the third person «se» («confundiéndose»), referring to «mis huesos», as if the most essential aspect of the poet's being, the support of his body, that which most patently belongs to his land of origin, also contained the essence of his mind; 2) a movement also from a temporally transitional condition (autumn) to permanence «para siempre»; 3) from «este bosque», separate from the speaker, indefinite, distant, so to speak, to «su tierra» specifically attributed, a relation of dependency; here also we note the «originating» role of «tierra» with respect to trees that grow on it, are nourished by it. In spare, objective language, Alberti organizes a sharp intuition into moments of growing intensity, transforming an alien, formless space into the precise tangible density of his home. It is in this formless space that Alberti finds the greatest threat to his being. The engulfing void at times seems overwhelming, the senses impotent against it, time itself absorbed: «Nada se escucha y nada / se ve. Parecería / que todo se ha marchado / o que nada ha existido» (*Aguilar,* p. 1110). In several compositions Alberti seems to create out of this void as if solidifying it in sharp forms, highly plastic images that are all the more vivid because of the indefiniteness that surrounds them. The evidence of things is captured in its pristine state:

> Una vaca llovida,
> angustiada, anhelando
> la alta rama de un álamo.
> Un carro de ruidos cruza las nubes. Tiembla
> el mundo. Cae un rayo.

(*Aguilar,* p. 1108)

A very careful use of attributes of graduated force draws the animal's anxious upthrust head. The crossing of the heavens by thunder extends along the fourth, much longer line, whose last word «tiembla» further expands the action to cosmic limits. The last line is the counterpart of the opening, ascending movement, an instantaneous return to earth. The poem's activity is concentrated in its final two lines with three verbs in the active present contrasting with the passive attributes of lines 1-3 («... llovida / angustiada, anhelando» — «... cruza... Tiembla / ... Cae...»). Alberti uses here the resources of his pictorial sensibility, creating with language a painting as vivid as that of any «paysagiste». Our perceptions are guided in such a way that we seem to scan a canvas from a central point: «Una vaca» upwards through intermediary space («la alta rama») to the stormy heavens («... cruza las nubes»). Verbal focusing sharply highlights the landscape's central element: the animal is described with three increasingly intense words that also duplicate the general vertical criss-cross pattern of the whole —cow's upward yearning, lightning's fall—: «llovida» suggests a kind of fallen solidification of the rain («llovido» also means «unexpected»): «angustiada», an element of emotion enters with this adjective, initiating the rising spiritualization; «anhelando», this gerund has greater emotional content and seems to elevate further, to abstract to a higher plane, the animal's presence. To render the sense of equivalence given in a landscape, for instance, to all its elements, so that the background and the foreground interact to form a cohesive, significant whole, Alberti reverses the expected semantic distribution. Thus, the foreground forms, (cow, tree) are linked by abstract words («llovida», «angustiada», «anhelando»); «a» is the most frequent vowel and contributes to the connotations of openness, flight, a certain spirituality, mostly, of course, in contrast to the rumbles of the last two lines; the background elements, by nature somewhat more diffuse, receive highly concrete treatment: rapid active sentences, strong alliteration («carro», «ruidos», cruza», and «tiembla», «el mundo»), a synesthesia (all of line four to «nubes»), with sound acquiring movement.

We have come to expect such sophistication in Alberti's ecphrastic technique since A la pintura. Here, the poet has managed equally striking expression with a willed parsimony of means. This simplicity, though it recalls the clarities of Marinero en tierra, La amante and so on, is the result of a highly polished art. There is no need for discursive introspection. The poet presents the tableau by itself, sufficient in its presence. It remains open, to some extent, to a range of emotional and intellectual connotations, though the range is defined by the general turn of the chapter — the yearning to be elsewhere, the need to etch out of the mist a livable space, the fear of things ending. We may, if we wish, transform the vignette into a correlative of the poet's condition, but there is no significant gain in such specificity. It is a portion of distinctness and order wrested out of the deliquescent void.

In restructuring the space around him —and within himself— those conditions that demand such ordering are the same that impose its limits. If all considerations of space must needs lead us to considerations of time, as they surely do, then the limits under which Alberti must labor are doubly stringent. Autumn, as we suggested earlier, is transitional as to space; there is a loss of definition in reality, so to speak, a disintegration of all forms, no longer the vividness of summer, not yet the decisive stability of winter; it is also transitional as to time, for we witness impending, though not quite achieved cessation, the anxiety of time growing short joined to the loss of vitality that prevents our filling it as we would wish. Against time, the poet opposes persistence in his enterprise, in moments of anguish, «—¿Cómo no hablar, y mucho y con nostalgia, / si ya pronto va a entrar en el invierno?» (*Aguilar*, p. 1111) in moments of rebellion: «tú te vas incendiando / —¡ay, a tus años, a tus muchos años!— / como un joven demonio entre las sombras» (*Aguilar*, p. 1111). Against nothingness, he hones his senses to their most acute, makes them join towards unitary expression: «Puedo decir que oigo, más que miro, / crecer fija la esfera / áurea de las naranjas» (*Aguilar*, p. 1111). Here, language captures hearing, sight, touch, and, by implication, also the taste and smell of the fruit.

Near the chapter's conclusion, Alberti returns to imagery that he used at the beginning; autumn appears wounded in both sides, its enfeebled body unable to offer any resistance. And though the winter is to be «triste, duro, inclemente...» (*Aguilar*, p. 1115), its threat may be less insidious. In this sequence the poet was still frequently overcome by a powerful yearning for other spaces, past regions. The very appearance of things was unpropitious to a disposition whose true home is in sundrenched shores. As the time it considers, the sequence is transitional; it looks both at the poet's present state, his present situation, and at those long past.

In *Abierto a todas horas* the moment of clearest openness to the surrounding world is captured by the seventeen aphoristic pieces of «El mirador de Mira-Al-Río» in Chapter 3. Here, the principal element is light in all its phases; the landscape grows out of it and persists to sight even in shadow: «... luz de transparentes / morados que se van hundiendo, oscuros» (*Aguilar*, p. 1135). The poet's recovered inner light reponds again, reflecting its own transformations: «También, la luz sin luz, según el tiempo, / o según el estado de alma que me sube / de los ojos y expando sobre todas las cosas» (*Aguilar*, p. 1135). In this quick sketch, all the elements of the first two lines are pure abstractions: «luz sin luz» is understanding or interior vision; it varies with «el tiempo», duration more than externally defined time, that is to say, with intuition and «estado de alma», which is emotion (as opposed to «estado de las cosas»). The result of this conjunction of forces is the poetic vision that links Alberti's inner space and the outside world.

In contrast to «El otoño, otra vez», Alberti's perception finds pleasure now in sharp differentiations, seizing forms amid movement and apparent uniformity:

¡Qué precisos los árboles! Se puede,
aun a pesar de su monocromía,
dibujar el perfil de cada uno,

        separar claramente cada ola
        del oleaje verde de sus cumbres.

                            (*Aguilar,* p. 1137)

Here again he uses verbal focusing to render the undulating sea of green in both its total impact and the distinctness of each treetop. Line 1, to «árboles», renders through the use of the plural both detail and multiplicity of line. «Se puede» at the end of the line begins the isolating focus but is interrupted by the generalized effect of line 2; the focusing is completed as to design in line 3, as to individual mass in line 4. The opening impression and the specific forms converge in the last line: «oleaje», movement, «verde», color, for the first time, sharp and brilliant because anticipated over the first four lines, «cumbres», design, distinct and multiplied. A graduated alternation of panoramic and close-up views produces a perfectly integrated picture in which individual elements and general contours fuse and yet stand apart as in the landscape of a master.

Alberti is now fully intent on considerations of light and space. As the title of the collection suggests, he is «abierto a todas horas» to the evidence of existent things. His language has become direct. Already in *Baladas* there was a noticeable preference for a simpler vocabulary, a preference that became even more marked in «El otoño, otra vez». Words are shorter, there are fewer abstractions — though abstraction itself is not eschewed, but allowed to come forth by means of word order and contrast. As we proceed in *Abierto a todas horas,* a certain lightness, reminiscent in tone of earliest Alberti begins to emerge; exclamations and questions are used more frequently, compositions are terse and aphoristic. The collection concludes with a sequence of nine calligraphic pieces, «Escrito en el aire», prepared for a series of nine drawings by a friend, León Ferrari, playful, light pieces that demonstrate the poet's new interaction with extension taken to its most concrete consequence.

III.  «*Roma, peligro para caminantes*»:   The Frame
       and the Picture

This collection manifests Alberti's newly intensified attention to his present, to the reality he happens to be in, a reality now only infrequently limned by that of his Spanish past. After the «openness» to other spaces of the preceding book, the next step is one of involvement, a plunging into the immediacy of daily living. Italy —and Rome— not unlike Andalusia in the nature of the people and in its geography, part of Alberti's inner world because of some remote ancestors as well as its Mediterranean character, strongly solicited this involvement. But Alberti is now ready to join the battle on new terms, regardless of similarities or reminiscences. Rome *qua* Rome beckons, and the absurd, joyful, earthy people of his neighborhood, the Trastevere; all this, he says, was «Lo que me hacía falta. Los poetas, los escritores en general se han detenido casi siempre ante los restos grandiosos, han narrado y cantado la Roma monumental, histórica, que naturalmente es extraordinaria, fantástica. Pero yo amo sobre todo a la gente, la gente viva, y la del Trastevere es la más viva y auténtica del mundo».[2]

The book is dedicated to the Italian poet, Giuseppe Gioachino Belli.[3] A thematic overture is followed by two series of ten and eleven sonnets separated by a chapter of «Versos sueltos, escenas y canciones»; the last part entitled «Poemas con nombre» contains pieces on contemporary Italian artists. The axis of the introductory poem «Monserrato, 20» is also a central notion in the whole book: Monumental, grandiose Rome is but the inert frame encompassing the city's true presence in vigorous art, an art that is life itself in all its threatened, sullied but dynamic splendor. «Monserrato, 20» is one of the longer compositions in the book, sixty-two hendecasyllables in assonant and occasionally full rhyme. From the point of view of the poem's «narration», its structure is a form of the «revelation plot»: the speaker comes to realize fully the double nature of the admired city, awakens from a dream of its past glories to its complex present. This awareness does not detract from his poetic endeavor, for the misery and grandeur that Rome offers in concentrated form, the poet has lived with and worked with for most of his life.

From the outset, the duality is anticipated: «Desciendo la escalera de mi casa, / mirado de relieves. ¿Dónde sueño?» At this point, the poet's questions suggests that his vision is inwardly directed rather than objective. The next few lines describe what he actually wants to see, figures of myth and art, the fulfillment of a dream: «¡Oh Roma deseada, en ti me tienes, / ya estoy dentro de ti, ya en mí te encuentras! / Me agrando o adelgazo por las calles y plazas». The city's extension and the poet's inner space merge. Alberti seems to have reached a moment of complete communion with the external world.

The twofold nature of Rome is at first overshadowed by the dream; reality is easily transformed. The poet can see his neighborhood «... embanderado, / como una barca, de tendidas ropas». But, as he approaches the moment of discovery, evidence penetrates the vision, «gatos» and «basuras» appear, though they are dwarfed by «muros de potentes hombros, / puertas de colosales estaturas». The risks of being a pedestrian also befall the dreamer, but jubilation transforms them into a promising invitation: «renacido a la vida a cada instante».

The speaker's amble is not aimless, his desire to become familiar with the city's extension has an esthetic purpose not merely in the passive but in the active, creative sense: «en ti me muevo, nueva lengua tuya». He wants to join his song to that of so many others who have celebrated the ancient city. He is also searching for someone to join him in such celebration: «Ando buscando compañía...» It is here that the second moment of the poem begins. The preceding lines had ended with the poet's avowed wish to become the city's singer. At this point the evidence of the city's present begins to gain ground, and this transitional moment ends with

2 Cf. *Bayo*, p. 94.
3 A popular, 19th century satirist.

the repetition of «Ando buscando...» Now the poet meets the unknown: a stranger observes him. The poem's even flow is interrupted by a sudden ellipsis and a series of questions «¿Quién se para mirándome...?» «¿Quién insiste...?» «¿Qué me mira, señor...?» «¿Qué oculta...?»

A new Theseus, the poet has reached the center of the labyrinth and encountered doubt. A being of double nature stands awaiting: it is Belli, in his hand Alberti's last sonnet. In the dialog that follows, Belli mourns the times and the city's plight in his very personal style: «e llibertá, e ddiluvi, a ppeste, e gguerra...». At the heart of the maze we come face with ourselves; Belli is here but that other aspect of himself that Alberti had forgotten for a moment in his joyous discovery of eternal Rome. Minotaur or Sphinx, the being at the center —or the gate— demands an effort of interpretation, his nature must be understood, his utterance translated. But here no battle is waged; recognition is sufficient. Awakened from the dream and recovering the unity of thought and perception necessary for the task at hand, the Spanish poet, bearing within him his own tradition, the roots of his personal art, offers his verse to the great city as it is now, with its history and its living people:

> Deja, mi Belli, amigo, que en tus manos
> te ponga ahora, ya perdido el miedo,
> sus sonetos romanos
> un hijo de los mares gaditanos,
> nieto de Lope, Góngora y Quevedo.
>
> (*Roma*, pp. 7-9)[4]

To begin his exploration of Rome, the poet chooses the classical sonnet, a form of Italian origin, of course, but which quickly became a favorite of Spanish poets since the sixteenth century. In selecting such a traditional, historically significant meter and using it to describe down-to-earth Roman life from the sordid to the inconsequential, Alberti portrays precisely that essence of the modern city, as he came to perceive it in the opening poem in which daily refuse and ancient grandeur are found side by side. This contrast also becomes one of the sources of the poet's humor, infrequent since his exile and now again freely indulged. Still, we must not expect the kind of exuberance that led José Bergamín to call him «El Alegre» in the days of *La amante*. Alberti's laughter acquires a more Quevedesque turn, with satirical overtones often and occasional sarcasm.

The first sonnet, «Lo que dejé por ti», is of particular interest because it stands somewhat apart from the rest. In it, Alberti still looks back across the Atlantic to what he left behind, and in a petitionary conclusion offers these separations to the city as tokens of his devotion, and merely in exchange for similar and henceforward inevitable losses. This is one of the most decidedly classical of the book's twenty-one sonnets (first and third chapters): the rhyme scheme of its tercets, cde, cde, was Garcilaso's

---

4 RAFAEL ALBERTI, *Roma, peligro para caminantes* (México, 1968).

favorite —that of the quatrains remained basically unchanged (abba, abba) until Modernism and predominates still— and its correlative construction is reminiscent of the great Golden Age *conceptistas*. The litany-like recension of bereavements is organized in a compact four-fold pattern through the first eleven lines (two quatrains and one tercet), interlinked by the same verb, «Dejé». The first quatrain refers to aspects of memory, elements of his previous life that became intimately linked with the passing of things and their remembrance, «mis bosques», «mi perdida arboleda», with reiterated loss, «mis perros desvelados». The second quatrain focuses on departure as the poet's abiding condition of existence:

> Dejé un temblor, dejé una sacudida,
> un resplandor de fuegos no apagados,
> Dejé mi sombra en los desesperados
> ojos sangrantes de la despedida.

This departure, though its imagery seems to refer to the violent days of 1939, pertains also to the more recent instance, the removal from America.

Images that came to signify immobility, imprisonment and separation —as in *Baladas y canciones del Paraná*— combine in the first tercet to conclude the enumeration at a peak of connotative power: «palomas tristes junto a un río», «Caballos sobre el sol de las arenas», «de oler la mar», and «de verte». The dove and the horse (denied their natural direction), distance from the sea, a dead horizon, all were central images in the poet's sense of confinement for long periods of his stay in Argentina and Uruguay. They also represent a multiple threat to poetic expression, that is vision (dove) and purpose and also vigor (horse). The smell of the sea is a more encompassing iteration of the horse image. Moreover, these images are direct references by Alberti to his own poetry: the second to last line of «se equivocó la paloma» is «ella se durmió en la orilla». The forgotten or immobile horse is frequent in Alberti's exile poetry, for instance in the «Balada de lo que el viento dijo», eternity might well be «un caballo olvidado» or in «Canción 1» (*Baladas*), «Los caballos como piedras» and so on. So that what the poet is referring to here is not only his existential past, but his past work as a poet. In retrospect, all previous images of loss are also poetic referents. That is what he has left behind and what he offers the city asking in return «Tanto como dejé para tenerte» (*Roma*, p. 13). This possession in then a possession through language, the purpose announced in «Monserrato, 20».

In his effort to seize the topsy-turvy accumulation of people, mores and machines that bustles daily across the Eternal City, Alberti, through the first series of sonnets, often resorts to «chaotic enumeration».[5] This stylistic recourse of long tradition is frequent in Quevedo and other

[5] A term coined first by Helmut Hatzfeld with reference to the Baroque and later used by Leo Spitzer in his «Enumeración caótica en la poesía moderna», in *Lingüística e historia literaria* (Madrid, 1968).

Baroque writers concerned with presenting the threat of a multifarious, disintegrating reality. Alberti puts the device to use in various manners: in the proliferation of objects (Sonnets IV and VII), of actions (V, X), or both in Sonnet II; through multiplied identical action (VIII) or variations of the same theme (III). In Sonnet IV, «Campo de' fiori», on the open-air market that takes place at that site in Rome, objects, people, and food jostle in happy promiscuity. As in most «chaotic enumerations», the initial impression left by the lists of items is one of pell-mell juxtaposition, a manifold fecundity: «Perchas, peroles, pícaros, patatas, / aves, lechugas, plásticos, cazuelas, / camisas, pantalones, sacamuelas, / cosas baratas que no son baratas». The last line of the quatrain gathers this profusion in an equalizing sweep: all items, people and objects together, are seen not in terms of their intrinsic value, their use, shape, color, or nature, rather they are devoid of all character except their monetary worth. The second quatrain ends with a similar leveling action, all things have become «Liras que corren...» These «flowers» of our modern times, those that now people the «Campo de' fiori», all are available for the right sum. Presiding over the profusion is Giordano Bruno — a monument to the sixteenth century Hermetic philosopher, burned as a heretic on the Campo de' fiori in 1680, stands now on that same spot: «Como el más triste rey de los mercados, / sobre tus vivos fuegos, ya apagados, / arde Giordano Bruno todavía» (Roma, p. 19). Thus has this most idealist thinker been reduced to surveying our daily barters. Still, he is the only true, perennial flower in the field and still burns, for the kind of thinking that sacrificed him then prevails still, epitomized by the transactions of the market place.

The «Versos sueltos» of the collection's second part are quick vignettes on aspects of the Eternal City, separated by several series of concentrated poetic aphorisms. The poems are generally short, often humorous and playful, passing glances at Rome and stray thoughts. Alberti sees Rome as the ancient, beating heart of Europe, full of mysery and greatness, contradictory. And everywhere is felt the dominating power of Roman Catholicism which the poet enjoys attacking or mocking: «Los curas, de tres en tres, / como paraguas andando / del revés» («La terna», Roma, p. 37). Alberti in Rome is a poet of the street, not so much in the political sense —his collected political verse is entitled El poeta en la calle— but as a frequently popular poet who walks down the sidewalks and uses the language of the people, often harsh or vulgar, always concrete. Alberti's awareness of «monumental» Rome is never lost, but he likes to emphasize the notion that the city and its historical remains have been appropriated by the people, that they live within it and enjoy it with easy familiarity or even indifference. It is this condition that he seeks to attain and to express in his poetry. That is why next to poems on the city's fountains we find an equal number on the innumerable streams of urine that also seem to flow down to the Tiber, or why he likes the linguistic contrast between the classical and the colloquial: «¡Fuentes que sin disimulo / bañan en agua a las ninfas / desde las tetas al culo!» («Invitación para el mes de agosto», Roma, p. 45).

But the tone it not invariably close to the ground. In some of his aphorisms, the poet delves on the city's true, lasting beauty, beyond that of her statues and her buildings: «Otoño en Roma. Empieza a coincidir / el oro de las hojas de los árboles / con el dorado de la arquitectura» (*Roma,* p. 57). The coincidence highlights a contrast between nature, whose aging is a temporary, necessary stage and man's artifacts, irremediably old, outside the cycle of rejuvenation. Inevitably the notion of time imposes itself on the poet, as a vital reality —he is growing old— and through the various layers of temporality that he sees concretized around him in the city: Roman Catholicism's claim to eternity, the remains of a lengthy history, the passing of days. The second sequence of sonnets opens with a composition that highlights the lack of significance of all these indices of history:

> Ya nada más entre tus sacros cantos
> Se oyen bocinas, pitos y sirenas,
> Y se ven por el cielo más antenas
> Que alas y palmas de ángeles y santos.
>
> (*Roma,* p. 89)

The phonetic contrast between the forms of yesterday («sacros cantos», «alas y palmas de ángeles y santos») with the broad «a's» that seem to spread as flat surfaces and those of today («bocinas, pitos y sirenas») with sharp vertical «i's» emphasizes the vigor of the latter (besides the onomatopoeia) as if they were growing out of the former, sapping their strength. The evidence of technique, man's control over his environment, has superseded those earlier efforts to propitiate nature that religion had offered. The second quatrain expands this idea further: man, who is now able to control the Tiber's flow, is no longer awed by the Church; his loss of fear allows him to see things in a truer perspective: «Y las Venus ya son menos obscenas / Que un Cardenal rendido a sus encantos». The very creative gifts that had made of the city a capital of art have been debased to the production of knicknacks for tourists. Here the poet is tempted to seek some measure of greatness in the remains of antiquity, but they too have become meaningless: «... laureles que a nadie ya coronan» (*Roma,* p. 89).

And yet, the spirit of Rome, the greatness that it achieved in spite of historical upheavals and retains amid present indifference, continues in the work of its artists now as it did always. The last chapter of *Roma* is devoted to them as the persevering embodiments of a seemingly inexhaustible tradition. The very first of these pieces, «Ugo Attardi, pintor», is of particular interest because Alberti, by means of a painting, turns his eyes again to Spain, from his closer, Roman exile. The poem's epigraph, «España hoy», probably refers to the title or the subject of the work that provides the point of departure of this pictorial meditation. In this poem Alberti sees Spain still in the throes of tragedy; though the conflagration of the Civil War ended over thirty years earlier, its aftermath, under a dictator's yoke, is but a protracted, still deadly reenactment. But a possibility of change, of movement —and any change, he feels, could not fail to be an improvement— appears at the poem's conclusion, for there are still in Spain signs of life.

At the outset the poet considers the inevitable recurrence of Spain on his horizon of concern: «Siempre habrá que nombrarte, España, hablar de ti, / trayéndote a la boca /.../ en cualquier parte donde esté». Time and space necessarily conspire to keep the homeland's image vivid before his eyes. Between the references to time («Siempre») and space («en cualquier parte») is conceptual focusing, the presence of Spain is reiterated six times: «nombrarte», «España», «hablar de ti», «trayéndote a la boca»,[6] «con amor», «con ira». The poet now situates himself before the present image of Spain, in a spatial reiteration that parallels the preceding emotive focusing: «como aquí, hoy, en Roma, ante esta imagen tuya, / esa que no quisiera que existiese / ni en el más triste oscuro de los sueños». The emotional intensity of remembrance is transferred to its present spatial coordinates —the poet in front of the painting— «aquí... imagen tuya». The poem now will fill the space between «esta imagen tuya» and «esa... en... sueños», the image represented in the painting, and the image that the poet bears within him. For neither time nor space, the poet's travels, his life now still away from Spain, have mitigated the suffering of Spain and that of the poet; distances and years are filled with death: «No han bastado, no bastan treinta años / para que el mar no sea el de la sangre».

The poet's voice rises to banish from his vision of the homeland all enduring images of suffering and repression. A picture of Spain emerges whose components are negated time and negated space (darkness and imprisonment): «... caras / de pálidos a fuerza / de tan largas condenas a no mirar la luz!», «... insomne pupila / tras de cerraduras», «... puertas que se desploman como losas / de sepulcros...», «tu muda noche», «¡tus ecos sordos!». Anguished questions wonder at the length of the torture, the pervasiveness of death. Alberti uses traditional religious images to render the sacrifice of Spain in terms of Christ's own suffering since, he believes, religious fanaticism played a considerable part in fomenting the Civil War and motivating subsequent retaliations. Spain rises in an endless torment as «... esta visión siniestra, / ... estos clavos, / esta herida sin fin, esta agonía». Still, the poet chooses to see some light in the future: «... tú estás viva, / hay signos en tu cielo...», even though the country's present image remains a crucifixion «... que nos trae / cada mañana el viento» (*Roma*, pp. 103-104).

Even in the midst of the tumult of Rome, perhaps because he is so close to home, the poet's exiled condition manifests itself with extraordinary force, in this one of his strongest, at times bitterest, invectives —apart from his purely political poems— against the forces that caused it. But the majority of the «Poemas con nombre» that conclude *Roma* are celebrations of artistic creativity and maintain the note of exultation

---

[6] The expression «traer en boca» means to speak ill of. Alberti, in changing its meaning, turns the current phrase into a more concrete image, mitigating its negative connotations.

and praise for the teeming city that flows as a strong undercurrent through most of the book's compositions, even in moments of irony or satire. In Rome, also, Alberti wants to remain «abierto a todas horas», receptive to all echoes and looking outward to present spaces and their opportunities more often than back to the enclosures of the past.

III. «*Canciones del alto valle del Aniene*»:
    «con un manso ruido...» [7]

The volume containing this collection of songs also includes the prose accounts of «Visitas a Picasso» (1968-1972), a group of poems on fellow artists assembled under the title «Otros versos», «El desvelo» (1970-1971) —prose meditations interspersed with short poems— and poetry preceding *Marinero en tierra,* some of it previously unpublished. Nearing seventy, Alberti seeks in his surroundings the serenity that will assuage his still strong anxiety to escape time and the occasional angers that some memories still elicit. Works of art, those of other creators, such as Picasso and the several writers, painters, musicians who are celebrated in *Otros versos,* are sources of wonder and occasions for generous praise, representing also moments of calm and lasting form erected against the erosions of passing days. For even at this stage, Alberti feels solicited by the same antagonistic forces that have given shape to his poetry since *Sobre los ángeles*: «... Sigo siempre viviendo entre el clavel y la espada... Dejadme hablar, por favor, escribir de ese pequeño río que va feliz, lleno de truchas y cangrejos, moviendo en sus cristales un finísimo paisaje de alamillos a punto de cantar iluminados de hojas... Y de pronto se entran en lo oscuro, sin quebrar las paredes, las voces frías, tajantes de la espada...».[8]

This is why in *Canciones* the occasional somber memory continues to appear, why it is as a resolute movement away from these voices drawing his attention still that this latest poetry should be viewed. Such a concern is posited in the last poem of the collection, «Carta a Horacio». The reader of Alberti's poetry recalls an earlier piece, «Carta abierta» in the last part of *Cal y canto,* in which was projected a poetic program. As was «Carta abierta», «Carta a Horacio» is a «fragment», making the reminiscence clear; to those youthful, confident anticipations now corresponds the yearning for tranquillity, a quieter ambition. Whereas the earlier letter was a joyous salute to modern discontinuities, the clashing accelerations to which poetry was to conform, the latter «fragment» represents all that this same world allows the poet, halting, incomplete dreams.

«Carta a Horacio» is particularly important because, in retrospect, it epitomizes and makes clear some notions underlining the poems that precede it in *Canciones.* The poem opens with a quotation from Horace on

---

[7] From FRAY LUIS, «La vida apartada».
[8] Not collected in Aguilar: RAFAEL ALBERTI, *Canciones del Alto Valle del Aniene* (Buenos Aires, 1972), pp. 159-160.

the pleasures of the country life. The great poet's estate has become a tourist attraction of sorts, to which Alberti is also drawn on occasion. But waiting there for him is the shadow of Fray Luis, great admirer and translator of Horace, and himself author of a famous poem on the «retired» life. Memories of Fray Luis's own orchard at La Flecha are interspersed with citations from Horace so that the three poets seem to contribute to the elaboration of this *locus amoenus*. The countryside now is altogether different, what remains of that Roman's estate is «... apenas / un esbozo extinguido de tu sueño». As he returns home, the present poet anticipates a feast to which he shall invite the ancient poet and other artist friends, a pleasant evening such as those enjoyed by Horace in his later years. It does not matter that these friends are ghosts: «Soñar un sueño fue nuestro destino. / Mas ¿quién puede ya hoy / ni hasta soñar que está soñando un sueño?» [9] (*Canciones*, pp. 61-64). And though a creation of the mind, which is what the «secluded spot» really is since language and imagination must effect both a temporal (historical) and spatial abstraction (joining the Villa Sabina to La Flecha and Alberti's own vision of both), it shimmers on the verge of disintegration, sustained by a construction of words upon words. It is in this light that one should read many of the compositions of *Canciones*, as conscious efforts to recreate and abstract from time short moments, pictures of a fragile *locus amoenus*, still protected, high above the plain.

The collection begins as it ends with the fusion of a literary reminiscence and a quick landscape, in which this concrete core of perception seems to merge with the poetic reference, almost become absorbed by it:

> Este valle
> hubiera sido soñado
> por Juan Ramón, este valle
> por donde corre escondido
> el Aniene,
> donde álamos y sauces
> con el susurro del agua
> mueven un son de arias tristes
> y pastorales lejanas.
> Este valle...
> ¡Oh, cuánta pena este valle,
> si hubiera sido soñado
> por él!

(*Canciones*, p. 11)

At the outset, the present site and its imagined poetic dream are one; in fact, the potential dream seems more palpable than the reality, but before the latter escapes thoroughly into the dream, Alberti restates its presence: «... este valle». Yet, the valley's principal element, the

---

[9] Cf. ANTONIO MACHADO, *Poesías completas*, 4th ed. (Buenos Aires, 1958), p. 163, XXI: «... soñé que soñaba».

river, is hidden; and the water and trees are seen through their «poetic» voice. Finally the landscape dissolves wholly in the possibility of another poet's dream, that is to say, it turns into a memory of language, into what remains of other potential words.

In *Canciones,* seeing is often more a mental than a perceptual activity. The world as viewed through and recast in language is a counterpart of its true aspect. This is true, of course, of all literary endeavor that takes reality as its point of departure, but here Alberti throws into sharp relief the distance between what things are and what they need to be for him:

> Tanta luz, es verdad, destruye todo.
> Cae como un inmenso
> polvo resplandeciente,
> borrando los perfiles, diluyendo
> las formas, los volúmenes,
> dejándonos
> como una nebulosa fulgurante
> que nos hubiera traspasado el sueño.
>
> (*Canciones,* p. 38)

The immediate juxtaposition of light and truth establishes also the old equation 'light = reason', and emphasizes the paradoxical nature of «destruye todo». What sort of destruction is this? For while the phenomenon is a recognizable, not uncommon, picture of blazing light changing the contours of objects, its effect seems an attack upon the speaker's world. It penetrates reality first, to change it, and then, by means of these transformed appearances, burns into the poet himself in blinding clarity. The dream of stable «formas», «volúmenes» is no longer possible. For an instant, light has revealed the transitoriness of all reliable objects and proportions. Here, the dream of the *locus amoenus* disintegrates at its most solid foundations.

This conflict, or rather the distance between the world as seen and the world as rendered by language, is a frequent preoccupation of Alberti's in *Canciones.* He speaks explicitly of «Reinventar un paisaje / después de visto» (*Canciones,* p. 40). The impossibility of capturing the ceaseless novelty of things, though it underlines the usual anxiety over time passing, elicits wonder at the minutest gradations of beauty from the simplest scenes to the most impressive landscapes. In these instances the poet's vocabulary returns to painting, his eyes linger over surfaces and shadows: «El rosal / estampa su sombra inmóvil / en la cal verde velado / del muro.» It is the transformations of color within the «sombra inmóvil», the lightborne transition between «rosal» and «muro», hovering across the spectrum from darkening green to white, that cannot be seized because of being a movement and not a shape or a hue: «Era así, pero no es eso» (*Canciones,* p. 41).

At times, it seems as if the poet has caught an interval of time, when past and present merge in a quiet, contained picture:

Agua redonda, inmóvil,

... ... ... ... ... ... ... ... ... ... ... ... ... ...

Suspenso estoy, llevado por los aires
a un momento o jardín que no pude habitar
y ahora me creas

agua redonda, inmóvil.

*(Canciones,* p. 47)

He can achieve an instant of repose through the abstraction of a portion of himself from the present, allowing the waters of the round pond to contain him as «mudas, nocturnas ramas sumergidas» *(Canciones,* p. 47).

Though the past cannot be shed, it may be hushed, or its clamor may be diverted. In this collection, composed with the purpose of creating a landscape that might at last alleviate the poet's restlessness, Alberti succeeds in capturing not so much the space itself that will receive him but the endeavor to reach it. And at the book's conclusion, the «Carta a Horacio», he joins this awareness to that of those two ancestors whose poetically wrought retreats were more real than their actual ones. Still, though he is aware of how much of his «hidden garden» is a dreamed image, his glance rests lovingly on its components, trying to seize shadings, movements, reverberations. When the past returns, it is mitigated by the forms of the present: this attention to reality and the task of turning it into language, he realizes, is perhaps the only *locus amoenus* that a poet can expect: «Soñar un sueño fue nuestro destino» *(Canciones,* p. 64).

## CHAPTER 8

# COMMITTED POETRY AND THE THEATER: «DE CARA AL HOMBRE DE LA CALLE» [1]

Alberti's interest in the theater and his commitment to Communism asserted themselves at the same time, in 1930. The social and political upheavals through which Spain was passing moved him to what he considered a more active employment of his talents. While the stage would provide him with the opportunity to objectify his poetic intuitions and to widen his audience, his political involvement required of him that he put his pen at the service of the «revolution». These activities meant a decisive turn outward for a considerable portion of his work; they necessitated the apprenticeship of a new form, for the theater, and the application of his imagination to a new purpose. But, Alberti remained a poet throughout. His dramatic efforts are uneven, and the circumstantial demands of his political persuasion, including the duties of the struggle against Franco during and after the Civil War, imposed limitations on his lyricism that were at times very difficult to overcome. Nevertheless, Alberti's later drama as well as his public poetry remain literature of high quality. It is only because of the excellence of his purely lyrical invention that they must take second place, and we devote only this final chapter to that work because Alberti's is principally a lyrical voice.

## I. *Political Poetry*

Alberti's first politically motivated poem is the «Elegía cívica», «Con los zapatos puestos tengo que morir», dated January 1, 1930. In it Alberti attacks the decaying monarchy and its supporters in strong, often colloquial, language and in a somewhat prophetic tone. There follow, in chronological order, *El poeta en la calle*, 1931-1936; *De un momento a otro*, 1934-1939; *Vida bilingüe de un refugiado español en Francia*, 1939-1940; *Signos del día*, 1945-1955; *Coplas de Juan Panadero*, 1949-1953, and *La primavera de los pueblos*, 1955-1957.

Juan Cano Ballesta says of Alberti that he is «the unequivocal initiator of revolutionary poetry in Spain» and that he became immediately

[1] From BLAS DE OTERO, «Cantar de amigo», *Expresión y reunión* (Madrid, 1969), p. 124.

«the visible leader of this new orientation in literature».[2] In fact, Alberti's first decidedly political poem, his «Elegía cívica», was immediately recognized as a work that broke ground by no less than Azorín, who praised it almost extravagantly.[3] In the magazine *Octubre,* Alberti attracted the early efforts of other poets in the same direction —notably Cernuda, who published the poem «Vientres sentados» therein— and was able through it to diffuse the new concepts and win great prestige for them. Alberti's first committed poetry is principally poetry of rebellion. Looking back upon his childhood and upbringing, and upon the Spain around him later, he is overcome with iconoclastic anger. In «Un fantasma recorre Europa» [3bis] from *El poeta en la calle,* he anticipates the triumph of Communism, pictures the greedy pusillanimity of the wealthy: «... Y las viejas familias cierran las ventanas, / afianzan las puertas, / y el padre corre a oscuras a los Bancos / y el pulso se le para en la Bolsa».[4] «La familia», written in 1934, is Alberti's unrelenting indictment of his own family. He accuses them of blighting his childhood in concert with the Jesuits, who taught him, and of being accomplices with those in power in the enslavement and destruction of the country. Although Alberti's viewpoint is here extremely personal, the poem speaks for an entire radicalized generation that looks back in disgust and despair over decades of criminal incompetence and of selfishness: «Hay que huir, / que desprenderse de ese tronco podrido, / de esa raíz comida de gusanos» (*P.C.,* p. 64).

Not all the poems of *El poeta en la calle* are successful. As always, Alberti's verse falters when abstractions take the place of his attention to the sharp, objective image, when his physical contact with the world becomes problematic. Still, the general quality of these committed pieces is surprisingly high. The intensity of his emotion often helped him to avoid the great dangers of political verse: rhetoricism and too great a reliance on ideology. Alberti's best pieces are those that seize upon specific events, or in which a very personal view of reality sets such events in a new context. Such is the case of «Monte de El Pardo» in *De un momento a otro,* when, in a reversal of the «pathetic fallacy» the poet inveighs nature for its indifference to war:

> Tanto sol en la guerra, de pronto, tanta lumbre
> desparramada a carros por valles y colinas;
> tan rabioso silencio, tan fiera mansedumbre
> bajando como un crimen del cielo a las encinas;
>
> (*P.C.,* p. 100)

The poet refuses to accept the distance seemingly insulating nature from man-made disaster. It is the opposition between the fire of the sun over

---

[2] JUAN CANO BALLESTA, *La poesía española entre pureza y compromiso* (Madrid, 1971), p. 195. My translation.
[3] Cf. *La arboleda perdida,* p. 291.
[3bis] First words of the *Communist Manifesto.*
[4] RAFAEL ALBERTI, *El poeta en la calle* (Madrid, 1978), p. 9. This volume contains the collected political writings: poetry, prose and theater. Hereafter as *P.C.* after quotes.

the landscape, its aloof keeping of time, and man's own incendiary ways, the fury that ought to affect even the passing of days that Alberti wants at first to abolish, as in a final holocaust. The disjunction is first expressed in terms of distance, physical and emotional, but the poet tries to conjoin forcibly natural and human elements, in his effort to achieve this concord in despair. The broad juxtaposition of line 1, «sol en la guerra», all that is light, reason, life overlooking the very epitome of death and darkness, becomes increasingly acute; the poet transfers his emotion to the indifferent components of the landscape trying to infuse them with his own anger. That the alliance is unstable is apparent in the inner conflict revealed by the oxymorons of line 3, «rabioso silencio», «fiera mansedumbre», reaching a peak of intensity in line 4 «bajando como un crimen del cielo a las encinas». This first stanza represents a species of verbal wish fulfillment, an effort to create in the poem the antagonism belied by the landscape. In stanza 2 the heavens' imperturbability must be viewed as willful unconcern, as worthy of blame as a mystic's transport amidst human suffering. In the final stanza the poet returns to the source of these dislocations within himself, to plumb the darkness that such external exuberance of sunlight produces in his mind, and to realize his own guilt in this attempt against nature, the guilt of all men. It is this inner awareness, this discovery that allows him truly to see: «La soledad retumba y el sol se descompone» (*P.C.*, p. 100). Now he can achieve the unity impossible before, realizing that the source of violence as well as the source of apparent indifference that he attributed to the elements lay within himself, that he is responsible, as we all are.

In his political poetry, Alberti is at his best in these intense moments that bypass all special commitments and, though historically precise, move rapidly beyond history's circumscription to become a human cry valid for all time. This universalization is achieved in a surprisingly large number of poems, given the circumstances and purposes of their writing; most of them, in the first part of his political work prior to 1939, were meant to be read aloud and were written to praise and to give heart to the combatants of a lost cause. It is a measure of Alberti's understanding and love of his fellow soldiers that he rarely felt the need to simplify. Nevertheless, some of these pieces suffer from the general failings of momentary verse: the imagery is at times weak, and, on occasion, the desire to create immediate effects as well as too urgent a need to denounce overcome the poet's customary excellence. Such is the case in «13 bandas y 48 estrellas», a chapter of *De un momento a otro,* in which the contrast between the inexhaustible power of lush nature, of the subjugated peoples of Spanish America, and «Yankee imperialism» is not a sufficiently strong theme to raise many compositions to the level that we have come to expect from Alberti.

The most successful of Alberti's militant poems written in exile belong to *Signos del día* (195-1963). Among these, «Nocturno español» stands out because of the intensity of emotion that drives it, owing to its sustained metaphoric strength and as another link in the chain of compositions lamenting the country's plight. In the twentieth century, Alberti wants to reiterate in his own idiom and with his own bitterness the same desperate dirge, now harshly focused on Franco's Spain, that sounds across the centuries in Quevedo's famous sonnet on the instability, decay and death that surrounds us. This piece —«Enseña como todas las cosas avisan de la muerte»— whose first line is quoted in the epigraph to «Nocturno español», renders Alberti's indictment even more relentless: for what in the *conceptista* poet was a general consideration of the times and of an inevitable decay towards death, a transcendent disillusionment, is gathered in Alberti's poem to form part of his accusation of the present regime and to give its evil not merely historical but metaphysical reverberations. This is also why the poet selects the traditional *silva* as the vehicle for his meditation. This classical form provides a frame to contain the poem's vehemence while recalling the country's spirit against which Franco and his cohorts stand as a massive denial. In the first *silva,* the poet invokes his new «muses» —«Ira» and «pena»— again referring to a traditional *topos* but revising it to fit the untypical circumstances:

> Ira, sosténme, pena, dame altura.
> Que no haya horror que al hombre vuelva manso,
> miedo que ponga grillos
> a la sangre, ya diente y mordedura,
> para llorar, para gritar cuchillos
> por tanta noche y muerte sin descanso.
> Porque, en verdad, allí nadie reposa,
> nadie cierra la luz sin que despierte
> viendo al alba otra cosa
> que el calculado rostro de la muerte.

After the appeal of the first line, the stanza divides into two parts, each controlled by its respective final line (lines 6 and 10) towards whose perception of death the syntax of the preceding lines is funneled. The first part of the stanza centers around the image of «grillos / a la sangre» in enjambement precisely to suggest its role as a link — a linking that is denied, at the same time, by the sense of the sentence. This axial metaphor joins the series of images under a) «Ira»: «horror», «diente y mordedura», «gritar cuchillos», and under b) «pena»: «que no haya horror», «miedo», «llorar», «noche». The second half of the stanza develops line 6 in terms of denial of rest and of light, contrasting its pall with the preceding anguish and concluding with a line that suggests the imposition of cold, careful evil over agonized resistance.

The second stanza considers death's prevalence through imagery of negated time and natural cycles undone, leading to the notion of death in its reign: «allí la muerte reine coronada». Stanzas 3, 4 and 5 further define this empire of death by developing other aspects of reigning death: a) power over the powerless, death as darkness, light denied — that is, reason denied; b) death as secret sapping, excavation; c) a reversal of the concept of growth in nature, where digging is destroying instead of planting.

In the final two stanzas, Alberti turns inward as he did at the outset.

145

In stanza 6 his own light fails before the black fog of death that covers his homeland as a lid. In stanza 7 (corresponding to lines 7 to 10 of the first), death has extended its domain to impose an eternal nightfall. The poem concludes with Quevedo's line —«los tristes muros de la patria mía»— now incorporated into the poem. But Alberti did not want to remain with so hopeless a vision. As a postcript, in willed anticipation of renewal that the poem did not allow for, several lines manifest confidence in the future of Spain: «Mas sé que tanta noche y agonía / tras de tan tristes muros, / serán capaces de alumbrar el día...» (*P.C.*, pp. 153-155).

Alberti wrote *Coplas de Juan Panadero* between 1949 and 1953 and *Nuevas coplas de Juan Panadero* in 1976-1977. Both the title (*Coplas de Juan Panadero*) and the intention of these songs refer us to a long tradition that reaches back to the medieval *copla* of satirical intent. From his exile he inveighs against Franco's Spain and those who have allowed it to exist, while praising leftist, specifically Communist politics. Within this denunciatory context, principal topics of the earlier *coplas* —there are twenty independently titled groups— are a self-portrait, several installments of a poetics suited to the popular tone of this verse, and the life of the exile. The *coplas* of the second and more recent series, *Nuevas coplas* —eight titles— are almost all occasioned by current events. Of the entire sequence the most interesting are the three attempts at defining a «popular poetics» and *coplas* on exile and return.

For this down-to-earth poetry, Alberti has chosen a three line stanza —a few of four lines— of assonant octosyllables. His first considerations of this new art of poetry center on the idea of simplicity. He begins by linking his present writing to Antonio Machado's *Juan de Mairena*. One of the first statements in «Juan de Mairena Talks to his Students» is: «Day by day, gentlemen, literature is becoming more written and less spoken. As a result, day by day, writing deteriorates»; he praises Bécquer in the same vein as «... he of the meager rhymes».[5] Thus Alberti begins:

> Digo con Juan de Mairena:
> «Prefiero la rima pobre»,
> esa que casi no suena.
> En lo que vengo a cantar,
> de diez palabras a veces
> sobran más de la mitad.

> (*P.C.*, p. 215)

And yet this assertion does not stem from his desire to be understood by the «people» for, he goes on, he refuses to «talk down» to them. And although, if he wished, he could turn out songs like «torres de pavos reales» (*P.C.*, p. 216), circumstances demand straightforward language: «Por eso es hoy mi cantar / canto de pocas palabras... / y algunas están de más» (*P.C.*, p. 217).

[5] ANTONIO MACHADO, *Juan de Mairena* (ed. and tr. by Ben Belitt, Berkeley, 1963), p. 1.

Juan Panadero's second sequence on poetry pursues the idea of simplicity, though now he emphasizes the capacity of poetry to transform the commonplace into the beautiful, still with the barest means. «Mas la sola condición / es que la estrella y el barro / dejen de ser lo que son» (*P.C.,* p. 230). One of the basic tenets of this poetry for the people is that it be seen also as poetry of the people, that is to say, that the people are now and always have been capable of making poetry.

Essentially, all of Alberti's political verse is that of a «Poeta en la calle».[6] In this he also follows specifically the reminder of Juan de Mairena «that our most enduring allusions to the human condition are always made in the language of Everyman».[7] In his third sequence on poetics, Juan Panadero insists on his *willed* simplicity, on the beauty that can surge from what is clear and evident to all men: «Buscar lo claro es tener / el perfil siempre dispuesto / a ver el amanecer» (*P.C.,* p. 275). He wants a language as plain and definite as a gesture, words of almost concrete strength. His verse, blunt or sharp, must be a goad or a weapon, not to be silently pondered but to urge us to action. Its distinctness must convince as incontrovertible evidence, making patent what is obscure and almost palpable what is obvious. It is not a poetry of syllogism or reflection but one where facts are added one by one, an ineludible array of conclusive determinations.

There are dangers in this *art poétique*. We have mentioned the most patent, prosaism. Another, too heavy a reliance or rhetoric, is less frequent because of the poet's great gifts of expression. Also, the obvious importance of repetition, the need to nail home the point, endangers the poems and at times monotony is not altogether avoided. Similarly, simple language, though it can be forceful, may also merely be the vehicle of trite notions. Yet there are some groups of *coplas* that achieve the aims that Alberti has set himself. The short «Coplas de Juan Panadero por los que mueren desterrados» conveys in strong, economical language the multiple separations that converge upon the exile to compound the final disjunction of death. The initial statement encompasses the deaths of all exiles. «¡Muerte de los desterrados! / Hay noches que por la mar / van y no vuelven los barcos». In this stanza only «Muerte» and its corresponding image «mar» are singular, for it is the same death —one that began when their exile began— for all outcasts. Stanzas 2 to 4 follow the departing inner gaze of a dying expatriate, in single, isolated pictures, from one room and one bed, empty, through the garden. Nearer death, he sees a river dragging down a broken bridge. In the fifth stanza, all movement ceasing, the boats over the sea have become one stationary windmill standing on a plain: «Ve también una llanura / con un molino sin velas, / rota ya la arboladura» (*P. C.,* pp. 231-232). In the final strophe, the exile sees as he dies alone the multitude of those who waited in vain for the doors to open.

The spare imagery of the poem has succeeded in capturing both the

6 Cf. Note 4 above.
7 *Op. cit.,* p. 115.

gradual oncoming of death for the individual exile and its symbolic resonance. Equally simple syntax emphasizes the idea of isolation, with few
connectives, relying on juxtaposition rather than linkage. A unitary mood
is maintained unabated by variously reiterated images of the initial couple
«muerte» — «mar»; absence: «una alcoba sin nadie», «una cama vacía»;
abandonment: «un limonero caído», «un rosal casi muerto»; severance:
«... un río / que arrastra, rota, una puente»; immobility: all of stanza 5
quoted above; rejection and denial: «una puerta cerrada». There is little
in this poem that would clearly label it as political. were it not for its
inclusion in this particular collection. It presents the poet's deeply felt
vision of a condition that is the result of political facts, but it transcends
such historicity and achieves universal significance because its vigor
depends neither on rhetoric nor invective, but rather on genuine existential anguish.

The collection, *La primavera de los pueblos,* encompasses political
poetry written by Alberti from 1955 to 1968. The first part arose from
a trip to eastern Europe and the Soviet Union, the second part «Sonríe
China» from a trip to China. In general, the quality of the poetry is
marred by the circumstantial element and the need to proselytize. Earlier,
Alberti's verse was often saved by the strong emotion that drove his
denunciation of the Franco regime, of war or injustice. But the impulse
to praise that he feels now, when viewing what he considers to be the
Communist success of those countries, seems not strong or lofty enough
to save his work from rhetoricism.

When he can establish a link between his present concern and more
personal levels of his being, Alberti's poetry becomes more interesting.
Such is the case with «Volando sobre Hungría», in which he remembers
his earliest impression of this country represented, by the young Gypsy
girl idealized in the sequence «La húngara» from *El alba del alhelí* (see
pages 40-41). He recalls in that first image beauty escaping inevitably
as the seasons pass: «Dos ojos que se llevaban / el sol en un carro verde / y en sombra al mundo dejaban.» Now, the poet seems to possess the
country as he flies over it and with it the girl's mature form: «Una
llanura morena, / una rosa joven llena / de poderoso rocío» (*PC.*, pp. 346-
347).

On the whole, Alberti's earlier committed poetry was of a higher
caliber. It responded to his immediate and deeply felt need to condemn
repression while his very personal vision of catastrophe had no need of
rhetoric to assert itself. Perhaps his growing interest in painting and in
the theater during these years redirected his energies away from poetry,
especially from the type of «manufactured» verse which obeisance to a
cause demands.

## II. *Theater*

Alberti's interest in the theater began quite early in his literary career.
In 1925 he wrote *La pájara pinta,* the same year he received the National
Prize for *Marinero en tierra* and began *La amante.* Alberti subtitled his

little play, of which he wrote only the prolog and the first act «guirigay lírico-bufo-bailable». It was inspired by the marionette theater of the Italian Podrecca on tour in Spain at that time. The prolog consisted of rhymed nonsense syllables accompanied by music and in the first act «distintos personajes de narraciones y coplas populares».[8] The links between this *divertissement* and Alberti's poetry of that time are obvious: simplicity, the recasting of traditional motifs, the importance of old songs and ballads, fantasy. Such a relationship between the poet's lyrical and dramatic expressions is not surprising; what is more interesting is to find that it remains strong throughout his career, from *La pájara pinta* to *La lozana andaluza*, from *La amante* to *Roma, peligro para caminantes*. In this study of Alberti, the lyrical poet, an overview of his theater will emphasize those aspects of it that are counterparts to his poetry.

Alberti's dramatic production may be divided into three epochs, no more than roughly chronological in their development. First, there were apparently several dramatic attempts of a minor nature akin to *La pájara pinta*, mostly left incomplete and still unpublished, such as *Ardiente y fría, madrigal dramático*, 1924, based on the poem of the same name in *Marinero en tierra. La novia del marinero*, 1924, and *Santa Casilda, misterio en tres actos y un prólogo*, 1930. These earliest pieces were never staged and have been lost. In the 1930's Alberti wrote what he was to call his «teatro de urgencia», quickly put-together works of a political intent, calculated to have an immediate impact. They were written at the time when Alberti's commitment seemed to him most necessary, when he felt that he had to devote his creative energies to an attack on the conservatism of the far right first and then, more intensely still in 1936-1939, to the struggle against the rebel Nationalist forces. In 1934 he published *Dos farsas revolucionarias: Bazar de la providencia, Farsa de los reyes magos*. The Teatro Español produced in 1936 *Los salvadores de España* with music by Acario Cotapos. In 1938 *Radio Sevilla, cuadro flamenco* appears in *El mono azul* (No. 45), a revolutionary serial, published by Alberti himself. This «teatro de urgencia» labored under self-imposed restrictions that limited its reach and durability to the immediate moment of presentation. It was intended, as was much of Alberti's committed poetry, to be more in the nature of a summons, a strong statement with little room for psychological shadings or literary refinement. The poet gives us his own understanding of this sort of work in his short essay «Teatro de urgencia»: «Una pieza de este tipo no puede plantear dificultades de montaje ni exigir gran número de actores. Su duración no debe sobrepasar la media hora. En veinte minutos escasos, si el tema está bien planteado y resuelto, se puede producir en los espectáculos el efecto de un fulminante».[9]

Although more ambitious in scope, it is to this group of plays that we should add *Fermín Galán, romance de ciegos*, Alberti's very first

---

[8] MANUEL BAYO, «Rafael Alberti y el teatro», in prolog to *El adefesio* (Madrid, 1976), p. 15.

[9] RAFAEL ALBERTI, «Teatro de urgencia», in *Prosas encontradas, 1924-1942*, ed. by Robert Marrast (Madrid, 1973), p. 196.

dramatic foray in to the world of politics. It was created by Margarita Xirgu and the Teatro Español in Madrid in 1931. By then, the poet's ideological commitment was clear, and he selected a recent political event for the plot of a play intended as an unrelenting indictment of the Spanish Monarchy and of the reactionary forces that sustained it: In December of 1930 two young officers at the Jaca garrison, Fermín Galán and García Hernández, led their troops in revolt. The revolt failed; two days later the two leaders were condemned to death and shot. Alberti's main problem was the event's contemporaneity. He thought he could bypass the lack of historical perspective by presenting it as a «romance de ciegos». This tradition, whereby events of a sensational nature were turned into popular ballads and recounted from town to town by blind men or beggars, generally with the aid of lurid illustrations,[10] offered him, he believed, a useful technique for generating adequate distancing. But the political climate was still too volatile and Alberti's dramatization too inexperienced for the play to have been well received. The principal criticisms were aimed precisely at the lack of perspective, but objections were also raised about the play's failure to move the audience and about moments of poor taste. Perhaps Alberti's error, as Robert Marrast indicates, was to offer a play meant for the masses to the sophisticated bourgeois public of Madrid.[11] On the other hand, Alberti wrote it to cause anger and indignation, as an «urgent» statement, not a carefully elaborated literary piece.

The two next full-length plays written by Alberti may be described as transitional in that, although a political and iconoclastic intent is still central to their development, their links to his more specifically lyrical work are more evident. *El hombre deshabitado,* 1930, and *De un momento a otro,* 1938-1939, are no longer agit-prop pieces. They refer to moments of crisis in the poet's life which he believed reflected equally critical concerns in Spanish society of the day. In this sense *El hombre deshabitado* expresses a prevalent rebellion, especially in intellectual circles, against established religious and metaphysical ideas, while *De un momento a otro* represents the rejection of bourgeois values.

Alberti has left us the record of his profound spiritual crisis in *Sobre los ángeles* and the same upheaval is at the source of *El hombre deshabitado.* The play is a modern auto sacramental (subtitled by Alberti «Auto in a Prolog, One Act and an Epilog»); in dark, negative hues, an accusing finger points at the transcendental deception practiced on man by religious tradition. In *Sobre los ángeles,* however, there was no specific indictment of religion — unless one considers Alberti's special angelology as a calculated reversal of Catholic lore; the poet considered his forsaken state, aware of the loss of some dimly perceived innocence and in a terrifying postlapsarian chaos. He sought the origins of this loss within himself now or in his past. *El hombre deshabitado* focuses Alberti's anger

---

[10] VALLE-INCLÁN's «El crimen de Medinica» is an interesting «esperpentic» poem in the genre.
[11] ROBERT MARRAST, *Aspects du théâtre de Rafael Alberti* (Paris, 1966), p. 60.

on the idea of a creating divinity that condemns man, his creature, to temptation. At the end of the play, The Man inveighs against the Nocturnal Watchman: «¡Mi creador! ¡Un criminal, Señor, un criminal! Tú, en vida, me rodeaste de monstruos sólo para perderme».[12] The loss of innocence is more acutely defined in *El hombre deshabitado* than in *Sobre los ángeles* and situated in its religious context. But The Man's spiritual state, shorn of these specific components, is not unlike the speaker's own in several of the poems *Sobre los ángeles,* in particular, the series entitled «El hombre deshabitado».[13]

In the play's prolog, The Man is an empty being, aimless, unaware of anything but the dark, subterranean surroundings from which he appears, immensely tired. The Nocturnal Watchman promises him a soul, if he will only beckon it: «¡Llámala! ¡Grítale! ¡Suplícale que descienda hasta tu cuerpo!» (*Teatro I,* p. 12). He then grants him the five senses and a female being that The Man is to turn into a woman, his wife, with whom to attain felicity. During the single act, The Man, The Woman and the Five Senses —as allegories— live in happiness and innocence until the appearance of Temptation in the form of a beautiful, apparently deathly tired, woman who implores their assistance. Moved by pity and curiosity they do not reject her. The Man, though he realizes obscurely the danger that she represents, cannot defend himself against her and ultimately succumbs to the desire to possess her. She leads him to murder his wife. At the end of the act, The Woman appears as a ghost and kills The Man in the arms of Temptation. In the epilog The Man has passed from the state of betrayed innocence to that of rebellion and returned to his primitive condition of the prolog. His previous emptiness, however, is now replaced by the awareness of his horrifying loss and of his Creator's deceit. Each step taken by The Man since he was invested with a «soul» at the outset has been both a gain in knowledge and a loss of innocence in the thirst for further knowledge that ensues.

Aspects of *Sobre los ángeles* center around this very notion. Suddenly the poet felt that his spiritual supports had given way, that he was defenseless against the onslaught of destructive instincts, enslaving passions; his very reason was threatened. The loss of innocence was the point of departure of his investigation. *El hombre deshabitado* would represent the allegorical prehistory of this loss. As a play, the *Auto* has many of the defects of an early effort. The symbolism is too heavyhanded [14] and the pace slow. The ideological content, while personally quite significant for the author, remains within orthodox lines of attack against the religious interpretation of free will. On the other hand, some of its elements were quite challenging, when we consider the prevalent conditions of the Spanish stage at that time. Alberti makes original use of Expressionistic

[12] RAFAEL ALBERTI, *Teatro* (Buenos Aires, 1959), p. 45. Hereafter quotes will be followed by *Teatro I* or *Teatro II*.
[13] Cf. C. M. DE ONÍS, *El surrealismo en cuatro poetas de la generación del 27,* pp. 172-178.
[14] In this respect the play is reminiscent of some of Jacinto Grau's «parables».

settings — the epilog takes place in an abandoned construction site, desolate and harsh; The Man climbs out of the depths of a sewer. The language reaches moments of strength, especially in the Man's invectives against The Nocturnal Watchman. Finally, the play's message is one of hope: Man is alone on Earth, but his future is his alone and he can shape it, for his will is truly free. After struggling out of the despair of *Sobre los ángeles,* Alberti would reiterate his rebellion and his anger at the great deception in *Sermones y moradas,* and his song to innocence in *Yo era un tonto...*

*De un momento a otro,* 1938, is subtitled «Drama de una familia española, en un prólogo y tres actos». Its poetic companion piece is the collection of committed poetry with the same title and more specifically, its first poem «La familia», bearing the date 1934 and subtitled «Poema dramático». In it, Alberti recalls with sadness and anger the stagnating, ultra-conservative ambience of his Andalusian home. One of the pieces of this sequence is especially relevant to the play, for it would seem to contain its dramatic source. «Balada de los dos hermanos» explores the unbridgeable ideological and psychological chasm separating the speaker from one of his brothers:

> Pero tú te marchaste con los santos,
> las engañadas vírgenes
> y los hombres extáticos.
> El oro imaginario de los cielos
> se convirtió en el oro de los Bancos.
> Las alas de los ángeles se volvieron cuchillos
> y tú,
> hermano,
> un rico militante reaccionario.

> (*P.C.*, p. 61)

In the play, the protagonist, Gabriel, tells his brother, Ignacio:

> «... qué quieres... ¿Que debo ir a misa? ¿Que mis amigos deben seguir siendo los mismos reaccionarios, hipócritas y mediocres de hace cuatro años? En una palabra: ¿que debo pensar como tú, ser como tú, hacer lo que tú, vivir como tú? Todo eso lo sabía. Pero yo nunca seré como *vosotros...*» (*Teatro II,* pp. 121-122)

Much of the play is autobiographical, though the action has been compressed and conflicts emphasized for dramatic ends. At the conclusion, as the town's people revolt, led by Gabriel, we are to assume that Ignacio shoots his brother.

Though written much later, the play is linked to *El hombre deshabitado* and *Sobre los ángeles* through its dramatization of the more external, social sources of Alberti's rebellion and sense of loss, the feeling that in the light of reason and of compassion for the downtrodden, the moral and ideological foundations of his life have collapsed. An active political commitment was the only answer, especially in the midst of the Civil

War (1938). Alberti expressed it both in his poetry and in this imperfect, but revealing, play.

The first two plays written by Alberti in exile have specifically lyrical sources. *El trébol florido,* 1940, is reminiscent in its avowedly mythical overtones of Alberti's Gongoristic moment. Both Robert Marrast and Louise Popkin, in their studies of Alberti's theater, mention a probable source of the drama in a Góngora fisherman's ballad «in which the fisherman Alción is spurned by a beautiful woman of the sea named Glauca».[15] In *El adefesio,* 1944, Alberti remembers the episode of «La encerrada» during his stay in Rute, the topic of nine short lyrics in *El alba del alhelí* (see pp. 40-41).

Marrast sees *El trébol florido* as «perhaps the most perfectly achieved of the plays of exile. It is the first term of what we might call 'the trilogy of the soil': *El adefesio* is the drama of superstition; *La Gallarda,* the tragedy of jealousy evoked through the myth of the bull; *El trébol florido* is the struggle of the Earth and the Sea».[16] The mythical atmosphere is set from the outset; the curtain rises on the eve of the Feast of St. John the Baptist, and Alberti has chosen as epigraph a song from Lope de Vega's *Peribáñez* — which also recreates the Feast: «Trebolé, ay Jesús, como huele! / ¡Trebolé, ay Jesús, qué olor!» The plot is rather straightforward: on an island a young girl, Aitana, daughter of Sileno, the miller, is wooed by two brothers, Martín and Alción, sons of Umbrosa, a fisherman's widow. Aitana pretends to love Martín, but secretly she loves Alción. Sileno and Umbrosa are adamantly opposed to the union of the families. Aitana prefers to toy with the brothers' feelings. (The lucky four-leaf clover, sought by all on the eve of St. John's, is obviously the symbol of Aitana's affection.) Officially, Martín and Aitana are engaged, but she has promised Alción to run away with him; they plan to leave during the long-delayed wedding ceremonies for Aitana and Martín. Sileno and Umbrosa have postponed the date in the hope that affections may change, but the event finally cannot be put off further. On the day of the wedding, passions converge; Sileno, apparently drunk, seeing that he will lose his daughter, strangles her at the height of the festivities.

The archetypal pattern is strongly underlined. The names of the characters are symbolic rather than real: Sileno, with his weakness for wine and his appearance —rotund, jowly and flatnosed— acts out his Dionysian role in its elemental components as god of earthly fruits, basic discord and riotous desire. Umbrosa recalls the shadow depths. Martín and Alción are both names of the kingfisher —a phallic symbol. The activities of the two families— fishing, milling of wheat— are also primordial representations of the antagonistic elements, land and sea. The language is frequently metaphorical, and its imagery leads us directly to the two telluric opponents: Aitana — «Te quiero, Alción, te quiero, como sólo la tierra puede querer lo que no tiene. Ya me siento de espuma, de sal fresca a tu lado» (*Teatro I,* p. 99). Through the use of highly figurative

---

[15] Cf. POPKIN, *The Theatre of Rafael Alberti,* p. 105.
[16] MARRAST, *op. cit.,* pp. 103-104. My translation.

speech, the effective stylization of characters and the careful pacing of the action towards an inevitable climax, Alberti has created a forceful play in which the dramatization of a cosmic struggle by means of well-defined human counterparts acquires truly poetic form.

*El adefesio* is Alberti's most frequently performed play. It was first staged by Margarita Xirgu [17] in 1944 in Buenos Aires. Lately, in 1976, María Casares [18] went to Spain expressly to present Alberti's play, its first performance in the poet's homeland. The play is subtitled «Fábula del amor y las viejas», and Alberti set it «en cualquier año de estos últimos setenta y en uno de esos pueblos fanáticos caídos entre las serranías del sur de España, cruzados de reminiscencias musulmanas» (*Teatro I*, p. 114).

The play's origins in provincial obscurantism and its description as both an «adefesio» and a «fábula» prepare us for a certain stylization of the characters and action as well as the exaggerated contrasts of a Valle-Inclán *esperpento*. Alberti felt great admiration for Don Ramón and may have had his later plays in mind when he conceived the characters of the three old crones. The plot itself is simple in outline: A young girl, Altea, lives secluded under the guard of three old maids, Gorgo, Uva and Aulaga. Gorgo is Altea's aunt and in her ruling of the household invokes the authority of her dead brother, Don Dino —Altea's father— going to the extreme at times of putting on a false beard and assuming masculine gestures. She and her two acolytes alternately fawn upon and torture Altea. Gorgo is intent on preventing any possible contact between Altea and Castor, the suitor. Finally, she has Altea falsely believe that Castor has committed suicide; as a consequence Altea kills herself. Gorgo then reveals that the marriage was impossible because Castor was Altea's half-brother.

Altea's innocence and her suffering present a revealing, guileless background to Gorgo's complex role-playing, to the multiple masks that she wears, exchanging in quick succession flattery for cruelty, gentleness for violence, self-flagellation for imperiousness. Ultimately, there is no substantial *persona* behind these masks, for she —as well as Uva and Aulaga— is at the mercy of the demands of an empty tradition. At the end, she admits defeat: «Mira, hermano, en qué abismo me hundiste... De nada me sirvió tu autoridad, el símbolo de mi varonía...» (*Teatro I*, p. 171). She sees in herself only an extravagant representation: «Yo no soy más que un monstruo, una pobre furia caída, un adefesio...» (*Teatro I*, p. 172).

In this play, Alberti evidences a growing mastery of dramatic technique, using to great effect the very concept of play-acting as a central element in the drama. To attack the dehumanizing effect of frozen traditions and the subtle variations of our willing acceptance of such rigidities, the central characters —with the exception of Altea— express themselves

[17] Margarita Xirgu founded the 'Teatro español'. She also went into exile.
[18] Actress born in Spain but who left for France as a young girl. She has become a star performer of the 'Comédie Française'.

through multi-leveled parody and reflex-like reactions, watching themselves perform and surrendering to the fascination of the performance. The forms of religion and of social intercourse merge into hollow ritual while opening a broad backward vista of similar enslaving manifestations and other antecedents from classical antiquity —the Furies— through the early Renaissance —Calixto and Melibea— to modern times. The stately, ritualized dance of the characters conveys the impression of a tragic ceremony replayed, crushing in its irrevocable iteration a true victim, the only character who is but herself, Altea. It is perhaps the straight-forward appeal of the young girl, her bewildered innocence, that, as Robert Marrast suggests,[19] sets the play apart from the «esperpentic» vision in the tradition of Valle-Inclán. The reduction of character into near grotesque mechanization is a necessary consequence, in Alberti, as well as in Valle-Inclán, of the forces that both wish to attack, but Alberti's form and his vision are largely his own.

The distorted reality that unfolds in El adefesio was born of Gorgo's commanding will and her obsession, and its links to our more common grounds are easily recognizable. La Gallarda (1944-1945), however, takes us entirely into the world of the poetic irrational, where the protagonist's humanity seems a thin veneer over ancestral, almost telluric passions: her destiny belongs exclusively to the world of myth.[20] A point of contact between the two plays is the power exercised by an absent character.[21] In El adefesio, Gorgo refers to wishes of her dead brother, Don Dino, as the justification for her tyrannical antics. In La Gallarda the young bull Resplandores is the symbolic focus of the entire play, representing for each character a means of reaching La Gallarda; to her, it remains the unattainable object of a confused mother's tenderness mixed with darkly erotic attraction. Thus, the animal's figure, filled with these multiple yearnings, especially transformed by La Gallarda's passion, transcends its physical presence to achieve a semi-divine status while alive —in fact, La Gallarda has built a small altar to the animal's sire in her room— and complete divinization as astral form upon its death. Its divine emergence, the earthly history of its attainment of such an exalted state, is the substance of the play. Like all divine births, it is shrouded in mystery, and this mystery remains at the heart of the play, concretely represented by La Gallarda's unearthly passion.

Alberti's interest in the bull as a mythical animal of the Mediterranean world, but particularly of Spain, suggests many sources for the play in his own poetry. A poem in Entre el clavel y la espada begins: «Mamaba el toro, mamaba / la leche de la serrana» (Aguilar, p. 484) and parallels La Gallarda's own wishes: La Gallarda — «¿No es el hijo, Manuel?˙ Yo en mis entrañas / soñé que en una noche me crecía / y que luego a mis pechos lo criaba» (Teatro I, p. 188). Her choice of the carnation as one of the principal images to describe the animal or its wounds is also

[19] Cf. MARRAST, op. cit., pp. 126-127.
[20] Cf. POPKIN, op. cit., p. 133.
[21] Ibid., p. 141.

reminiscent of similar descriptions throughout the poetry and invests the animal with clearly phallic references.

To sustain this sense of mystery, besides the poetic language which surrounds the action with an aura of stately ceremony, Alberti presents the play's events as having taken place already —and yet about to happen— as if it were some inevitably cyclical occurrence. This he accomplishes by means of Babu, a character who introduces himself in the prolog as the perennial forces of nature in human form: «Soy todo. / Todo he venido a ser al subir los cien años. / ¿Oís el árbol? Soy árbol. ¿Veis el viento? Soy viento...» (*Teatro I*, p. 176). He is seer and interpreter of the action he simultaneously forewarns and laments; in short, his role is that of the chorus in ancient tragedy.

As he did in *El trébol florido* and *El adefesio,* Alberti found within his own lyricism the sources of the play. His handling of dramatic material, his effective manipulation of distancing techniques and of temporal coordinates suggest, without revealing it, the ineffable mystery at the core of tragedy and of myth. This powerful and tightly elaborated play has never been performed. It awaits, to quote Robert Marrast: «... a director of genius (...) to give it life on the stage».[22]

In *Noche de guerra en el Museo del Prado,* 1956, Alberti uses again a prolog in which a character introduces the play, as did Babu, but here the character presents himself as the Author, and his role is to situate the action within a personal history. The most immediate effect of this technique is to create a distancing of the action and to set a slightly didactic or rather exemplary tone.[23] In the Museum and its works, mainly those of Goya, converge and wage battle the forces that have shaped Spanish history. Through multiple historical duplication, the play contains aspects of the poet's personal history, of the recent Civil War, of the earlier resistance to Napoleon, of the Spain of the Austrias. The defense of the Museum suggests thereby that of perennial values against barbarism. In this sense the historical vista is vastly broadened when Titian's «Venus and Adonis» joins the action, for it echoes the same struggle in the Renaissance and in antiquity. Likewise, the animation of painted figures suggests a confluence of both historical and artistic interior duplications in endless reflections.

*Noche de guerra* is subtitled «Aguafuerte en un prólogo y un acto», and although published three years after the main body of *A la pintura,* 1953, it is a continuation of Alberti's renewed interest in pictorial art, and more specifically of his attempts to relive intense moments of communion with his most admired artists. Ricard Salvat, who staged it in 1972, underlined this aspect of the play by having the «Author» recite part of Poem 3 of *A la pintura*'s introductory trilogy, as well as portions of other poems of the collection (segments of the poem to Titian, to Veláz-

[22] MARRAST, *op. cit.,* p. 146.
[23] Cf. ALBERTI's statements on Brecht, in *Noche de guerra en el Museo del del Prado* (Madrid, 1975), p. 68.

quez and others).[24] As for Goya, characters from several of his paintings are central to the entire action to the extent that, as Louise Popkin suggests,[25] he may be considered a «collaborator» of Alberti in the play's creation. The Author recalls in the prolog the night during the Civil War when he and some militiamen had been entrusted with the duty of saving the Museum's treasures from the possible ravages of battle. It is then a different sort of remembrance from that undertaken in *A la pintura;* to the latter's reflective mode corresponds the «active», politically-committed view of the Prado in the play. Still, the concept of art remains central to the staged action: it is to take place within a frame, and directions are given to have the Museum's central hall projected on a cinema screen while the Author talks. The figures of Goya's paintings come to life to defend the Museum against Napoleon's troops, while the militiamen undertake the same defense against those of Franco. Venus and Adonis pursue an action of their own under the threat of Mars. In parallel development, Philip IV and his famous dwarf, Don Sebastián de Morra (Velázquez), cower under the crash of weapons while two archangels (San Gabriel from a painting by Fra Angelico and San Miguel from an anonymous *retable*) lament their plight at being prisoners on a hellish earth, their way back to heaven forgotten. All these actions proceed independent of one another, but linked to the underlying theme of human values threatened by unchained barbarism.

Alberti brings to bear here the techniques of stylization that he used brilliantly in *El adefesio,* and his strong sense of irony, to create a total esthetic spectacle as well as a piece of historical-biographical commentary, whose intellectual content retains its significance through effective distancing. Much of the play's success, however, depends on staging effects and on the vision of the director who may integrate seemingly disparate levels of action. To the extent of such dependence, it must suffer from overemphasis on its didactic components at the expense of those purely artistic.

In 1963 Alberti was in Rome. He fell under the spell of the city and its inhabitants —in particular, the people of the Trastevere, where he lived— and, as we saw, celebrated both later (1968) in *Roma, peligro para caminantes.* The collection reflects the city's vitality through a seemingly indiscriminate mixture of historical reminiscences and of today's bustling colloquialism, the shameless or absurd together with the monumental and sublime. This lively, topsy-turvy world seemed not much different to Alberti from that of Francisco Delicado's *Retrato de la lozana andaluza* (1524); one of the collection's compositions is, in fact, an imaginary encounter with this heroine's reincarnation or perhaps her very same self, still saucily ambling down the city's streets, gracing the marketplaces and garden:

> Señora, la conozco. ¿Dónde vive?
> Por Dios, que he visto esos dos ojos negros,

---

[24] Introduction to *Noche de guerra en el Museo del Prado.*
[25] POPKIN, *op. cit.,* p. 162.

esas caderas anchas, esa forma
de culear andando, esas dos tetas...

(«La puttana andaluza», Roma, p. 38)

When he decided to turn Francisco Delicado's picaresque novel into a play, *La lozana andaluza*, 1963, Alberti's first concern was not to weigh down or lose the heroine's lustiness and exuberant charm, so that «el retrato de la andaluza, al levantarse en una escena, [respondiese] a la calidad que reclama de mí la antigüedad y prestigio de su talento» (*Teatro II*, p. 9). Nevertheless, a long multifaceted novel with over one hundred characters had to be reduced to representable proportions. Alberti subtitles it «mamotreto en un prólogo y tres actos».[26]

The emphasis of Alberti's adaptation is to show Aldonza's (La lozana's) growth into almost the proportions of myth. In a city where vice and corruption are rampant, Aldonza's vigorous, direct attitude towards her daily business, her joining of the happy use of her body to the art of curing secret ills and of maintaining youth and beauty, seem by contrast a clear, healthy profession. The character of Rampin, in Delicado merely a rogue and an object of satire, becomes more differentiated as befits Aldonza's lover; he shows himself capable of real jealousy and devotion to his mistress. To maintain the impression of effervescent activity, Alberti has kept a large number of characters (thirty-two) interacting on several levels of the stage in a rapid succession of scenes with a background of noises, shouts and laughter. The plot simply follows Aldonza's rise in Rome's world of courtesans and her growing fame not only as a beauty but as one gifted in other arts, all this on the eve of the Emperor Charles's sack of the city. Delicado had his heroine fleeing Rome and retiring to the Island of Lipari. But at the play's conclusion, Aldonza arouses her fellow prostitutes to the task of dispersing the advancing troops' destructive impetus through the ardors of love; as a large company of men and women hailing the heroine go forward to sacrifice themselves for the sake of the city, Rampin, wounded, searches for Aldonza in their burning house, calling for her. Alberti suggests: «¡Lozana, Lozana! — puede corresponder a esa final y necesaria sed inextinguible del hombre de salvarse en el lucero errante de la madre Venus» (*Teatro II*, p. 12).

## III. *Conclusion*

Alberti's effort to reach a wider audience was first anchored in the need to communicate the sources and outcome of a personal upheaval. This upheaval was caused, in part, by the realization that long-held values were empty and stultifying at the level both of personal ethics and of social intercourse. The situation in Spain at that time demanded of everyone and of intellectuals in particular that they take political positions.

---

[26] A «mamotreto» originally was a book of memoranda or notations, but it has come to mean an accumulation of near formless, disconnected comments.

Alberti's option against conservatism led him directly to the Communist Left. Later, during the Civil War, the vastly more immediate need to act as a writer, as well as a participant, imposed even greater strictures on Alberti's art.

The almost contradictory requirements of art and proselytizing were at times left unresolved in Alberti's public poetry. Numerous poems are effective propaganda and less than successful art. They seem more *pièces sur commande* than carefully thought-out works. But even among those poems that hail the coming of the Communist revolution, there are some where the message's intensity is sufficient to overcome the obvious obstacles of didacticism, and effective committed poetry results as in «Un fantasma recorre Europa». Still, the most successful pieces of *El poeta en la calle* are those where the poet's emotion takes him beyond the specificity of politics and allows him to reach universality through his revealing vision of obscurantism, suffering and war. Here he finds again his personal idiom, and abstractions give way to immediate contact with the real as anguish pours forth with strength as it did in *Sobre los ángeles*. There is a significant number of such poems in *El poeta en la calle*. In *Fermín Galán* and *El hombre deshabitado,* written as the 1930's began, the ideological burden has perhaps not been clearly dramatized and the characterization is not sufficiently differentiated. The same may be said of *De un momento a otro,* with its heavy doses of autobiographical material. In the 1940's, however, Alberti returns to lyrical resources. In addition, he now has technique well in hand and is able, as in *El adefesio,* to integrate thoroughly his social commentary within the dramatic framework. This latter play, together with *El trébol florido* and *La Gallarda,* constitute his great mythopoetic trilogy and the apex of the poet's theatrical oeuvre. Here again, it is when Alberti assumes his personal poetic voice that he creates his most accomplished works.

CHAPTER 9

CONCLUSION

In conclusion, it seems an amazing feat of misreading that Alberti,
along with other members of the group of 1925, should have been criti-
cized as being too much the esthete, the pure poet. For always, while his
commitment to his art remained total, he was both echo and augur of
an age.

Alberti's poetic resolve has been unwaveringly focused on a bridging
of the distances that existential and historical predicaments imposed upon
him. At the outset, as he tried to recapture the luminous image of a
childhood sea from the landlocked Castilian plateau or to etch a personal
itinerary across the peninsula against the background of its litorals,
a pristine map seemed to open before him, inviting his imaginative survey.
Soon this distance would grow and disjunctions that had seemed fleeting
would become radical. Earlier there had been invention, a world of
available, revealing imagery accessible to his language, a possible reshaping
of existing space. Now with *Sobre los ángeles,* Alberti's energies converge
on an accelerated effort to see, merely to name or define blind impulses,
to circumscribe at all costs the threatening forces that cloud his vision.
His angels surged forth as anticipations of later cataclysms as if he under-
went his baptism by fire in advance of history.

The chasm that this bout with the negative forces of his spirit
revealed to him was more profound than that which had been the early
source of his inspiration: what had seemed a temporary separation was
now a permanent expulsion from possible felicity. And soon after, as the
poet was regaining an equilibrium of sorts through social and emotional
commitments, the Spanish Civil War would make permanent for him an
alienated condition which his spiritual crisis had adumbrated.

As he left the coast of Europe on the night of February 10, 1940, Alberti took with him the unfinished manuscript of *Entre el clavel y la
espada,* poetic reflections on love and violence, on the erotic metamorphosis of reality and on its vulnerability. This collection, begun in Spain in
the last days of the Civil War and completed on the other side of the
Atlantic, also delineates the poet's wish to span the two shores of his
creative activity, imaginative and historical, lyrical and committed, joyful
song and somber accusation. But the double symbol of its title already
hints at the unitary mainspring of all his work and affirms the transforming

power of language as well as the malleability of the real to its constructions. Apart from its intrinsic value, *Entre el clavel y la espada* is significant because the poet, while moving from the metamorphoses of love
to those of death, encompasses both, and though the power of death
seems pervasive, he feels strong enough still, and confident, to oppose
to pervasive disaster his single lover's voice.

For Alberti, time is a category of space. The far past is simply far
away and thus still, at times, accessible. His expression seems ever an
exploration of broad expanses of reality, his encounters first visual and
tactile. Unmoored from familiar regions, he needs initially to realize the
new topographies, to incorporate these boundaries within the compass
of his imagination. That is why his first encounters with the vast American continent result in a near emotional paralysis until he can capture
within the land echoes and images familiar from before, can merge the
landscape with the legend behind it. And his full vigor will return to
him only in trying to seize the most passionate moments of his past as
in *A la pintura* and *Retornos de lo vivo lejano* — doing so, even then,
more in terms of spaces to reimagine or resituate than to relive. A word
will recapture a scene, the scene becomes a poem.

The genesis of Alberti's poetry is in language first, that is to say, that
in him works seeking a form create a thought. The structure of his poems
depends on a web of echoes, analogies, rhythms, tightly encasing a vision,
an intuition. He is probably the most accomplished craftsman of his
generation, the one whose language can achieve the most complex, semantic, phonetic, musical interrelationships, all this done with suppleness
and elegance. But behind such brilliance there is also passion and thought.
The first to do so in Spain, he forged a new idiom to capture the chaotic
spirit of his times in *Sobre los ángeles,* one of the great books of the
century. He was also the first to write revolutionary poetry, socially committed poetry, establishing a tradition that has found echoes in the best
poets of the following generations. Alberti developed an extraordinarily
subtle pictorial technique, bringing to bear all the resources of expression
in the evocation of painting and wrote the most poignant poetry of exile
and yearning. His work has always been distinguished by consummate
craftsmanship and the happy compliance of exuberant, chaotic or fundamental language to challenging form.

# SELECTED BIBLIOGRAPHY

PRIMARY SOURCES [1]

a) *Poetry*

*Marinero en tierra.* Madrid: Biblioteca Nueva, 1925.
*La amante.* Málaga: Imprenta «Litoral», 1926.
*El alba del alhelí.* Santander. Edición para amigos de José María de Cossío, 1927.
*Cal y Canto.* Madrid: «Revista de Occidente», 1929.
*Sobre los ángeles.* Madrid: Ediciones de la Compañía Ibero-Americana de Publicaciones, S. A., 1929.
*Consignas.* Madrid: Ediciones «Octubre», 1933.
*Un fantasma recorre Europa.* Madrid: Ediciones «La Tentativa Poética», 1933.
*Verte y no verte.* México: Impresor Miguel N. Lira, 1935.
*Poesía, 1924-1930.* Madrid: Cruz y Raya, 1955. Contains previous collections: *Marinero en tierra; La amante; El alba del alhelí; Cal y canto; Sobre los ángeles; Yo era un tonto y lo que he visto me ha hecho dos tontos;* poems published around 1929, gathered under one title for the first time, *Sermones y moradas* (previously unpublished).
*De un momento a otro (poesía e historia) (1932-1937).* Madrid: Ediciones «Europa-América», 1937.
*Poesía, 1924-1937.* Madrid: Editorial Signo, 1938.
*Entre el clavel y la espada (1939-1940).* Buenos Aires: Losada, 1941.
*Vida bilingüe de un refugiado español en Francia (1939-1940).* Buenos Aires: Bajel, 1942.
*Pleamar (1942-44).* Buenos Aires: Losada, 1944.
*Selected Poems of Rafael Alberti* (tr. by Lloyd Mallan). New York: New Directions, 1944.
*A la pintura, cantata de la línea y del color.* Buenos Aires: López, 1945 (Private, limited edition).
*A la pintura, poema del color y la línea (1945-1948).* Buenos Aires: Losada, 1948.
*Coplas de Juan Panadero (Libro I).* Montevideo: «Pueblos Unidos», 1948.
*Buenos Aires en tinta china.* Buenos Aires: Losada, 1951.
*Retornos de lo vivo lejano (1948-1952).* Buenos Aires: Losada, 1952.
*Ora marítima, seguida de baladas y canciones del Paraná (1953).* Buenos Aires: Losada, 1953.
*Baladas y canciones del Paraná (1953-1954).* Buenos Aires: Losada, 1954.
*Sonríe China* (in collaboration with María Teresa León). Buenos Aires: Jacobo Muchnik, editor, 1958.
*Poesías completas* (with an autobiographical index, and a bibliography by Horacio Jorge Becco). Buenos Aires: Losada, 1961.
*Poemas escénicos.* Buenos Aires: Losada, 1962.
*Abierto a todas horas.* Madrid: Afrodisio Aguado, 1964.
*El poeta en la calle (poesía civil) (1931-1945).* Paris: Colección Ebro, 1966.

[1] Largely based on Manuel Bayo's Bibliography in his *Sobre Alberti,* Madrid: CVS Ediciones, 1974, pp. 211-217.

*Fustigada luz (1972-1978).* Barcelona: Seix Barral, 1980[2].
*Rafael Alberti. Selected Poems* (tr. by Ben Belitt; introduction by Luis Monguió).
Berkeley: University of California Press, 1966.
*Concerning the Angels; Rafael Alberti* (tr. with an introduction by Geoffrey Connell). London: Rapp & Carroll, 1967.
*Roma, peligro para caminantes.* México: Joaquín Mortiz, 1968.
*Poesía (1924-1967).* Madrid: Aguilar, 1972. Edited by Aitana Alberti. Contains no political poetry. First of four planned volumes of Alberti's works.
*Canciones del Alto Valle del Aniene. Poesía y prosa (1967-1972).* Buenos Aires: Losada, 1972.
*Marinero en tierra; La amante; El alba del alhelí.* Madrid: Castalia, 1972. Ed. by Robert Marrast, with introduction, notes, variants and bibliography.
*The Owl's Insomnia* (tr. by Mark Strand). New York: Atheneum, 1973. A selection of Alberti's poetry.
*El poeta en la calle (obra civil).* Madrid: Aguilar, 1978. Ed. by Aitana Alberti. Contains Alberti's committed works.

### b) *Prose*

*La arboleda perdida (Libro primero de memorias).* México: Editorial Séneca, 1942.
*Imagen primera de...* Buenos Aires: Losada, 1945.
*La arboleda perdida (Libros I y II de memorias).* Buenos Aires: Compañía General Fabril Editora, 1959.
*Prosas encontradas, 1924-1942.* Madrid: Editorial Ayuso, 1970. Presented by Robert Marrast.
*The Lost Grove* (tr. by Gabriel Berns). Berkeley: University of California Press, 1976.

### c) *Drama*

*El hombre deshabitado (Auto en un prólogo, un acto y un epílogo).* Madrid: Editorial «Plutarco», 1931.
*Fermín Galán (Romance de ciego en tres actos, diez episodios y un epílogo).* Madrid: Editorial «Plutarco», 1931.
*Bazar de la providencia (negocio), seguido de Farsa de los Reyes Magos (Dos Farsas revolucionarias).* Madrid: Ediciones «Octubre», 1934.
*Radio Sevilla, cuadro flamenco.* (In 'Teatro de urgencia', collective work.) Madrid: Signo, 1938.
*Numancia.* Buenos Aires: Losada, 1943. Cervantes's play modernized by Alberti.
*El adefesio (Fábula del amor y las viejas).* Buenos Aires: Losada, 1944.
*Teatro.* Buenos Aires: Losada, 1950. Contains: *El hombre deshabitado, El trébol florido, La Gallarda.*
*Noche de guerra en el Museo del Prado (aguafuerte en un prólogo y un acto).* Buenos Aires: Ediciones «Losange», 1956.
*Teatro II.* Buenos Aires: Losada, 1964. Contains: *La lozana andaluza, De un momento a otro, Noche de guerra en el Museo del Prado.*

### SELECTED SECONDARY SOURCES

BAYO, MANUEL: *Sobre Alberti.* Madrid: CVS ediciones, 1974.
BOWRA, SIR CECIL M.: «Rafael Alberti, 'Sobre los ángeles'», in *The Creative Experiment.* New York: Grove Press, 1948, pp. 250-253.
— *Poetry and Politics, 1900-1960.* Cambridge: Cambridge University Press, 1966, pp. 125-127.

[2] This collection appeared after this essay was in press.

CANO BALLESTA, JUAN: *La poesía española entre pureza y compromiso*. Madrid: Gredos, 1971, pp. 112-122; pp. 195-200.

CIRRE, J. F.: «Sublimación de elementos populares en la poesía de Rafael Alberti», in *Forma y espíritu de una lírica española*. México: Panamericana, 1950, pp. 71-84.

CRESPO, ANGEL: «Realismo y pitagorismo en el libro de Alberti, *A la pintura*», in *Papeles de Son Armadans*, XXX (1963), pp. 93-126.

DEBICKI, ANDREW P.: «El 'correlativo objetivo' en la poesía temprana de Rafael Alberti», in *La palabra y el hombre* (Revista de la Universidad Veracruzana), No. 45, pp. 89-107.

DEHENNIN, ELSA: «Rafael Alberti», in *La Résurgence de Góngora et la génération poétique de 1927*. Paris: Didier, 1962, pp. 143-179.

DÍEZ DE REVENGA, F. J.: *La métrica de los poetas del 27*. Murcia: Universidad de Murcia, 1973.

DURÁN, MANUEL (editor): *Rafael Alberti*. Madrid: Taurus, 1975.

FEAL DEIBE, C.: «Rafael Alberti, de la nostalgia a la esperanza», talk delivered at MLA Convention, Chicago, 1977.

GULLÓN, RICARDO: «Alegrías y sombras de Rafael Alberti (Primer momento; Segundo momento)», in MANUEL DURÁN, *Rafael Alberti*, pp. 65-74; pp. 241-264.

HERRERO, JAVIER: «The Sun Against the Moon and the Birth of the Sea: Rafael Alberti's *Marinero en tierra*», in *Studia Hispánica in Honor of Rodolfo Cardona*. Madrid: Cátedra, 1981, pp. 97-129.

LLORÉNS, VICENTE: «Rafael Alberti, poeta social: historia y mito», in *Rafael Alberti*, Manuel Durán, editor, pp. 297-307.

MANTEIGA, ROBERT C.: *The Poetry of Rafael Alberti: A Visual Approach*. London: Tamesis Books Limited, 1978.

— «Rafael Alberti's 'Poesía taurina': A Visual Perspective», in *Hispanic Journal*, I, 2 (1980), pp. 73-88.

— «Color Synthesis and Antithesis: The Parallel Construction of Color Images in Rafael Alberti's Early Works», in *Crítica Hispánica*, III, 1 (1981), pp. 21-36.

MARRAST, ROBERT: *Aspects du théâtre de Rafael Alberti*. Paris: Société d'édition d'enseignement supérieur, 1966.

MAYORAL, MARINA: «Se equivocó la paloma (Comentario a un poema de Alberti», *Insula*, No. 282, pp. 3, 14.

MONGUIÓ, LUIS: «Rafael Alberti: Poetry and Painting», in *Crítica Hispánica*, I, 1 (1979), pp. 75-86.

MORRIS, C. B.: *A Generation of Spanish Poets (1920-1936)*. Cambridge: Cambridge University Press, 1969.

— *Surrealism and Spain (1920-1936)*. Cambridge: Cambridge University Press, 1972.

— *Rafael Alberti's Sobre los ángeles*. Hull: University of Hull Publications, 1966.

NANTELL, JUDITH: «Alberti's *Yo era un tonto y lo que he visto me ha hecho dos tontos*; Close-up: The Keatonesque Fool», in *Anales de Literatura Española Contemporánea*, 6 (1981), pp. 141-159.

— «Poetry for Politics' Sake: Rafael Alberti's *Consignas*», in *Crítica Hispánica*, V, 1 (1983), pp. 47-58.

ONÍS, C. M. DE: *El surrealismo y cuatro poetas de la generación del '27*. Madrid: José Porrúa Turanzas, 1974, pp. 151-207.

PANCORBO, LUIS: «Rafael Alberti; más años fuera que dentro de España». Interview in *Revista de Occidente*, No. 148: 41-77.

PÉREZ, CARLOS ALBERTO: «Rafael Alberti: Sobre los tontos», *Revista Hispánica Moderna*, No. XXXII, pp. 205-217.

POPKIN, LOUISE B.: *The Theatre of Rafael Alberti*. London: Tamesis Books Limited, 1976.

PROLL, ERIC: «Popularismo and Barroquismo in the Poetry of Rafael Alberti», *Bulletin of Spanish Studies*, XIX, pp. 58-83.

— «The Surrealistic Element in Rafael Alberti», *Bulletin of Spanish Studies*, XXI, pp. 70-82.

SALINAS DE MARICHAL, SOLITA: *El mundo poético de Rafael Alberti.* Madrid: Gredos, 1968.

SPANG, KURT: *Inquietud y nostalgia: La poesía de Rafael Alberti.* Pamplona: Ed. de la Universidad de Navarra, 1973.

STIEM, BRUCE G.: «Derivación léxica como recurso poético en algunas poesías de Rafael Alberti», in *Cuadernos Hispanoamericanos,* 360, pp. 585-592.

TEJADA, JOSÉ LUIS: *Rafael Alberti, entre la tradición y la vanguardia.* Madrid: Gredos, 1976.

VIVANCO, LUIS FELIPE: «Rafael Alberti en su palabra acelerada y vestida de luces», in his *Introducción a la poesía española contemporánea.* Madrid: Guadarrama, 1957, pp. 221-258.

WARNER, I. R.: «Subjective Time and Space in Alberti's 'Baladas y canciones de La Quinta del Mayor Loco'», *Bulletin of Hispanic Studies,* Vol. L, 1973, pp. 374-381.

WINKELMANN, ANA MARÍA: «Pintura y poesía en Rafael Alberti», *Papeles de Son Armadans,* XXX, pp. 147-162.

ZARDOYA, CONCHA: «La técnica metafórica albertiana», in *Poesía española del '98 y del '27.* Madrid: Gredos, 1968, pp. 294-336.

— «El mar en la poesía de Rafael Alberti», in *Poesía española contemporánea.* Madrid: Guadarrama, 1961, pp. 601-633.

ZULETA, EMILIA DE: «La poesía de Rafael Alberti», in *Cinco poetas españoles.* Madrid: Gredos, 1971, pp. 273-395.